Building Total Quality

Building Total Quality
A guide for
management

Tito Conti

CHAPMAN & HALL

London · Glasgow · New York · Tokyo · Melbourne · Madras

Published by Chapman & Hall, 2–6 Boundary Row, London SE1 8HN

Chapman & Hall, 2–6 Boundary Row, London SE1 8HN, UK

Blackie Academic & Professional, Wester Cleddens Road, Bishopbriggs, Glasgow G64 2NZ, UK

Chapman & Hall Inc., 29 West 35th Street, New York NY10001, USA

Chapman & Hall Japan, Thomson Publishing Japan, Hirakawacho Nemoto Building, 6F, 1-7-11 Hirakawa-cho, Chiyoda-ku, Tokyo 102, Japan

Chapman & Hall Australia, Thomas Nelson Australia, 102 Dodds Street, South Melbourne, Victoria 3205, Australia

Chapman & Hall India, R. Seshadri, 32 Second Main Road, CIT East, Madras 600 035, India

English language edition 1993

© 1993 Chapman & Hall

Original Italian language edition – *Costruire la Qualita' Totale* – © 1992, Sperling & Kupfer Editori, Milan
Translated from the Italian by Jane Simpson

Typeset in 11/13 pt Times by Excel Typesetters Company, Hong Kong
Printed in Great Britain by Clays, St Ives Plc, Bungay, Suffolk

ISBN 0 412 49780 8

Apart from any fair dealing for the purposes of research or private study, or criticism or review, as permitted under the UK Copyright Designs and Patents Act, 1988, this publication may not be reproduced, stored, or transmitted, in any form or by any means, without the prior permission in writing of the publishers, or in the case of reprographic reproduction only in accordance with the terms of the licences issued by the Copyright Licensing Agency in the UK, or in accordance with the terms of licences issued by the appropriate Reproduction Rights Organization outside the UK. Enquiries concerning reproduction outside the terms stated here should be sent to the publishers at the London address printed on this page.

The publisher makes no representation, express or implied, with regard to the accuracy of the information contained in this book and cannot accept any legal responsibility or liability for any errors or omissions that may be made.

A catalogue record for this book is available from the British Library

Library of Congress Cataloging-in-Publication data
Conti, Tito.
[Costruire la qualità totale. English]
Building total quality: a guide for management / Tito Conti. – English language ed.
p.   cm.
Includes bibliographical references and index.
ISBN 0–412–49780–8
1. Total quality management.   I. Title.
HD62.15.C6413   1993
658.5'62–dc20   93–14850
                                                            CIP

LEEDS METROPOLITAN
UNIVERSITY LIBRARY

1700 58639 X
BIO
49662   10·3·94
658.562 CON
15·3·94   35·00

Contents

CONTENTS

CONTENTS

Foreword

The quality crisis of the 1980s stimulated a massive response by American companies, and an associated flood of books by American authors. Most of these books focused on tools and techniques, despite the claims of their titles.

The European response to the quality crisis was on a more limited scale, as was the number of books authored by Europeans. This came as a surprise to those of us who lectured and were consulted extensively in Europe. In my view, the European companies, no less than their American counterparts, needed drastic revisions in their approach to managing for quality. In addition, I could see no difference in the authorship capabilities, American or European.

The present book is by Dr Tito Conti, a European manager whose credentials are impressive. His experience in the field is international in scope, and at the highest levels of organisation. He has produced an authoritative book on how to manage for quality.

Conti undertakes to meet three objectives:

- to offer a guide to the construction of a company quality system;
- to offer a guide for assessing and diagnosing such company quality systems;
- to propose a model and examine the criteria to be used in assessing the situation of a company in relation to its quality mission.

Within the overall concept of TQM (total quality management), Conti focuses on several key subconcepts:

- competition in the ratio of value to cost, as perceived by the user;
- process quality;
- the internal customer/supplier relationship within a company;
- continuous improvement;
- extension of the approach thoughout the company (to Conti, 'total' in TQM really means 'total').

The book meets its objectives brilliantly. It does so through its mastery of the subject matter, its challenge to conventional thinking and its explanations by use of lucid text and models.

An example of a challenge to conventional thinking relates to the topic of 'quality costs'. Conti makes clear the distinction between (a) investments to add value and (b) costs incurred due to failures. In addition, he points out that the costs due to poor quality of **goals** exceed the costs due to poor quality or **execution**. As a result, he exhibits little interest in manipulating the out-dated quality cost categories.

A second example of challenge to conventional thinking relates to the criteria which have emerged as the basis for the ISO 9000 series of standards, plus the various national and international awards, chiefly the Deming, Baldrige and European awards. Conti is well qualified to criticise these – he was one of the architects of the European Award. His analysis of these criteria deserves careful study.

A striking feature of Conti's book is its insistence on clear definition of the key concepts. For example, 'positive quality', which provides added value for customers and which generates income, is distinguished from 'negative quality', which produces customer dissatisfaction and increases costs. Products for sale in the market are distinguished from products for internal use in the company.

Equally striking is the use of models to explain the complex interrelations between the numerous elements which make up total quality management. Conti does not blind the reader with bewildering, complex models. Instead, he mercifully builds up the model, step-by-step, accompanied by step-by-step explanations. Such an approach holds the reader's interest and can be followed easily.

Yet another impressive feature of the book is Conti's determination to advance the state of the art. He is not content to rewrite what others have written. He does his work at the cutting edge. This determination is evidenced by numerous findings and insights.

An important example is seen in the tangled thicket of standards, assessment and certification. Conti classifies assessment into subspecies and examines the respective purposes (and cross-purposes). His examination yields insights and nuances which shed much new light on the subject. Such insights and nuances appear throughout the book. To paraphrase some of these:

- Process quality must be distinguished from product quality. Product quality is a result; process quality is the means to that result.
- Corporate quality goals must be validated by the deployment process.
- Certification to standards wins a hunting licence.
- Europe's preoccupation with certification to standards may divert attention from the need to be competitive.
- Training details usually consist of lessons in the use of tools and methodologies, rather than education about total quality.

Conti's broad focus is on managing for quality. He is clearly well versed in the functions which comprise the organisational structure of our enterprises: technology, human relations, finance and so on. He is equally comfortable at all levels of the hierarchy. However, he focuses on managing for quality. Only occasionally does he get into the tools and techniques which are the main focus of most contemporary books in the field of quality.

Those who undertake to read this book should prepare themselves for an intellectual experience. The book is not designed for surface reading. Neither is it designed as a source of entertainment, or as a form of comic relief from the serious business of managing for quality. This is a high density book, providing fresh thinking, incisive reasoning, lucid explanations and a global outlook. It demands patient study, in digestible amounts, and at a deliberate pace. Those who undertake such study, and who stay the course, will be richly rewarded.

J.M. Juran
Chairman Emeritus
Juran Institute, Inc.

Introduction

At a time when a great many books are being published on
quality, and on total quality in particular, what are the objectives that this book sets out to achieve?

As the title itself suggests, the first objective is to provide a
guide for the managers of companies starting out or already
moving along the road to total quality. General observations
have therefore been kept to a minimum – just one chapter. Their
function is to provide a framework for the points explained in
the following chapters and to ensure a 'conceptual alignment'
with the reader, an essential requirement at this still highly
fluid stage in the development of total quality. Full general,
anthological or historical information has already been provided
by other authors, to whom readers who wish to extend their
knowledge are referred in the bibliography and references.

Since this book is intended chiefly for managers attempting to
create the necessary cultural, behavioural and organisational
conditions for the generation of quality, the issues it considers
are essentially of a managerial nature: organisational models,
planning, process management, results measurement, communications, training, etc. Quality-specific methodologies and techniques are not dealt with here, although reference is made
where necessary, particularly in the bibliography.

Managers come from any number of cultural backgrounds;
and their main concern is rationalisation with a view to application rather than abstract speculation. For this reason, clear
exposition takes precedence when absolute formal rigour im-
pedes understanding. One example is the use of analogical,

1

captioned figures offering a step-by-step description of the development of the model, to ensure correct transmission of the message.

The 'model' is the key concept dealt with in this book. The aim of the second chapter is to construct a model capable of describing the company-market in relation to the **quality mission**, in other words, to the company's ability to generate and continuously to improve the satisfaction of its external and internal customers/users (in the extended sense), while simultaneously keeping costs and development and turnaround times to a minimum. This model is referred to in the subsequent chapters, which examine the organisation, planning and management of the quality mission.

The total quality 'models' adopted to date – by companies, specialists or national quality awards – are inductive constructions, based on the experience of those involved in their definition. The authors of these models have attempted to condense what, in their view, are the 'pillars' of a corporate total quality system into a limited number of 'categories'. Naturally enough, this empirical approach has led to the definition of a great many models, each one different from the next. The approach described here, which appeared in the proposals submitted by the author in December 1990 as a contribution to the definition of the European Quality Award (see Bibliography), is a combination of deductive and inductive elements. Its starting point is an **organisational model** geared to the quality mission, rather than the definition of the 'system pillars' (which would have led to yet another set of pillars, based on the experience and preferences of the author). The 'deductions' drawn from the organisational model are combined with the 'inductions' inferred from experience to give an open, non-prescriptive model of the **company quality system**, which can be adapted to individual needs (of a company, an area of commerce, a market, a national quality award, etc.).

Reference to a model implies a rationalisation and structuralisation of the concepts of total quality management. It means moving from the necessarily turbulent developments of the 1980s into a period of reflection and adjustment. The necessity of this will be obvious to anyone involved in the field. Total quality today is a banner for the most diverse interpretations, from the very latest theories to smartened-up versions of traditional codes, from conformity with the ISO 9000 standards to messianic solutions, a potentially damaging situation for the credibility and value of ideas of enormous potential. But in considering the total quality management model discussed here, the reader should guard against the danger of dogmatic or mechanistic interpretation.

A healthy dose of pragmatism, which regards the model as a 'working hypothesis' – a good attempt at interpreting and describing reality, a schematic approximation rather than a reflection of reality – will help to keep the risk of dogmatic interpretation at bay.

Greater caution must be exercised against the more insidious risk of mechanistic interpretation. It must be clearly understood that the model is a guide for management, not a formula that can be applied mechanically to guarantee a result. There is no formula for excellence. The company is a living organism. Attempts can be made to describe and interpret the anatomy, physiology, psychology, culture and behaviour of excellent companies, but it is not possible to 'clone' them.

Nevertheless, if management is well-informed and determined, it can attempt gradually to lead the living organism, through the necessary and always difficult changes involved, along the road to excellence. Determination cannot be transmitted via a model, but information can. The model is an aid to understanding, which is the first step towards action; it is a tool for clarifying the company's quality missions and for understanding the mechanisms that generate customer satisfaction, the methods of testing satisfaction, the relationship between satisfaction and the company processes, and the ways of managing these processes. Despite its intrinsic ambiguities, the model also helps managers understand and assess the company's situation in relation to those 'invisible characteristics' that play such a decisive part in the company's ability to achieve its quality mission.

This book's first objective, to offer a guide to the construction of a company quality system, incorporates the second: to offer a guide for assessing and diagnosing these systems. This second aim is clearly internal to the first because construction of a quality system is not a task that can be accomplished in a 'planning-implementation' cycle: it is an on-going process, based on constant repetition of the following sequence: assessment of results – diagnosis of causes of variations – new improvement planning/implementation, etc.

Nevertheless, the second objective is also important in its own right: while assessment of the company system may be self-assessment for the purposes of improvement, it can also be an assessment of the company's suppliers (second-party assessment) or a neutral assessment (third-party).

The demand for experts who specialise in the assessment and diagnosis of company quality systems is likely to rise strongly. These specialists will be involved both in company self-assessments and in second- and third-party assessments. While the market offers experts specialised in assessing quality systems in relation to standards (for example, ISO 9000/EN 29000), it does not as yet offer a significant number of specialists capable of assessing and diagnosing company systems in relation to total quality. By proposing a model and examining the criteria to be used in assessing the situation of the company in relation to its quality mission, this book can contribute to the development of the new skills required by total quality system assessors.

As far as external assessments are concerned, those conducted for the assignment of national or international quality awards will be the focus of increasing attention in the future. The growing interest in the Malcolm Baldrige Award in the United States confirms this: although the number of companies competing for the award is limited, very large and increasing numbers of companies wish independently to assess themselves using the Baldrige Award criteria.

This leads to the third aim of this book: to offer critical and constructive observations for a rationalisation of these criteria, so that the guiding role played by the awards in extending companies' knowledge and experience of total quality can be strengthened. This is an area that may seem restricted to a limited audience. But in terms of culture and information, it will be of undoubted interest to the vast numbers of managers and specialists who, sooner or later, will come into contact with quality awards: the European Quality Award, introduced in 1992, will hopefully exert an influence on European companies.

The contents of this book are based on lengthy experience, accumulated both directly, in the fertile environment of the large company of which for eight years I was Vice President for Quality, and indirectly, through constant contacts with many European, Japanese and US colleagues who, like me, are trying to give shape to the idea of total quality. Not everyone will agree with my conclusions, but I believe that a critical experience-based review of quality concepts – particularly those that have become commonplace – can provide useful pointers for many colleagues working in this field. And the need for a critical spirit, for a concrete approach and for a systematic comparison with other people's experience has never been so great.

Quality today | 1 |

1.1 TOTAL QUALITY

If **total quality** were an unequivocal, clearly defined concept today, this book could begin working towards its goal of providing a guide to the construction and assessment of a corporate **total quality system** right from the very first page. But this is not the case. A glance at the programmes of countless total quality conferences and round tables all over Europe shows that the term covers a variety of concepts; some are similar but not identical, while others may be quite divergent. So even a book that does not intend to examine general concepts or to compare the different schools of thought needs to start with a few brief remarks to ensure a conceptual alignment with the reader. In this way, room is left open for discussion of the legitimate differences that distinguish the current stage in the development of quality, but the author's position as regards total quality will be clear.

1.1.1 A succinct expression embracing a series of concepts

The full conceptual significance of the modern view of quality cannot be conveyed by such a succinct expression as 'total quality'. Moreover, the adjective 'total' is so broad that inevitably it becomes ambiguous: any plausible interpretation could be included (even that of absolute quality, free of defects). Conventionally, 'total' is used to indicate company-wide application, and terms like **total quality management** or, better still,

company-wide quality management (**company-wide quality control** in Japan) certainly convey more successfully the basic message of a quality system embracing the entire company and everyone within the company. But even these definitions reflect only one aspect – albeit an important one – of the modern view of quality. In fact, quality can be seen from two perspectives: the perspective of the market (primary) and the perspective of the company (derivative).

The underlying concept of the **market perspective** is that quality is a strategic competitive factor: customer satisfaction and value for money for the user with utilisation of the minimum resources (costs and time) are the areas in which companies compete. **Competitive quality** could therefore be the most appropriate definition of this view of quality.

Approaching quality from the **company perspective**, on the other hand, means defining a managerial strategy and a corporate culture capable of sustaining competition in quality and through quality. In other words, it means identifying the main elements of the quality approach the company has to adopt to meet the competitive challenge. Spreading the quality culture and quality practices throughout the company is certainly one of these elements, but it is not the only one: as will be seen, other elements are equally important.

Of course, it is difficult to condense a series of elements and concepts into a brief and necessarily conventional definition. Consequently, a choice must be made: either the market perspective, with its very general, results-oriented definition of competitive quality, which fails to qualify the approach; or the company perspective, with a definition that defines the approach but conveys only a part of the conceptual content and is open to ambiguity.

So that is the situation; 'total quality' is accepted usage and we may as well learn to live with it, taking care not to extend the ambiguity of the expression to its conceptual contents. In particular, the fundamental concept of competitive quality should never be forgotten. Otherwise, total quality runs the risk of being regarded as quality related to standards (for example, the ISO 9000 standards), overlooking the fact that compliance with

8

a standard is, if anything, a requirement to be met in order to enter the competitive arena, not a competitive differential.

The main concepts within the overall concept of total quality are:

1. competition at the level of the value/cost ratio perceived by the user;
2. focus on process quality;
3. the supplier/customer relationship within the company;
4. continuous improvement as a strategy; and
5. extension of the approach to every corporate sector, level and process.

All of these concepts are familiar; often they are not fully understood, or are trivialised or sometimes even (in the case of the fifth) provoke a rejection crisis among management. It is worth examining them one by one.

(a) Competition at the level of the value/cost ratio perceived by the user

The user of a product or service tends to assess his experience and the alternatives available on the market in terms of value for money, that is, in terms of the ratio

perceived global value/global costs

where global costs can often be calculated with a fair degree of accuracy (they include purchase price or depreciation rates, leasing, running costs, defect-related costs); value, on the other hand, is the sum of a series of global perceptions.

The main **value perception** is usually the degree to which (product + service) corresponds to the user's expectations. It is worth noting that, even when the primary object of the transaction is a product, the related service can alter significantly the user's perception of that product, for better or worse. In the age of competition on quality, an awareness of the importance of service in boosting value perceived by the user is critical to success. Companies should also be aware of the influence of corporate image on perceived value, when the user is making his

9

choice of product or service (image is a multiplying factor of the numerator of the (perceived value/global costs) ratio, which is lesser or greater than 1).

Investment in image (based on a solid foundation of quality) is worthwhile, because the notably delayed effect of the image variable can help to minimise damage from the upsets that inevitably occur (accidental quality problems with products/services).

Today, defectiveness, non-conformity or, more generally, any negative variation between product or service performance and the user's expectations is termed **negative quality**. **Positive quality** ✦ is any positive variance with expectations. Positive quality is therefore any area in which the product or service surpasses the user's expectations or competitors' offers; it is a **plus** value.

Competition in quality today aims to minimise negative quality, ideally to reduce it to zero; and to maximise positive quality, the value perceived by the user. Negative quality has a finite limit, a **zero defect rate** (although this is an apparent limit, which moves over time as customers' expectations rise). But there are no ceilings for positive quality. A product or service 'plus' can always be added to a particular range of basic capabilities and prices, to increase the value for the user, in terms of fitness for use or other areas that raise satisfaction (Fig. 1.1).

The figure suggests that the real area for competition in quality today is positive quality, and that negative quality consequently has a secondary role. In some ways, this is true: for certain types of product (though certainly not for services!), the market is becoming accustomed to increasingly low defect rates and therefore demands an 'almost zero' defect rate as a condition for entry. For companies already capable of competing at the level of negative defectiveness, that is, companies 'structurally' capable of keeping defect rates at the minimum sectorial levels, the competitive arena is positive quality.

Nevertheless, an offer of 'pluses' does not offset high defectiveness rates (high as compared with competitors' rates). For the user, defectiveness means expense and inconvenience. Users are pleased with 'pluses', but far more vociferous in their complaints about non-quality. So before a company can set out to compete in the quality arena, first of all it must 'get the

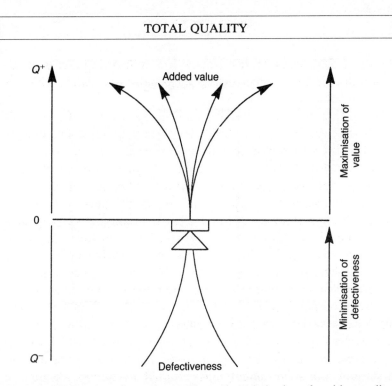

Fig. 1.1 Minimisation of negative quality and maximisation of positive quality.

house straight', making use of any tools that help reduce defectiveness; with the dual advantage of reducing costs and improving
customer satisfaction. From here, once the first hurdle of a
structural reduction in negative quality has been overcome, the
company will move into the vast competitive arena of positive
quality. In reality, other hurdles lie beyond the first. The zero
line of Fig. 1.1 gradually rises as 'pluses' turn into user expectations. This applies in particular to services, but also to manufactured goods (defect rates that were once considered acceptable
later become serious in the user's perception).

The primary concern of companies competing at the level of
positive quality is **quality of goals**, the maximisation of the value
of the offer as perceived by the user. Figure 1.2 illustrates the
concept: competition on quality is based on two pillars – quality
of goals and **quality of execution** – where the second pillar
represents the conventional dimension of quality: do things right

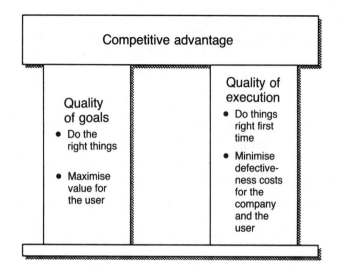

Fig. 1.2 The two pillars of competitive quality.

first time, minimise defectiveness and the costs of non-quality. The first pillar represents the new dimension, which sees quality as a competitive variable: do the right things; do what the market expects, consciously or not; maximise user value.

This raises a question that will be examined in depth in the section on process quality. It is true that the left-hand pillar is the more important in a market where players compete on quality; but the right-hand pillar is important because competition is also a question of costs. Quality of execution means better process quality and therefore lower costs and shorter execution time. The relative importance of the two pillars may of course vary, depending on the type of company and market. For companies that supply specific products to specific customers on a contractual basis, goals are established and quality is therefore essentially quality of execution. Generally speaking, however, both pillars are important as regards market competitiveness, one in relation to value and the other in relation to costs (for the company as well as the user).

A final observation about competition at the level of quality. The market tends to alternate between phases in which either demand or supply prevails: a **supplier's market** in the first case, a **consumer's market** (or a buyer's market) in the second. Sceptics tend to attribute today's 'consecration' of quality to the current extended buyer's market phase; it is a passing phase, they say, which will change when demand once again outstrips supply, as in the 1960s and 1970s, when in many market sectors consumers had no choice but to take what was offered and accept any negative quality.

A return to this situation is unlikely, unless some unforeseen upheaval occurs, for a number of reasons:

- In today's more advanced markets (whose size and number are growing), consumers have a greater say and occupy an increasingly high position in the **need pyramid** (where the quality of products and services is considered a pre-requisite for the quality of life). **The need for quality is tending to become a structural market factor**.
- When Japanese suppliers abandoned the tacit understanding (based on the view that quality comes at a cost) that 'if the customer wants higher quality, he must pay for it' (where quality, far from being higher value in relation to expectations, was simply lower defectiveness) and began to offer higher quality than that required by **de facto** market standards, at equal or lower prices, it became clear to companies capable of grasping the message that 'quality pays'. **It pays in terms of long-term market shares**, because when the customer has the upper hand, he tends to remember previous grievances and to choose the supplier with a consistent quality image; **it pays in terms of lower costs**.

In short, quality as a **strategic competitive variable** is the distinguishing concept of the new approach to quality, in terms of market results and customer satisfaction. The other concepts are a consequence of the first, they represent 'the means to the end', the characteristics the company has to assume to become more competitive in quality. Of course, these are not characteristics that can be acquired through a one-off reorganisation; a lengthy and costly process of change is necessary. They are related to the company's culture and its values – the most difficult characteristics to change – and require a wide-ranging long-term strategic vision.

(b) Focus on process quality

With the growing awareness that the quality of results (product or service quality and customer satisfaction) is determined by the quality of all contributing processes (section 1.4), it has gradually become clear that high-quality processes not only generate high-quality products and services, and therefore customer satisfaction, they also enable companies to minimise costs and execution time, thus also generating the satisfaction of the supplier.

It is incorrect to talk about quality without differentiating between products and processes; it is extremely restrictive to equate **process quality** with **product quality**. Process quality is more than product quality (Fig. 1.3): process quality is the **means**, product quality is **one of the results (effectiveness)**; the others are improved **efficiency** (minimum costs and execution time) and greater **elasticity** (ability to adjust rapidly to change). Figure 1.4 illustrates the relationship between process quality and results quality in terms of effectiveness, efficiency and elasticity (the '3 Es' of processes, Conti (1988)).

It is worth inventing a mnemonic acronym to remember the triple **Time-Quality-Costs** valency of process quality. Better still,

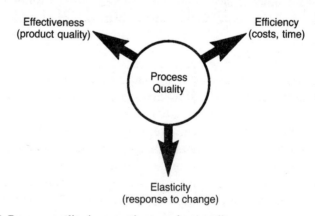

Fig. 1.3 Process quality is more than product quality.

14

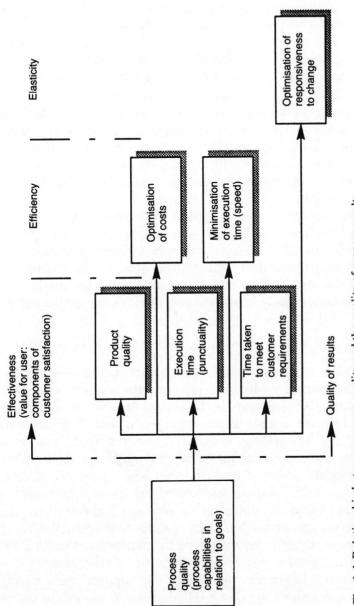

Fig. 1.4 Relationship between process quality and the quality of process results.

the TQC acronym (which some people, particularly the Japanese, use to indicate total quality management) can be adopted.

People who tend to discount references to the Japanese and Japanese quality should consider the way in which the Japanese have analysed and exploited the different valencies of process quality: first and most obvious, as the chief means of obtaining sharp reductions in product defect rates; then as a way to cut costs, to minimise execution time and working capital; and, today, to reduce time-to-market. These results are different, but they have a common root: process quality, a shift in management focus from results to the means by which results are obtained, from target-oriented management to ends-and-means management.

The concept of **quality applied to processes** follows hierarchically from the concept of competitive quality in the list of the concepts of total quality: not only because it constitutes the chief means of creating competitive quality, but also because it links the first fundamental goal – quality for the market – with the second, equally important goal of efficiency for the company.

(c) The supplier-customer relationship inside the company

The idea of using the supplier-customer relationship as a model for the company's internal relationships was introduced by K. Ishikawa (1985). Naturally this is a **sui generis** relationship, since the customer cannot usually change supplier. The necessity of satisfying the customer is therefore dictated not by market laws, but by the realisation that a supplier-customer relationship (in the modern sense of a partnership which provides advantages for both sides, not the old conflictual, fiscal relationship) can enhance value and minimise the company's global costs. Clearly this type of partnership does not develop spontaneously in a company, it has to be supported by management and the assessment/recognition systems implemented by management.

In this relationship, the goal of the 'supplier' must be similar to that described in point 1 on competitive quality: to maximise value for the 'customer' and simultaneously minimise costs. But since in this case both the costs of the supplier process and the costs of the customer process are costs for the company, it is the 'value for the user/global costs' ratio that has to be maximised.

The supplier-customer combination is particularly valuable when it is associated with the view of the company as a series of processes. The process chains are seen as supplier-customer chains and the supplier process must provide the user process with the expected value; all the processes in the chain must work together to minimise global costs. Applied to processes, the supplier-customer relationship is a **horizontal** partnership, because it tends to be between 'equals' (section 1.4 and Fig. 1.14). It is one of the fundamental concepts of total quality because, if correctly applied, it helps create process chains that generate maximum value on the market (not just for the internal customer) at the minimum cost to the company.

The supplier-customer approach also functions **vertically**, through the hierarchical manager-staff chains. The manager acts as a supplier for the legitimate expectations of his staff: supplying clear goals and the means to achieve them; providing support, training, praise for results and so on. The staff members supply the manager with results, transparency, exhaustive information, respect for his role and so on.

(d) Continuous improvement as a strategy

Continuous improvement was the first key total quality concept to emerge, at the beginning of the 1950s, thanks to the work of J.M. Juran (1954). This concept is so central that many regard the term 'total quality' as incomplete because it lacks a reference to continuous improvement, and prefer to use the expression **total quality improvement** instead.

Continuous improvement is the basic tool for competitive quality, for the **gradual** elimination of defects (negative qualities) from products or services and the introduction of 'pluses' that enhance value as perceived by the user. It translates the primary concept of competitive quality into terms of corporate strategy. When applied **systematically to processes**, continuous improvement also helps the company gradually to identify and eliminate costs with no corresponding value for users, to reduce transit times and inventories, improve customer support services (speed, response times) and accelerate capital turnover.

J.M. Juran, the master of **continuous quality improvement**, maintains that the following conditions are necessary to achieve useful improvement:

1. It must be planned.
2. It must be achieved **project by project**.
3. The breakthrough phase, which modifies previous balances, must be followed by a 'holding-the-gains' phase, when new standards are established to consolidate the improvement and prevent regression.

Many companies embraced the idea of continuous improvement in the 1980s, but rarely applied the conditions for success correctly and fully. In particular, a failure to meet the third condition and standardise the new level meant that the benefits of immediate improvements were not maintained.

Continuous improvement is like a down staircase: each down-step in defectiveness (the 'breakthrough' or structural change in processes) is followed by a horizontal phase of stabilisation (standardisation of the new process and the new balance).

Figure 1.5 illustrates this concept. The Deming PDCA (**Plan-Do-Check-Act**) wheel represents the improvement process and the SDCA (**Standardise-Do-Check-Act**) wheel represents the standardisation process.

An even more frequent shortcoming among companies that claim to have adopted continuous improvement is related to planning. Even though these companies draw up annual improvement plans, they often adopt a bottom-up approach, where the company plan is a consolidation of the individual plans drawn up by managers for their own sectors. This makes it difficult to link the company's macro-goals on the market (competitive quality) with the sectorial goals of the individual plans. These macro-goals – the most important improvements needed in the company – generally lead to **interfunctional processes**, which are a step above the sectorial plans created through bottom-up processes and therefore cannot be included within them.

It is impossible to compete in quality without a **strategic**

18

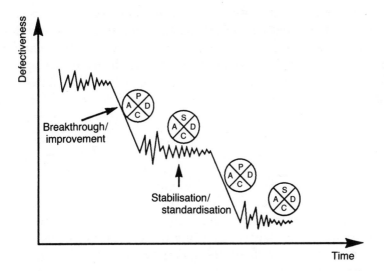

Fig. 1.5 The continuous improvement staircase.

approach to improvement and this requires strategic planning at the very highest level to launch a top-down process (an interactive top-down process, like the vertical policy/goal deployment processes described in Chapter 3), which extends to both interfunctional and sectorial operating improvement plans. Strategic improvement planning is one of the main themes of this book and is dealt with in depth in Chapter 3, which is based on original and innovative experiments in this field.

A clarification is perhaps needed at this point: only an extension of the improvement concept can justify the strategic dimension discussed here. Initially, the concept of 'improvement' suggested the idea of aiming at a definite limit, the limit of perfection or zero defectiveness. But in the modern context of positive quality, this would be restrictive. Today's target is a moving target, and improvement therefore also means continuous realignment in relation to this target; in other words, continuous improvement **in goals** and consequently in performance.

How can top-down planning be reconciled with the Juranian idea of incremental project-by-project continuous improvement? This question is examined in Chapter 3, too, and in Chapter

19

4, which deals with process management. A brief answer is provided here, with a preliminary observation. The top-down process must be highly interactive. All the ideas of the company's employees regarding the current situation of processes and the possibility of improvement must be allowed to flow up to meet the macro-improvement goals coming down from the top. Interaction becomes effective when the improvement goals cross over with the company processes: this occurs in the planning and deployment phase (Chapter 3). But it is during the operating phase that incremental, continuous improvement can be achieved, project by project, as long as the company sectors involved in the functional and interfunctional annual improvement plans truly embrace the idea of continuous improvement and organise themselves accordingly. Permanent interfunctional process management teams (Chapter 4) and formally constituted (not voluntary) improvement groups must be operational. Given the macro-goals of the improvement plans and growing experience in process management, incremental continuous improvement can be achieved through identification of opportunities, microplanning and execution of individual initiatives (PDCA cycles). Figure 1.6 illustrates the links between the macro-

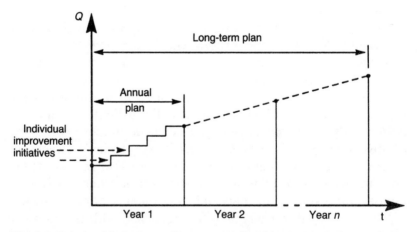

Fig. 1.6 Relationship between the macro-goals of long-term and annual plans and the micro-goals of individual improvement initiatives.

goals of the company's plans and the micro-goals of individual improvement initiatives.

(e) Extension of the approach to every corporate sector, level and process

This is the concept that led to the definition 'total quality'. Introduced for the first time by Feigenbaum in 1956 with the name **Total Quality Control** (TQC), though within a heavily Western (hierarchical-functional) context (Feigenbaum, 1956, 1961), the concept was later embraced by the Japanese, who adopted a more interfunctional approach with distribution of responsibilities (although the Japanese still prefer the definition **Total Quality Control**, they have coined the much more meaningful **Company-Wide Quality Control**).

Attentive observers of quality developments generally agree that of all total quality concepts, extension to the entire company and to everyone in the company is the most difficult for Western managers to accept and often causes a rejection of total quality.

The concept of competitive quality is accepted, though sometimes only in the form of lip service, in anticipation of a return to a supplier's market.

The concept of quality applied to processes is convincing as far as processes that create and distribute products or services are concerned, less so for other processes. Great enthusiasm is expressed for the supplier-customer approach, although acceptance still tends to be theoretical rather than practical. The concept of continuous improvement is accepted, too, even though insufficient direct involvement of senior management – and the consequent absence of strategic planning – often creates a body without a head. In short, the first four concepts are often poorly understood or poorly translated into company practice, but they are not rejected.

The idea of extending the new quality approach to all levels and to all company sectors and processes, even to those that do not generate products or services for the market, is often regarded as an exaggeration, an extreme result of the current 'obsession' with quality, a loss of contact with reality.

The irony is that the new quality approach takes its name from this fifth and most difficult concept, extension to the entire company; with the curious result that when senior managers find themselves having to pay the now obligatory tribute to the new quality approach, even the most unconvinced are forced to use a terminology based on what is the most controversial issue of all.

In practical terms, extension to the entire company means many things, all of which require considerable management effort and considerable disruption to traditional organisations. First of all, it means **horizontal extension** to all corporate functions. This is where the arguments begin: 'What's quality got to do with us?' 'What have we got to do with administration or with personnel?' (Hopefully, these questions won't be asked by sales process managers; if they are, an analysis of surveys of customers' perception of quality should provide a sufficient answer.)

If anything, the theoretical answer to these questions is too easy. Staff functions do not generate products or services for the market, but they do generate products or services for the company, the quality of which is sometimes crucial to the stream of market-oriented processes. (Management information systems are a case in point!)

Without doubt, viewing 'products and services for the company' in terms of fitness for use, of value to the customer, is rational and beneficial. Just as it is rational to manage the processes that generate these products or services to ensure the greatest effectiveness, efficiency and elasticity. And if the supplier-customer approach can benefit market-oriented processes, there is no reason to suppose it would not be equally beneficial for support processes.

The theoretical answer can be backed up by examples of practical experience, such as that described by J.C. Abegglen and G. Stalk, Jr in **Kaisha. The Japanese Corporation**, which gives the results of a comparative productivity analysis between a Japanese and a US automobile manufacturer. The productivity of the first in relation to the second was higher by a factor of

2.5, but this arose from a 1.5 factor in direct personnel and a factor of 6 in indirect personnel (Abegglen and Stalk, 1985).

This result applies not just to production, but to every company sector. Company inefficiencies, historical stratifications caused by an inability to deal with problems at their source, parochialism, multiple controls and red tape mean staff functions grow much more rapidly than line organisations. A process-oriented quality approach, which begins with 'value' for the user and monitors the growth of costs in relation to the growth of value throughout the chain of processes, will reduce and even eliminate areas of corporate inefficiency, especially at staff levels. Generally, however, neither theoretical arguments nor practical experience can overcome objections to the horizontal extension of quality. In fact it is best not to insist, because rejection may lead to lengthy delays in the move towards total quality.

In these cases, the best approach is to focus on the functions and processes involved in the generation/distribution/sale/post-sales support of the company's products or services. This limits extension, but covers the fundamental areas as far as customer satisfaction is concerned. Within these limits, however, determined efforts must be made to establish the first four concepts within the company. If even this cannot be achieved (or it is impossible to involve all the functions that contribute towards external customer satisfaction, beginning with commercial functions), then the company may as well abandon total quality, because management evidently fails to appreciate the importance of the first concept, competition on quality.

If the first four concepts are accepted, then it is likely that the direct commitment of a significant proportion of the company's managers (and its office and factory staff, although they do not constitute the main problem) will assist the creation of a new culture and practices that will gradually spread to the rest of the company.

The critical points of horizontal extensions have been examined at length and prudent suggestions for removing obstacles have been offered. Vertical extension – up to the apex of the company pyramid and then down to the base – is even more critical.

But it does not require lengthy discussion, because there is no room for exceptions or compromises in this area.

Whereas horizontal extension can be implemented gradually, vertical extension is an on-off concept: either the company's top officers lead the changeover towards competitive quality or the company forgets about total quality. Concepts 1 to 4 (and horizontal extension) will not be able to take root unless the changes in organisation and attitude that only top management can initiate are implemented, with the support of middle managers. The direct, personal involvement of senior management (the chief executive officer and his first line) is a *conditio sine qua non*. It is essential, but not in itself sufficient.

Difficult changes must be made if total quality is to take root: management styles, attitudes, organisation structures and value scales must all be reviewed. It is vital that all managers, particularly at the second level, support or even champion the change. Top management must combine determination with a search for the best ways to assist the changeover and avoid or overcome the inevitable pockets of resistance.

Finally, company-wide quality means **integration**, at both horizontal and vertical levels. Extending quality to all company sectors is not enough if these sectors fail to integrate with one another in interfunctional processes; involvement of all levels is not enough if these levels are not linked with one another through communication channels and operating methods that encourage effective decision-making and rapid, effective policy/ goal deployment.

1.1.2 How the company's approach to total quality can change as product/market characteristics change

The characteristic elements of a competitive approach to quality, in jargon 'total quality', apply in full to companies that produce goods or services for the market (that is, for an open group of users not known individually beforehand), in accordance with the rules of free competition. For this type of company, a **reactive** approach (dictated by problems, by customer complaints, by what the market no longer tolerates) is counter-productive today. A long-term market presence can only be achieved through a **proactive** approach (aimed not only at preventing problems, but at meeting customers' requirements in general), through dynamic quality focused on continuous improvement, with the **primary mover** of improvement located at the top of the company.

Other companies produce goods or services for specific customers on a contractual basis. Until now, standards have been the guideline for these companies. How can they apply the concepts of total quality?

For these companies, competitiveness is related above all to execution. The immediate temptation is to say that in Fig. 1.2 the left-hand pillar disappears: goals are those required by or agreed with the customer; quality is conformity with those goals. In practice, the supplier can take a more active part in working with the customer to define goals, differentiating himself from competitors with proposals aimed at improving the product or service's fitness for use and the efficiency of the customer's processes. This type of differentiation is often useful and appreciated as regards the service supplied with a product (delivery schedules and methods, application support, data and information on supplier processes, and so on).

Nevertheless, while goal-related opportunities should be exploited to the full, the 'quality of execution' pillar is the main focus for this type of company, and the left-hand pillar is of secondary importance. Elimination of defectiveness in products and services is the principal area of competition for these companies.

With this qualification regarding competitive quality, all the other concepts described previously also apply to companies working on a contractual basis.

Total quality is a challenge for this type of company, whose quality culture is based on standards (section 1.2): in fact, the key concepts of continuous improvement and an internal **supplier-customer** model are a consequence of a competitive quality approach rather than of a standards-based approach.

A third category of companies operates in a monopoly regime or in a heavily protected environment. These companies lack the fundamental spur of competition on quality. Uncorrected, the aberrations this can cause lead to **Total Non-Quality**. Examples include many public-sector service providers, which seem never to have heard of (or to have forgotten) the concept of customer satisfaction. In these companies, services are often supplied to suit the interests of the supplier rather than satisfy the expectations of the users (industry associations of individual private business enterprises sometimes adopt a similar approach).

As long as these companies operate in a protected environment, sheltered from the challenge of competition, they are unlikely to make any progress as regards either total quality, or quality in general. But if public opinion were strong enough to force the political sector to act, it would provide an incentive similar to that operating in the open market: the risk of losing a vote can in some ways be compared with the danger of losing a customer.

In the highly theoretical hypothesis of public opinion acting as a competitive stimulus, the managers of public-sector companies would have to adopt customer satisfaction as their main criterion, and the regular assessment of satisfaction as their basic quality indicator. Then all observations concerning total quality could be applied to the State sector, too, with enormous benefits for the public, in terms of costs as well as service quality.

Other special cases include companies that manufacture goods in accordance with pre-defined specifications (raw materials or chemical products) or those that manufacture mature products in which the full potential for product improvement has already been realised. For both categories, as for companies operating on a contractual basis, the 'quality of execution' pillar is predominant. The main objective is to reduce defectiveness for the customer and costs for the supplier by improving process quality. But in both cases, in particular for companies that manufacture mature products, the possibility that a careful analysis of user requirement trends and a search for competitive pluses will reveal new opportunities as regards goals, too, cannot be ruled out.

This book, especially the chapters dealing with the development of a model and its application in the construction and assessment of total quality systems, refers to the general case of companies that produce products or services for the market in a competitive environment. For these companies, the concepts of total quality, in particular the fundamental concept of competitive quality, apply in full. Nevertheless, as seen above, with the necessary modifications – most notably the weighting of the 'quality of execution' pillar in relation to that of the 'quality of goals' pillar – the concepts remain valid for other categories of company. So subsequent developments will be valid, too, allowing for the necessary adjustments, such as variations in the relative weights of the various components in the system.

1.2 STANDARDS-BASED QUALITY

Standards are usually intended to safeguard the interests of users: consumers, industrial users, the community. Quality standards first developed in the military field as a means of guaranteeing the quality of supplies, and were soon adopted in the space, nuclear and energy industries and in the area of large-scale procurements. As the US Military Standards (MIL) became more familiar, they, or conceptually similar standards catering for specific requirements, spread rapidly to a growing number of sectors in the vast area of contractual purchase transactions, in particular Original Equipment Manufacturer (OEM) supply agreements.

Standards were regarded as means of ensuring the quality of the goods acquired. Quality standards were originally concerned with the object of the purchase transaction, the **product**. They covered particular requirements (safety, disturbance of the environment, resistance to environmental forces, etc.), defectiveness on delivery (AQL) or during use (reliability) and methods of measurement.

A growing awareness that the source of quality lay in processes led to the gradual extension of standards from the product to production processes, and from there to all processes involved in the creation and support of the product. The principle is: **assess the company's entire product quality management and assurance system to obtain the maximum guarantee of the quality of supplies**.

27

1.2.1 Quality as perceived by the purchaser and by the supplier

Given their origin, the standards-based quality culture and approach are inevitably geared to the viewpoint of the purchaser. Equally inevitably, the supplier tends to adopt a reactive attitude, supplying what is required and nothing more, and simply 'passing the test' as regards assessment of his quality assurance system by the customer or a third party. The supplier's main concern is to meet his targets, there will be time for continuous improvement later (these are extreme cases, used to highlight the type of attitude induced by standards; exceptions obviously exist, particularly now that this attitude has been countered by a competitive view of quality).

In some ways, the development of the standards used for quality systems, for example ISO 9000/EN 29000, is certainly a step towards total quality (and forthcoming developments will move even further in this direction): their systemic perspective and responsibility attribution model confirm this. So does the incorporation in the standards system of a 'guide' to the construction of the quality system (ISO 9004), which approaches quality from the viewpoint of the supplier and is not linked to a contractual type of relationship. But although quality system standards play a fundamental role in relation to contractual relationships, in eliminating technical obstacles to international trade and in spreading a basic quality culture, they cannot nor should they claim to embrace the competitive aspects of quality.

The translation of the basic concepts of total quality into corporate culture and attitudes involves, in fact, company characteristics that, for the most part, are intangible and therefore cannot be assessed in objective terms. A reference model can be constructed (and this is the purpose of this book), but the model cannot be frozen into a standard, nor can its implementation be monitored with checklists to give the assessor a sufficient degree of confidence about the company's capabilities in terms of results.

Total quality, moreover, is dynamic, while a standard, by definition, is static, even though it may be part of a sequence of steps designed to keep pace with a constantly changing scenario (Fig. 1.7). The belief held by many people today that total

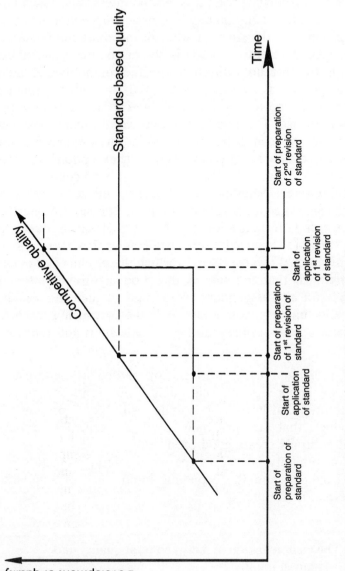

Fig. 1.7 Development of quality and development of standards.

quality and standards-based quality can be combined into a single vision is unworkable; it is also pointless, since each has its own role to play. Total quality is a proactive view of quality, the view adopted by the supplier who, in the continuous search for competitive differentials, regards standards, or any established result, as the threshold for entry into the competitive arena: but real competition is open, it has no fixed points of reference and is based solely on the supplier's ability continuously to improve his performance. The standards-based view of quality has developed from the conventional viewpoint of the purchaser and cannot be entirely separated from its origins – and this is just as well.

The ISO 9000 development guidelines laid down by the ISO TC 176 committee for the 1990s (Marquardt *et al.*, 1991) provide, correctly, for diversifications at the level of the product (hardware, software, materials, service). This approach is concerned with the purchase transaction, of which the product is the object. An approach that focuses on the product – and to that end provides for the assessment of the system that creates, distributes and supports that product – is the correct approach for a standard, whose primary aim is to safeguard the interests of users:

- the individual user, who is not particularly interested in the supplier's view of total quality, but wants the maximum guarantee that he will be supplied with 'good' products (and products that are 'originally good', generated by processes that naturally create good products);
- the community, as regards personal safety, protection of the environment and the economic importance of standards in international trade.

1.2.2 The complementarity between total quality and standards-based quality

Instead of trying to blend the two approaches to quality into an unlikely combination (apart from anything else, this would only undermine standards, which need a certain period of stability

30

to realise their full potential and therefore cannot match the rapid conceptual development of total quality), it is better to emphasise their complementarity, optimising each approach in relation to its specific objectives and guaranteeing consistency between the two. Total quality – or competitive quality – is important because it is closely linked with the principles of competitiveness and the free market. Once quality has been identified as a competitive factor (at the double level of quality of goals and quality of execution), corporate creativity has no limit, it cannot be regulated or even guided by standards.

Standards, as has been seen, play a fundamental role. They mark the consolidated stages of competitive development for the benefit of the individual or community user. They represent platforms (the steps in Fig. 1.7) on which suppliers with no contractual obligations can freely build, and on which suppliers with contractual obligations can build in partnership with their customers. In both cases, the platform is a basic level that can be required of any supplier who enters the competitive arena, particularly the international marketplace, or of suppliers of companies competing on international marketplaces. But the fundamental role of standards, today, is also related to the fact that our industrial culture – at least in the West – is still predominantly reactive as far as quality is concerned. The maximum attention must be given to total quality as the direction in which we should be moving – and fast – but it would be wrong to act as though total quality were already a reality, as if all suppliers today adopted a proactive approach.

The international ISO 9000 standards therefore play a strategically important role today: for users, they guarantee that the supplier conforms to fundamental product quality assurance requirements; for suppliers, they provide a univocal point of reference (as long as a proliferation of variations is avoided: some may be justified by the inadequacy of standards, but others are based on the mistaken assumption that they are following the moving target of total quality).

Standards are strategically important also as a vehicle for spreading a quality culture and basic quality tools to the myriad small/medium-sized businesses that form the backbone of many

31

economic systems. Many of these companies know how to generate quality, but do not possess the cultural tools to optimise quality and costs simultaneously, to communicate on equal terms with their customers or to approach international marketplaces.

Standards also play a strategic role in helping to eliminate the technical barriers that impede the free circulation of goods on international markets.

1.2.3 The horizontal and vertical dimensions of quality

The emphasis on the role of standards in a book on total quality is necessary to avoid misunderstandings: the risk always exists that a deliberate focus on a particular aspect will be interpreted as a de-emphasis of other aspects. It also prevents misinterpretation of two expressions introduced in this section – the **horizontal dimension** and the **vertical dimension** of quality – which refer respectively to standards and to total quality.

In Fig. 1.8, standards are placed on the horizontal planes, with each plane corresponding to a step in Fig. 1.7. Standards are considered as a horizontal dimension because:

- they are basic platforms;
- they remain constant until they are replaced by new standards;
- conformity with standards is a prerequisite for competition, not a competitive differential. Standards are the basis on which competitive 'pluses' are built.

Standards are intended for the widest possible diffusion, preferably without variations, across all product/market sectors and all countries.

Total quality is considered as a vertical dimension because:

- it is a competitive dimension with no limits;
- it has no reference specifications or levels;
- the 'state of the art' evolves continually.

Some people insist that standards give a competitive advantage. For a company at a lower level, reaching the standard level is clearly a significant step forward; but since the standard is clearly defined and within the reach of the average company –

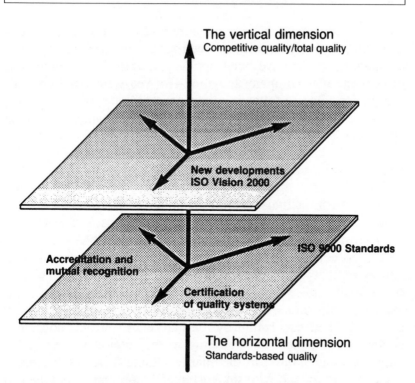

The vertical dimension
Competitive quality/total quality

New developments
ISO Vision 2000

Accreditation and
mutual recognition

ISO 9000 Standards

Certification
of quality systems

The horizontal dimension
Standards-based quality

Fig. 1.8 The horizontal and vertical dimensions of quality.

as it should be – it is more appropriate to regard standards-conformity – and certification in particular – as a 'preliminary qualification' for entering the real quality competition.

This is the situation for individual companies. In the case of an economic system, bringing the majority of small/medium businesses to a standard level could constitute a significant competitive advantage: not only would it remove restrictions as far as exports are concerned, it would help spread a basic quality culture through the business community. This is a major opportunity for Europe today. It should be clear, however, that for the individual company the real competitive advantages over the medium/long term can only come through competitive differentiation, in other words, through the vertical dimension of quality. Unless companies move beyond standards and adopt a proactive approach aimed at achieving maximum value for users, they will be unable to compete with or even act as suppliers to Japanese companies, which have been applying *Keizen* – continuous improvement of all company activities – for years, or to the Western companies who are following their example.

The vertical dimension is best suited to companies producing goods and services for a market of potential users who are not individually known beforehand, but whose individual requirements must be satisfied if they are to be won over.

The horizontal dimension is best suited to companies that work on a contractual 'customer/supplier' basis, where the main problem is to meet specifications and standards to ensure conformity with the user's requirements.

It is no coincidence that Japan and the West have diverging views of quality. As Professor Kume (1990) notes, Japan's main concern after the Second World War was to export, above all to export large volumes of goods whose level of quality would guarantee their absorption by the market. Electronic consumer goods, automobiles and cameras were manufactured not for large customers but for the market. Quality levels therefore could not be agreed with the customer beforehand, they had to be the best possible – and improve all the time. This fostered the growth of a proactive view of quality. The quality culture that evolved in the West, on the other hand, was fostered chiefly by the MIL specifications and the subsequent proliferation of standards. The view that quality means conformity with standards is still widespread, and certainly hinders the diffusion of a competitive quality culture.

1.2.4 The ISO 9000 standards

The real importance of the ISO 9000 standards (EN 29000 in Europe) is that they have produced a situation of international harmonisation, which hopefully will be maintained despite the current shortcomings. Previously, enormous differences existed between one country and another, one market sector or one company and another, with significant costs both for customers and suppliers.

The contents of the ISO 9000 standards reflect their age: although they were established as such in 1987, they are largely based on the British Standards Institute's BS 5750 standard, which dates from 1979.

The ISO 9000 standards are subdivided into criteria for corporate quality management and corporate quality systems (ISO 9004), and criteria for **external quality assurance** (ISO 9001/2/3). This second group is the basis for certification, while ISO 9004 is a guide to help suppliers build a company system in line with ISO 9000 requirements – which, incidentally, do not prescribe any implementation methodologies – and achieve certification.

The ISO TC 176 committee is hard at work on a new edition that will update the standards and prevent any new diversifications which would weaken their chief goal of universality. In particular, given that product quality assurance is the purpose of these standards, the plan to subdivide products into four categories – hardware, software, materials, services – seems a logical step, even if it is regarded as an intermediate phase towards achieving the *Vision 2000* objective (Marquardt *et al.*, 1991).

It is reasonable for a standard to examine and clarify all aspects of quality related to the life cycle of the product (hardware, software, materials, services) in terms of management, control and internal assurance, and to improve the 9004 guide accordingly. But, as was seen earlier, extending these standards to include characteristics that are less tangible and less easily verified through external assessments, like the most important characteristics for total quality management, is likely to do more harm than good.

This section on quality and standards can be closed with a specific observation on Europe. The 1993 deadline for the single European market has focused attention on standards as the means to remove the technical obstacles that impede the free circulation of goods among the EC and EFTA countries. The EN 29000 standards, certification of conformity to these standards and mutual recognition of certification have become important political objectives. For this reason, the early 1990s have witnessed a growing emphasis on standards-based quality. This

35

is both an opportunity and a danger for Europe: an opportunity, because, as stated earlier, certification is likely to foster the horizontal spread of a quality culture and basic quality tools; the risk is that this intensive focus on standards could divert European managers' attention away from competitive quality.

However well intended, the quality standard with its fixed, codified references tends to blunt the importance of continuous improvement. The balance in Europe needs to be re-adjusted to emphasise both the horizontal dimension of quality (a concrete dimension offering important technical, economic and political advantages over the short/medium term), and the vertical dimension of quality (already indispensable for companies competing on global markets and of vital importance for any economic system over the medium/long term). But the foundations for the medium/long term must be laid now: a proactive quality culture takes decades to become established. So, for Europe too, total quality is an urgent matter, not something that can be postponed until tomorrow because of the 'standards emergency'.

1.3 QUALITY IN SMALL AND LARGE COMPANIES

Before the specific issues involved in total quality are considered, the following questions must be answered:

- Does the question of quality vary according to the size of the company? If so, how? Is there a specific quality question for small companies and another for large companies?
- In particular, do the conceptual contents of total quality described in section 1.1 change in relation to small companies? If so, how?
- How does the relative weight of total quality and standards-based quality change when moving from a large company to a small one?

Figure 1.9 provides the answer to the first question. It makes no claim to provide a quantitative interpretation of reality, but simply provides a qualitative interpretation based on experience and observation of many company situations.

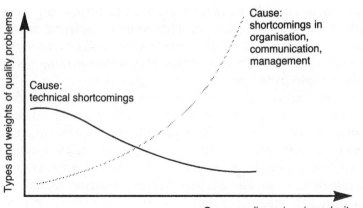

Fig. 1.9 How the weight of quality problems linked to technical causes and quality problems due to flaws in organisation/communication/management varies as company dimensions grow.

Figure 1.9 indicates that for the small company quality is essentially a technical-methodological question, a question of knowhow: familiarity with the techniques, methodologies and tools that will enable the company to obtain maximum quality at minimum costs and continuously improve this capability. This is a crucial issue for small companies, which generally lack specialist skills and the necessary information channels to keep up to date with developments in quality.

The large company can – and must – have specialist quality resources, whose task is to guarantee the necessary level and application of technical-methodological knowhow. The weight of the knowhow problem therefore tends to diminish as the company becomes larger. On the other hand, as the company's dimensions grow, so does the weight of quality problems that may appear to be linked to technical-methodological short-comings, but are in fact rooted in organisation, management style, communication and use of human resources.

It is even possible for a large company to obtain ISO 9000 certification without having resolved its main quality problems. For large companies, horizontal integration (interfunctional pro-cess management, teamwork), vertical integration (policy/goal deployment), involvement of the entire company, top management leadership in achieving improvement, internal customer-supplier relations – to list just some of the fundamental elements of total quality – are the precondition for turning technical expertise into excellence.

In other words, the large company is the area in which the conceptual contents of total quality can be applied in full; indeed, some of these concepts provide specific remedies for the specific inadequacies of the large organisation. ISO 9000 conformity certification, on the other hand, will give the large company a tactical advantage, but will not provide a cure for its structural problems.

On the other hand, the large company may have an interest in standards in relation to its purchasing policies, as an 'entry guarantee' for potential new suppliers.

Both the small and the large company need to assimilate the fundamental concept of **competitive quality**, which automatically leads to the concept of continuous improvement, 'how' the company interprets quality to become competitive. The third concept, which focuses on process quality, is as vital for the small organisation as for the large because it optimises the quality-cost ratio and represents the main route towards improvement. For the small company, process control is essentially a technical issue and therefore much more easily resolved than in the large company, where complex interfunctional processes require solutions in the area of organisation.

The other concepts – the internal customer-supplier model, the horizontal and vertical extension of the quality approach and organisation integration – are generally valid, although they tend to be present 'naturally' in small unstructured organisations, where interpersonal relations are direct and immediate and where the manager has direct, global visibility and control of the entire company.

To sum up, for small companies the total quality concepts of competitive quality, continuous improvement and process quality apply in full, while reconstruction of organisational integrity and total involvement are secondary concerns. Since these two concepts tend to resolve the problems of large organisations and restore the small-company functional model, they are not usually applicable to the small company until it grows to a size where it needs a functional structure.

For the small company, the answer to the last question – the relative weights of total quality and standards-based quality – is based on the consideration that the main role of the small company is to operate as a supplier to larger organisations, on a contractual basis. The ISO 9000 standards and certification are therefore of prime importance. But even though total quality can be trimmed of unnecessary concepts, it is still important for small organisations today. Competitive quality – in the full sense of the term for companies that operate directly on the market-place, in a reduced version, related chiefly to the quality of execution, for companies that work on a contractual basis – and the consequent logic of continuous improvement and process quality, should become universal concepts, the foundation for the strategy of any type of company.

Here, the small company and the large company have been considered, that is, the company without a functional structure and the fully structured company: a whole range of intermediate situations exists between these two extremes. The following chapters on the model and the construction and assessment of total quality systems will be concerned with the organisationally complex company, the most significant as far as total quality is concerned. The present section should provide useful indications for simplifying the model according to the organisational complexity of the individual company.

1.4 THE PROCESS: THE SOURCE OF QUALITY

Another conceptual alignment necessary before looking at the model concerns processes. This section provides a summary of the fundamental concepts related to processes. The reader is referred to other literature for further discussion of this point (Conti, 1991a; Pall, 1987; Tosalli *et al.*, 1990, Ch. 3) and to Chapter 4 for a discussion of process management.

A **process** is usually defined as any organised activity designed

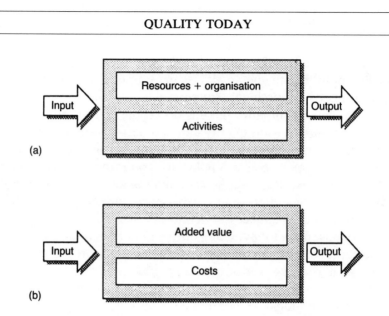

Fig. 1.10 (a) The process as an organised activity; and (b) as a link in the value chain.

to generate a pre-established output for identified users, beginning from the necessary input. There is general agreement that a process is an activity with these characteristics. Examples include: the product development process, the production process, the product distribution process, the sales process, the billing process. Allocation of the resources involved in these activities is where disagreement arises. Many people regard resources (people, equipment, etc.) as process input. Here, it is considered more helpful to include resources with the process, so that input consists only of the streams coming from other company processes or, more generally, from sources outside the process (the 'suppliers' of the process in question), just as output is directed towards the 'customers' or 'users' of the process in question.

Figure 1.10(a) illustrates this view of the process. Usually, the resources assigned to the process are distributed among one or more company functions: hierarchically speaking, they are part of the function, but they are dynamically associated with the activity, as and when required by that activity.

1.4.1 Process quality, added value and cost

The process is also a link in the value chains, the source of 'added value' (Fig. 1.10(b)). Of course, the activity has to generate value, but value for whom?

The company's activity is geared to achieving the results expected by its users, external and internal. The legitimate added value is therefore the **value for the users of the process**: first, for the end users of the value-added chain to which the process belongs; second, for the intermediate users (the subsequent links in the chain), as long as value is geared to end-user expectations and requirements.

The primary indicator of quality is the following:

$$\text{process quality} = \text{output quality/process cost}$$
$$= \text{added value for the user/process cost}$$

Process quality reflects the process's ability not only to generate the value expected by users but to do so at the minimum cost (the time factor has been excluded here, to avoid complicating matters; for a full picture, see Fig. 1.4).

The transformation cost is usually taken as the yardstick for added value. Nothing could be more misleading. Added value and cost are two separate and not always related concepts. A fairly high proportion of the process cost is related to activities that have no value for the user (Fig. 1.11). Value can be measured conventionally in terms of cost, that is, as the costs of activities that generate value. In the ideal reference process, value and costs thus coincide. In real processes, value is lower than costs.

Unlike costs, value cannot be assessed precisely, but it can be estimated through a joint analysis conducted by the managers of the supplier and the user processes; on the other hand, the 'costs delta' can be assessed *a posteriori*, after completion of an improvement initiative aimed at lowering non-value-adding costs (Fig. 1.12). Since the object is to estimate costs, but above all to identify those activities with no value for the user, this type of improvement initiative requires the involvement of the managers of all the processes in the chain, working as a team.

41

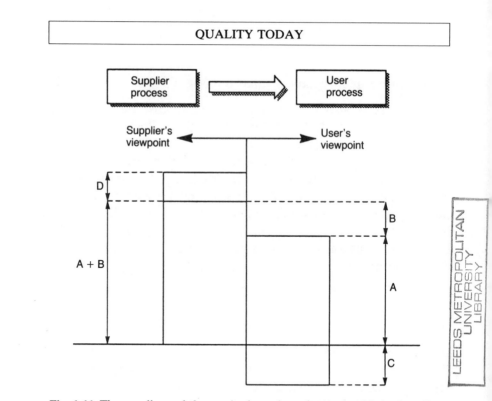

Fig. 1.11 The supplier and the user's viewpoints of process added value. From the supplier's viewpoint: D is activity wasted owing to internal process defectiveness; A and B are activities that generate value. From the user's viewpoint: A is value recognised by the user; B is non-value for the user; C is value expected by the user and not provided by the supplier. Costs correspond to A + B + D; added value corresponds to A; value expected but not provided (shortcoming in quality) corresponds to C.

Figures 1.11 and 1.12 illustrate a theory regarding the costs of non-quality, which is correct, but nearly always based on incorrect reasoning. The correct theory is that these costs can account for a very high percentage of a company's revenues (20–30% or more!); the incorrect reasoning is that they arise from defectiveness (internal and external), added to the costs of prevention and checking (the three classic categories). In fact, a company would have to be in very bad shape for the costs of non-quality **of execution** (which is what the costs of these three categories are, apart from prevention costs, which are certainly insignificant in relation to revenues) to reach double-digit percen-

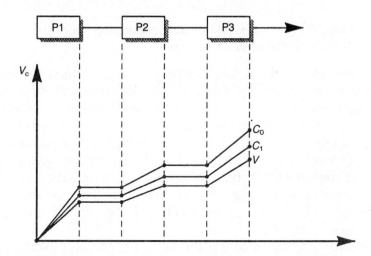

Fig. 1.12 The growth of cost and value (measured in comparable terms with costs) along a process chain. C_0 and C_1 are costs before and after an improvement initiative (with V unvaried).

tages. The chief non-quality costs are always related to the **quality of goals** ('doing the right things') rather than to the quality of execution ('doing things right first time') and, as Fig. 1.11 shows, they are related not only to the quality of end goals on the market, but also to the quality of intermediate goals (alignment of goals among the processes in a chain).

The disalignment of process goals with one another and with the market is the most serious and least understood cause of company inefficiency. It is a structural cause, because it is the almost inevitable consequence of functional division, of barriers between functions, of a breakdown in communications (see below). Remedies exist – as will be seen in dealing with inter-functional process management – but management is reluctant to accept cures that interfere with the company's functional-hierarchical structure and ends up in short-sighted pursuit of traditional non-quality costs, while the more substantial costs of non-alignment among processes is neglected. (See Chapter 6 for a discussion of the economics of quality.)

43

1.4.2 From the generalisation of the process concept to the generalisation of the product concept

The extension of the process concept from production to every type of company activity is now an established part of corporate managerial culture, and is reflected in the definition of 'process' given above. The conceptual route that has led to this generalisation is interesting, but it is not relevant for the purposes of this book (Tosalli *et al.*, 1990, pp. 117–20). At this point, for the sake of conceptual clarity, another useful generalisation should be examined, which may appear simply to be a question of definition. This is the generalisation of the product concept, illustrated in Fig. 1.13.

The first step (a) is to use the term 'product' for everything that leaves the company directed for the market: hardware, software, documentation, services, advertising, information. The second step (b) is to extend this concept to 'products for the internal use of the company'. These products are vital to the functioning of the company, to its ability to create products for the market efficiently and effectively. The most important example of a product for internal use is information, the typical product for management. The concept of quality, as value for the user at the minimum cost to the company, can be applied to information as to all other products for internal use.

The third step (c) is less immediate: it requires the company to have developed an approach that regards processes as a substantial company reality. Here, the product is **the result of every process**, not just the end result of the chain, but every intermediate result, the output of each different process in the chain.

Of course, the **end product** is the primary goal of all the processes in the chain, and the intermediate products are geared to the end product. But the concept of the intermediate product forces the company to adopt the supplier-customer approach at each process interface, and obliges supplier and customer to decide what 'specifications' the product should have and what value the customer expects. As will be seen, if this approach is adopted and quality function deployment is used as a tool to

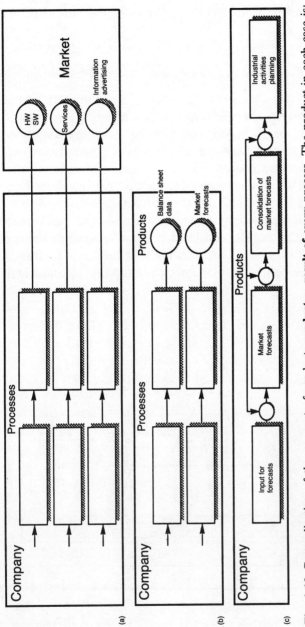

Fig. 1.13 Generalisation of the concept of product: **product = result of every process**. The product in each case is: (a) everything that leaves the company directed for the market; (b) what the company produces for its internal use; (c) the result of every process.

identify end goals and distribute them along the chain (Conti, 1989), the gap between value and costs in Fig. 1.12 will tend to close.

1.4.3 'Intrafunctional processes' and 'interfunctional processes'

An activity – a process – may be simple or complex, it may be performed within a single function (for example, preparation of wage sheets) or it may involve more than one function (for example, definition and development of a new product and related production processes).

The extension of company processes is illustrated, in simplified form, in Fig. 1.14. The triangle is a two-dimensional representation of a typical company pyramid, with the chief executive officer at the apex, the first-level heads of function, the second-level managers, and so on (the number and exact name of the levels will evidently vary from one company to another). The

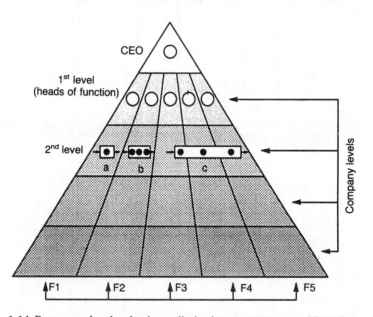

Fig. 1.14 Processes develop horizontally in the company pyramid, and may be intrafunctional or interfunctional. F1, F2, F3, F4, F5 are functions; a, b are intrafunctional processes; and c is an interfunctional process.

vertical lines in the figure represent the subdivision into functions (five in this case).

If the second-level managers are those responsible for the company's main processes, then (a) is a simple process, controlled by a single second-level manager within function F1; process (b) involves more than one second-level manager, but is still part of a single function, F2; (c) is a more complex process, involving a number of functions.

Processes (a) and (b) are intrafunctional processes, while (c) is interfunctional. Product development and planning is a typical interfunctional process, involving the functions of marketing, design and production.

Interfunctional processes are critically important not only to quality, but also to global costs and execution time. They are therefore one of the most important factors in total quality.

It should be noted that processes that generate 'products' for the market and the company are horizontal in relation to the company pyramid and the company functions, which develop vertically (vertical processes are related to the functional hierarchy and are thus not considered in this section, which focuses on processes that generate 'products' in a broad sense).

Horizontal company process chains can be extended towards external suppliers on one hand and towards external customers on the other (Fig. 1.19 below). Diagrams must therefore show suppliers and customers at the side of the company, with interfaces operating at different levels (Fig. 1.15).

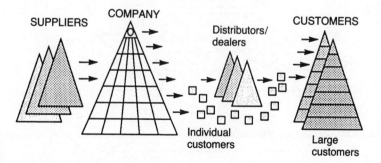

Fig. 1.15 The company interfaces with customers and suppliers at various levels.

As far as customers are concerned, a distinction can be made between small customers and large or corporate customers. While small customers usually interface with a relatively low level of the corporate organisation or with dealers, corporate customers (who can also be represented with a pyramid) interface at many different levels. Intermediate users (distributors, dealers) are also multi-interface corporate customers.

Figure 1.14 illustrates the horizontal extension of processes and chains, the complexity of the process. Processes also develop in a vertical direction to include resources and activities from different company levels. A project process, for example, can be considered at the level of the project sector manager (who is responsible for the project), the project group managers (Fig. 1.16), the designers, the prototype and test engineers. As far as the quality of the result and efficiency are concerned, each of these levels should interface, where necessary, with the corresponding level in the other functions, in this case with production and marketing.

The downward 'explosion' of the process can be seen as a segmentation into subprocesses, down to the lowest levels of responsibility.

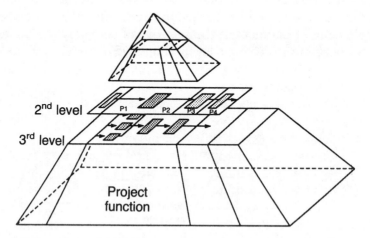

Fig. 1.16 Vertical explosion from the second to the third levels of process P2 within the project function.

This segmentation is useful as the process culture gradually takes root. It helps each manager, at whatever level, to regard his work as a process that can be governed by precise rules.

At the highest level of aggregation, it is important to consider how responsibility for the process is to be attributed and consequently whether and to what degree processes should be segmented horizontally.

Figure 1.14 clarifies the point: should responsibility for process (b) be divided between the two second-level managers involved in the process? Or should global responsibility for the process be maintained, and formally assigned to one person? And if so, to whom? The same question is even more important in relation to process (c), which involves second-level managers from different functions: F3, F4, F5. If sole responsibility is to be assigned for this process, the question of who should be responsible is even more critical than in case (b). In the latter case, responsibility could in theory be assigned to the head of function F2 (though in practice this should be avoided, because it would be a solely formal responsibility based on a hierarchical vision of the organisation rather than on an operational, process-based view) or to one of the managers who already share responsibility at function level. In case (c), it would not be feasible to make the head of the company responsible for the process, but it would not be unreasonable to consider formally attributing responsibility to one of the heads of function involved (F3, F4, F5).

This raises an issue of vital importance for complex companies with function-based structures, whose major processes are interfunctional processes such as process (c) in Fig. 1.14. The issue is vital because it concerns the company's ability to generate customer satisfaction at the end of complex processes and to minimise global costs and execution time.

The point will be examined later, and a full discussion will be made in Chapter 4 when dealing with process management. Here it need be noted only that in today's functional organisations, a single overall process manager generally does not exist and that there are at least as many managers responsible for the process as the number of functions involved.

Diagrams therefore have to segment the process into **at least** as many blocks as the number of functions involved. But this is just an initial, minimum requirement. The requirements of horizontal segmentation often go further. The criterion to be used to achieve correct horizontal segmentation is the **integrated process** (Conti, 1991a).

1.4.4 The integrated process

If a process is to give predictable results, all the process variables must be known and under control. A process is under control only if variability is contained within statistically known limits, and if sensors exist to indicate that a variable may be about to exceed the permitted limits and activate appropriate corrective feedback loops.

To keep a process under control, therefore, the first goal is to keep every variable within statistically defined limits (eliminating 'special causes' of variation); the second is to set up an appropriate control system (sensors, feedback loops) to monitor in particular those variables with the greatest influence on the result (**dominant variables**) (Tosalli *et al.*, 1990, pp. 124–9).

If this control model is applicable in full to production processes or, at a more general level, to repetitive processes with easily assessed quantitative parameters (in which case a state of statistical control can be achieved), then it can be applied **cum grano salis** to all company processes.

In any company process, the basic problem is to identify the dominant variables, those that require the greatest attention and control in order to improve the predictability of results. For these variables in particular, indicators will be established, sensors will be applied, measurements will be made, corrective action will be taken.

This is all very well as long as the variables are physical, in which case it is always possible, if not always easy, to identify and monitor the causes of variability. The real difficulties begin when the dominant variables are related to organisation, to the human factor, to relationships and even to 'political factors'. This can happen when functional barriers make communication difficult, when relationships are bureaucratic, when instrumental use is made of information.

Then the causes of variability move beyond the control of the process manager and it becomes difficult to predict results.

The term 'technical' can be used to qualify the variables over which the process manager has sufficient control to ensure they are kept within statistically predictable limits. Consequently, as long as the organisation variables that can affect process performance can be controlled by the manager in much the same way as the physical variables, then they can be combined with the technical variables.

Organisational variables are extremely sensitive to the dimensions of the organisation area involved in the process. The smaller the area and the greater its organisational integration, the easier it will be to assimilate the organisation variable with a technical variable and vice versa, as the organisational dimensions become larger.

Communication can be taken as an example of a variable. The process manager can usually ensure adequate control of the variable if the process is limited to a single function, but he may not be able to guarantee control if the process is part of a complex interfunctional chain.

The question of the organisation area leads to the definition of the expression 'integrated process' as used here (where the term 'integrated' refers to 'organisational integration', the cohesion among the different parts in the process): 'a process made up exclusively of technical variables'; or 'a process in which the manager has complete command over all variables, both technical, in the strict sense, and organisational, so that the latter may be considered, for the purposes of process control, on an equal footing with technical variables'.

The importance of the integrated process is related to the fact that when process variables are 'technical', their variability can be traced back to an aleatory level, in which only 'common causes' are present, since 'special causes' have been eliminated.

Process management is therefore a technical issue, for which established methodologies exist. This is the field defined by the 'Juran trilogy' (Juran, 1982, 1988): planning, control, improvement.

The integrated process concept is the criterion for the first stage in the analysis of complex processes, when companies have to decide how the process can be segmented horizontally. Functional segmentation, as has been seen, is the minimum level of segmentation: the reason for this is that the integrated process never (or hardly ever) exists when the process crosses the boundary between one function and another (a boundary that often becomes an **organisation barrier**). In some cases, organisational integration, which depends to a great degree on dimensions, is not even present within a single function, and so it may be necessary to divide the functional segment (type (b) in Fig. 1.14) into two or more parts operating sequentially and/or in parallel.

Segmentation turns a complex process into a **stream of integrated processes**, where the observations made earlier apply to each process in the stream, particularly as regards process management (planning, control, improvement). But, as a whole, the stream presents organisation management problems, which need to be examined separately.

1.4.5 The process stream

Process chains, value chains and supplier-customer chains have already been mentioned.

In practice, horizontal segmentation of a complex process rarely creates a simple chain. It is more likely to produce a multi-branch stream converging towards the final process, which interfaces with the user.

Figure 1.17 is an example of a process in which a product is made and delivered to a customer, beginning from the order. The process can be represented in two ways. The simpler and more obvious (Fig. 1.17(a)) illustrates the logical sequential flow of activities, at the expense of an orderly representation of functions. The second solution (Fig. 1.17(b)) is a cross-section at the appropriate level of the company pyramid in Fig. 1.16. The complexity of a three-dimensional graphic representation increases as the process stream becomes more intricate, so it is better to use a cross-section of the pyramid rather than the pyramid itself, specifying the level to which the section refers. Figure 1.17(b) is extremely useful when processes are analysed for the purposes of optimisation, because it highlights the winding course followed by the stream when process responsibility is not correctly assigned, and the organisation mazes this can create.

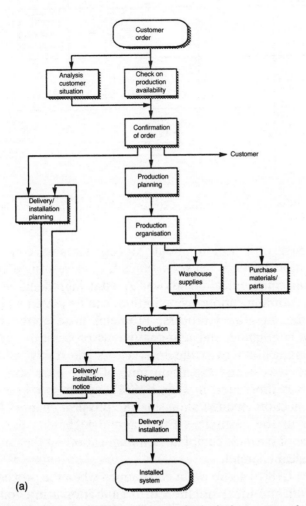

(a)

Fig. 1.17 (a) Example of a process stream: the logical sequence of processes.

53

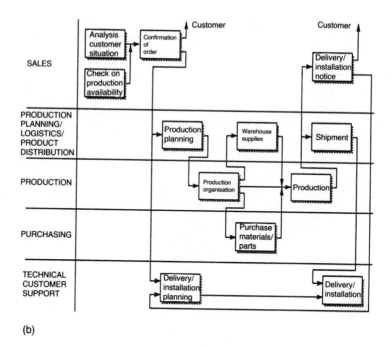

(b)

Fig. 1.17 (b) Example of a process stream: the process-function relationships.

The first observation about process streams concerns the organisation barriers between functions, to return to the comments on communication above. A vital ingredient in process quality, communication, by definition, can be governed correctly within the integrated process. Problems arise at the interface between contiguous and non-contiguous processes. Every lapse in communication over the interface is inevitably reflected in the quality, cost and execution time of the entire stream. This situation is illustrated in Fig. 1.18(a), which shows a two-way communication channel alongside the **physical channel** from the supplier to the customer. The diagram highlights the decisive influence of correct, complete communication on the contents of the physical channel.

Figure 1.18(b) shows what can happen when the process moves away from the ideal situation of organisational integration and is sliced up, with each slice assigned to a particular function.

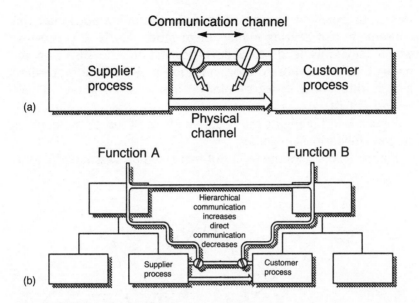

Fig. 1.18 Communication integrity is decisive to product quality: (a) restricting communication quantity/quality harms the products flowing along the physical channel; (b) as organisational distances lengthen, direct communication deteriorates while bureaucratic communication increases.

Communication, the vital sap of the process, no longer flows freely in a horizontal – and physiological – direction. Its quality and quantity are limited and it is deviated into vertical (hierarchical) channels. 'How to kill processes' could be the title of countless corporate case histories, where the growth of the company is accompanied by a gradual increase in functional powers and a corresponding rise in the height of the barriers between functions. It is no coincidence that the pyramid, the Weberian organisation model, is also known as the 'bureaucratic model'. It may have been valid for large state-owned, military or corporate organisations, where large uncultured masses were led towards usually stable goals fixed by a few (Taylorian model). It is certainly not appropriate in the present age of rapid change, of competition among companies and economic systems, of high levels of education. The classic organisation model needs to be adjusted. Today, a great deal is heard about **flat organisations**:

this is an excellent concept, but if the flattening out is not the consequence of gearing management more closely to processes, which inevitably leads to a deverticalisation, the suspicion remains that the corporate reorganisation may be little more than a reshuffling of a series of blocks, a sort of corporate 'Lego' (Conti, 1988).

Figure 1.19 highlights the negative effect of functional barriers on interfunctional processes.

Figure 1.20 shows the effect of increaséd process length, com-

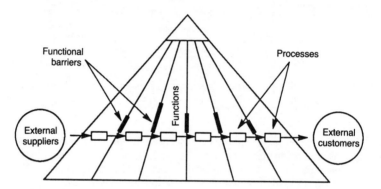

Fig. 1.19 The main process streams cut across the company. Functional barriers impede their effectiveness and efficiency.

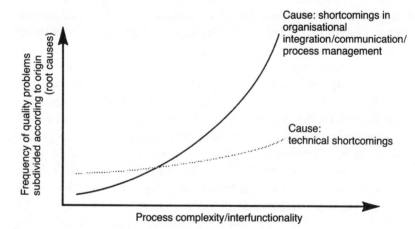

Fig. 1.20 The sources of quality problems in large organisations.

plexity and interfunctionality – in the absence of integration – on quality, cost and time.

The steeply rising curve refers to problems caused chiefly by organisation shortcomings (in particular, lack of communication); in fact, problems that at first sight appear to have a technical cause often turn out in subsequent analyses to have a structural, organisational root. Take the example of the modifications curve for a product during the first six months after mass production start-up: a series of technical defects and critical difficulties, clearly of a mainly technical nature. So much so that the chief executives of companies affected by this type of problem are likely to lay the blame with their designers and planners. If, on the other hand, the chief executives of companies that had managed to achieve significant improvements in the modifications curve were questioned, their answers would indicate that this success was due not so much to improved skills, motivation, or individual attitudes, as to organisational integration: making sure that marketing, design, production, purchasing and logistics staff worked together from the start of the project for the duration of the development process.

The curve in Fig. 1.20 (which is empirical and qualitative, but realistic) reflects a situation of structural non-quality, which can only be tackled with a total quality approach. The issues of horizontal integration, communication and teamwork, and interfunctional process control structures can be successfully dealt with only if they are tackled by top management, working together with the first line and with the cooperation of the rest of the company's management.

This is a question of key importance for the company, the *conditio sine qua non* for generating quality with the maximum efficiency which highlights the need for a total quality approach to finding a solution. It concludes this introduction and introduces the core theme of the book.

57

The total quality model | 2

2.1 THE QUALITY MISSION AND THE COMPANY-MARKET MODEL

Every organisation has its own long- and short-term goals. Some of these are permanent and fundamental: the purpose for which the company was founded, its raison d'être. These are the organisation's **missions**.

The main missions are specific and characterise the company at the deepest level. A company whose mission is high-precision mechanics, for example, will be profoundly different to a service company working in the hotel trade; it will also be very different to a company that manufactures semiconductors, because it utilises different technology, but the difference will be less marked because the two companies will share the production and market culture and values typical of the high-technology sector. Certain missions, however, are common to all organisations. Companies operating on the open market should all have a profit mission. Consequently, they should aim to **satisfy their customers**, which is the fundamental **quality mission**. As early as 1960, Ted Levitt noted: 'The awareness that the mission of the company is to satisfy the customer, not to produce goods, is vital to any type of entrepreneur'.

The quality mission can reasonably be regarded as the **common mission** of all companies that intend to remain on the marketplace. But, in a society whose needs continue to grow, the customer satisfaction mission extends to all organisations, including non-profit-making organisations. As will be seen later,

59

it also extends to all customers, to external and internal customers, and in particular to corporate employees. For the sake of simplicity, only profit-making organisations are dealt with in this book. The significance of the fundamental customer satisfaction mission may vary, depending on the situation of the market in which companies operate. This discussion is concerned with the current situation of global markets and competition on quality. It therefore refers to the concept of competitive quality, or total quality, as discussed in Chapter 1.

In a total quality environment, the quality mission can be summarised as follows: '**To achieve excellent results in terms of user satisfaction with minimum use of resources and to improve these results continuously over time**'.

It is implicit in the definition that excellence is relative to users' generally rising expectations of results and to the levels reached by competitors. The purpose of this chapter is: **to build a model that corresponds to the mission defined above**. A general model that can be used by any organisation **in relation to the quality mission**, independently of that organisation's specific missions. This general model will permit the adjustments necessary to cater for the specific characteristics of individual companies. The true value of the model lies in its role as a common conceptual matrix, which can be used by the most diverse types of organisation.

Since the total quality mission is concerned with competition at the level of 'user satisfaction' and therefore with continuous improvement – and only then with the way the company structures itself to compete – the model must be a **company-market model**. Relations with the market, and with users in particular, are fundamental, as is assessment of results on the market.

Before discussing how to build the model, a general observation is needed regarding the approach adopted here. Building a model does not imply a mechanistic view of the organisation. On the contrary, the approach described here is based on the firm belief that the human factor, culture, values, the **invisible resources** that make each successful company unique, cannot be confined within a model, nor can they be reproduced mechanically through application of a model. **There is no formula for**

excellence. A company is a living organism. Attempts can be made to describe and interpret its 'anatomy' and 'physiology'; an analysis of its 'psychology' may be useful to highlight the confines beyond which any further exploration is arbitrary. Nevertheless, the model is an indispensable guide for anyone trying to plan, assess and improve their company's quality system. To the extent that it offers a faithful interpretation of reality, the model can help the company identify its fundamental mechanisms and understand its current position and the direction it should take to accomplish its quality mission; it is certainly no guarantee of the excellence of results.

2.2 THE BASIC MODEL

2.2.1 User 'results': the first basic component of the model

For the sake of simplicity, the model will be built step by step. Many diagrams are included to clarify the different concepts involved, even if this involves use of analogical illustrations at the expense of formal scientific rigour.

Figure 2.1 illustrates the first step in building the model. The company is still shown as an undifferentiated block opposite a second undifferentiated block, the current and potential users of

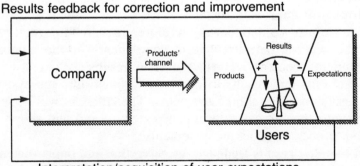

Fig. 2.1 Basic model of the company-users relationship in the context of customer satisfaction.

61

its products ('products' in the extended sense as defined in section 1.4 and explained in detail further on).

These user expectations, expressed or unexpressed, vary greatly and are influenced by the active presence of competitors (product offers, advertising, image . . .). The **interpretation/acquisition of user expectations** channel is thus extremely important. It is particularly critical for companies producing goods and services for the market, that is, for a set of potential customers with varying expectations and influenced by other parties, the majority of whom are normally not known to the company (note the substantial difference, discussed in section 1.1, with companies that produce for specific customers).

The 'products' channel represents the company's **response** to the expectations of the targeted user group. As used here, the term 'products' signifies not individual products but the **menu** offered by the company to meet the expectations of its target users. This menu will be matched against the expectations of each effective user and the comparison (the scales in Fig. 2.1) will reflect the level of satisfaction.

Results are the assessments given by the users: they can be measured with customer satisfaction surveys (using the method described in section 3.3), and are the **only legitimate yardstick for assessing the degree to which the quality mission has been accomplished**, as far as customer satisfaction is concerned. Although Fig. 2.1 as yet contains no specific elements relating to **continuous improvement**, regular monitoring of user results will provide an indication of improvement rates.

The 'results' component is therefore crucially important, and will be one of the three basic components in the company assessment processes. Here, the term **results** will be used to indicate only end results as obtained through user surveys, not the results of internal measurements. The latter, as will be seen, come into the 'processes/products' category and will simply be called 'process/product measurements'.

In Fig. 2.1, **results feedback for correction and improvement** is obviously the channel through which 'real' results (as defined above) are referred back to the company, together with the company's regular field assessments on its products, in particular on defects (if properly performed, these assessments approximate and, at diagnostic level, complete 'real' results), and customer complaints. In this elementary diagram, the 'company' block represents the company plus suppliers ('company system').

2.2.2 From the expectations menu to the offer menu and results

To achieve user satisfaction, the company must first of all identify the different classes of user (**according to types of expectation**) for which its offer is intended. Then it must analyse the expectations of each class and plan its response to each expectation (**offer characterisation**). The structured process for performing this analysis and characterising the offer is known as **product quality deployment** (where 'product' signifies the entire offer; consequently the process can also be called **offer quality deployment**) (Akao, 1990; Conti, 1991b).

The weighted expectations of each user class together form the user expectation **menu** or **tree** of that class, otherwise known as the **customer satisfaction menu** (or tree), because it contains all the expectations that would have to be satisfied, according to their weights, to achieve the maximum satisfaction of the users in the class as a whole (the two right-hand columns in Fig. 2.2, which takes computer system users as an example). Not surprisingly, expectations follow a hierarchical order (for example: **product quality/reliability** and **support quality** can be considered first-level expectations; **hardware quality** and **system software quality** would be second-level expectations, within 'product quality'). The first-level components (right-hand column in Fig. 2.2) can be called customer satisfaction **categories**.

The company's response to the **expectation menu** is an offer whose quality depends on the company's ability to interpret market requirements, to detect even those 'vague signs' that often indicate latent expectations; to match its reading to the possibilities offered by technology; to take competitive decisions on the basis of this comparison and its costs/revenues estimates. In principle, the **offer menu** column in Fig. 2.2 mirrors the 'expectation menu' column.

The concept of the offer menu as the company's response to

63

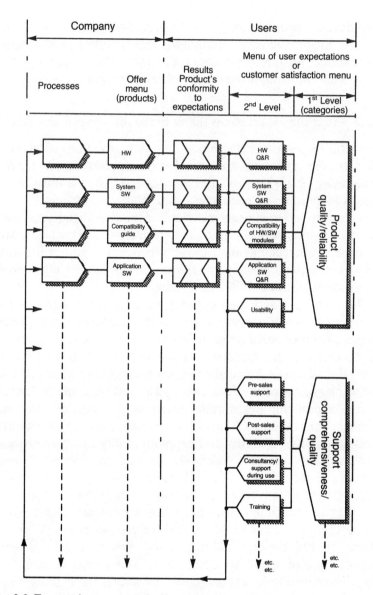

Fig. 2.2 Expectation menu and offer menu.

the expectation menu suggests a useful definition of 'product': **any response of the company to an element, or group of elements, in the expectation menu**. Consequently, the company's offer is a **product menu**, which, generally speaking, will not correspond precisely to the expectation menu, for two reasons: first, because the company's offer strategy may ignore certain expectations or amplify its response to others; second, because a single **company process** may respond to more than one elementary expectation or, conversely, a response to an expectation may come from more than one process (the reason for the qualification 'an element, or group of elements' in the above definition).

At this point, 'the process' is introduced, the **company quantum** of activities that generates each and every company product. The process completes the picture, as Fig. 2.3 shows. The company responds to the users' 'expectation' (or group of expectations) with a process, which generates a 'product'. On the market, the product encounters the users' expectations and produces a 'result', that is, the opinion of the user regarding conformity to expectations.

The significance of extending the product concept to every element in the customer satisfaction menu is based on the following consideration. Many companies find it difficult to keep pace with changing user expectations, especially hardware manufacturers (or companies with the mentality of the hardware producer), who consider the relationship with the customer

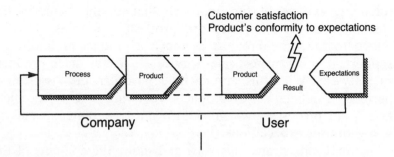

Fig. 2.3 The 'expectations – process–product–expectations' alignment is decisive to results from the users viewpoint.

almost exclusively in terms of the product, since direct contact is limited to the few unavoidable moments of the sale and delivery, and are slow to realise the growing importance of service in user expectations. Many companies lose market share because of the divergence between their offer menu and the expectation menu: management concentrates solely on products (in the strict sense of hardware and software), while the short-comings felt most strongly by the customer concern service.

The author was present at a discussion between a manu-facturer and some of his largest dealers on the reliability of a particular product line. The manufacturer continued to invest resources to improve the early-life reliability level of the line (breakdowns while the products were still under guarantee). Although the dealers appreciated the improvements, they con-sidered the products to be on an equal footing with competitor products as far as reliability was concerned; where the producer fell short was in providing support to resolve problems. The dealers said they would prefer to double the defect rate, but be sure of rapid and resolutive support. In their view, the company should have focused its efforts on service support, which was the most critical factor at that time. But inside the company, the lack of information on user expectations combined with a sec-torial approach meant that management was unable to see 'the wood for the trees'.

To be truly market-driven, companies should reject the view of products as tangible, deliverable objects, accompanied by a series of indefinable features related to service and customer relations, and adopt the approach that all the items in the customer satisfaction menu are products. Pre-sales activities linked to the offer are just as much a product as hardware; support, training or post-sales service are just as much products as software. With this approach, a miscellaneous assortment becomes a defined set of products, requiring precise 'specifica-tions' and processes, which in turn must guarantee results in line with user expectations.

Figure 2.2 illustrates this view and shows the contents of the 'expectations' and 'results' blocks of the basic model in Fig. 2.1. It also introduces the second step in the model, which begins to explore the fundamental elements of the 'company' block (processes and products), focusing attention on the link between these elements and expectations and results. There is a logical link, clearly illustrated in Figs 2.2 and 2.3, between the company's processes-products and user expectations on one hand and between processes-products and results on the market on the other. This link can be summarised as follows:

$$\text{expectations} \Rightarrow \text{processes} \Rightarrow \text{products} \Rightarrow \text{results} \Leftarrow \text{expectations}$$

2.2.3 Aligning processes/products with user expectations

Processes/products are aligned with user expectations through the 'interpretation/acquisition of user expectations' channel (Fig. 2.1), with which specific company processes are associated. These processes are shown in Fig. 2.4(a) as 'identification of expectations and definition of product goals'. They usually involve the institutional functions of marketing and/or product planning; in an integrated total quality approach, they should involve all the functions that contribute to execution, even if responsibility is assigned to the institutional function. In this connection, the competitiveness of the offer depends on both the ability of the company to interpret and assess market expectations – actual and latent – and its technological capabilities, which form the basis for the response to expectations. The quality of goals (Fig. 1.2) is therefore based on the company's ability to understand the market, its technological knowhow and its capacity for innovation.

In Fig. 2.4(a), the 'identification of expectations and definition of product goals' process terminates with a 'product' (see the generalisation of the product concept as the result of every process, section 1.4). This product consists of the goals of the product or offer developed by the company in response to certain specific user expectations (**product specifications** or **offer specifications**).

The 'product' sets in motion the execution processes, which, in the case of a **deliverable product** (hardware, software, finished deliverable services, see Fig. 2.4(a)) terminate with that deliver-

67

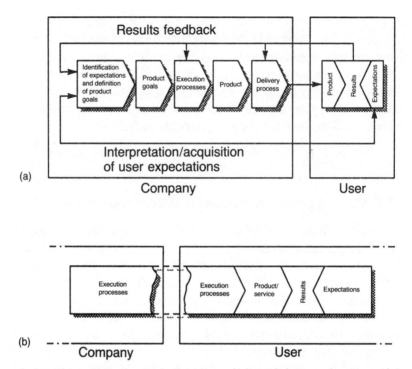

Fig. 2.4 The company processes/products chain and the users/company channels: (a) for a 'deliverable' product; (b) for a 'service' product.

able product. The **delivery process**, when the product is delivered to the user, follows. In the case of a 'service' product, where production is wholly or in part simultaneous with delivery, the execution processes terminate with the user (Fig. 2.4(b)). Although this is often a **virtual**, not physically identifiable product, it can always be logically defined in terms of 'result of the service process' and 'response to user expectations'.

Figure 2.4(a) shows that processes/products are also aligned with user expectations through the results feedback channel, that is, through corrective and/or improving action taken at various levels: the execution and delivery processes (mainly corrective action) and the goal redefinition processes (mainly improving action).

2.2.4 Processes: the second basic component of the model

'Results', as defined above, are the first basic component of the model. It is worth stressing once again that these are not the results of the company's internal assessments of its products, but the degree to which the offer menu matches the expectation menu; in other words, customer satisfaction.

This is a **customer-centric** view of results, as opposed to a **company-centric** view. In the company-centric view, the results of the company's own assessments of its products are pre-eminent, while customer assessments, if they are included, are of secondary importance.

In the customer-centric view – the only approach compatible with the quality mission defined in section 2.1 – the 'real' results are those obtained from customer assessments. Necessary but not in themselves sufficient, the company's assessments of its processes and its products are instrumental in achieving customer satisfaction. Their value, however, lies in the degree to which they correspond with and anticipate customer assessments. To ensure customer satisfaction, the company will have to establish adequate process and product indicators; it will have to check processes and products on the basis of the information provided by these indicators; it will have to perform periodic reviews on its indicators by comparing its internal measurements with external measurements (the results of the customer satisfaction surveys).

By now it will be obvious that, as Figs 2.2, 2.3 and 2.4 show, the **process-product** group is the second basic component of the model, the component that transforms expectations into results, with which ideally it should be aligned. This is the first internal company component in the step-by-step construction of the model, which, in the context of the quality mission, takes its cue from the market and the expectations of users.

The term 'processes' will be used from now on to indicate the processes/products component. This is not just for brevity; the term also underlines the fact that the significant company reality is the process. The process is where users' expectations are translated into company goals, where goals are translated into the

69

company's response to user expectations, that is, into products. The product is the **terminal point** of the process, the conclusive point at which the conformity of the process results with goals is measured. The product is extremely important, but it is always just the conclusion of the process.

Other considerations should be kept in mind:

- A lack of quality in execution is almost always due to short-comings in the assessments made during the process. Product assessments are simply the final assessments, the most signifi-cant assessments are those performed during the process. The latter must be continually correlated with product assess-ments, and product assessments with user-results.
- When processes improve to the point that product defect rates reach very low levels, product assessments become less significant and too expensive; at this point, process assess-ments are the only practical assessments.
- Where 'service' products are concerned, only in a minority of cases is there a deliverable product that can be assessed prior to consignment. In most cases, the supplier can conduct pre-liminary assessments on any finished products involved in the final service execution process, but only process assessments can be performed on the global result, since production is simultaneous with delivery.

To conclude, the 'process', standing for the 'process-product' group, is the **second basic component of the model**.

The greatest quality of the company process is the ability to create value for the user. Company processes, by which expectations are translated into goals, and goals into products (Fig. 2.4(a)), must maximise results, that is, user satisfaction. **The alignment of process-product assessments with results is therefore a primary requirement**. When internal assessments (process-product) offer a fair approximation of the user's judge-ment, then the company will be able to manage the strategic variable of quality consistently with its mission. So the most important aspect of processes-products is not the actual assess-ment ('results' in the company-centric view), but the degree to which the assessment matches the external customer satisfaction results.

2.2.5 The quality system: the third basic component of the model

'Results' indicate the company's current ability to satisfy customers (and its capacity for improvement if surveys are made at regular intervals).

Processes are vehicles, the tools for achieving results (customer satisfaction). The main vehicles (those with the greatest impact on customer satisfaction) must be carefully controlled to enable management to anticipate results and thus prevent problems occurring with users. (Processes are like rivers leading to the sea, that is, the market: along the course of the river it is possible to have early warning of what will happen at the mouth and take correcting action.)

But how can the company manage its processes so as to achieve excellent results? How can it obtain these results with the maximum efficiency or continuously improve its performance? The answer to these questions lies at the very source of quality and excellence. The foundation on which processes – and consequently results – are developed is solid or unstable, depending on the company system: whether it creates the right environment, culture, values and attitudes for excellence and continuous improvement.

These largely intangible factors cannot be measured in quantitative terms, but to a certain extent they can be assessed in relation to models (archetypes), usually experience-based models that analyse the characteristics of successful companies. These models are not objective, and are always largely opinable, but they do provide useful frames of reference, as long as they are continually checked, tested and updated. They are dynamic models, partly because of the objective difficulty of identifying the cause-effect links between the characteristics of the system and the quality of processes and attitudes, partly because the world outside the company is changing all the time.

The characteristics of the company system that are important in relation to the quality mission are defined here as the **quality system** (strictly speaking, it would be more correct to use the term **quality subsystem**, because the characteristics concerned are the elements of the organisation system that relate to the quality mission).

71

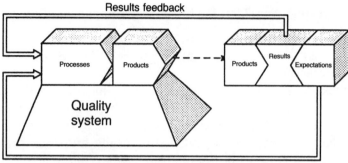

Fig. 2.5 The quality system is the foundation of process quality.

The quality system is assumed here to be the third basic component of the model. In Fig. 2.5, the quality system is the solid foundation of processes, which in turn are the source of quality and efficiency. Processes have been simplified here compared with the stream in Fig. 2.4(a), for greater immediacy. Processes are shown as a single block, which generates products for the user. For simplicity, this and the following figures refer only to deliverable products, and the delivery process is omitted. The main elements of the quality system will be described later. Here, it is sufficient to note that these elements cover the entire organisation system: the role of management, company values and culture, human resources, organisation infrastructures.

The highly simplified representation of the model in Fig. 2.5 shows the main blocks involved in the quality mission and the relationships between them. But although the customer satisfaction mechanism is clear, two other aspects of the mission are less obvious: **efficiency** and **continuous improvement**.

The role of efficiency can be clarified by introducing a few new details about users, who so far have been treated as a single group. Figure 2.6 introduces the **owner** user category: not only the company's owners/shareholders, but everyone with an interest in the company (stake-holders). The figure also shows the internal users of internal products (products in the extended sense, as defined in section 1.4).

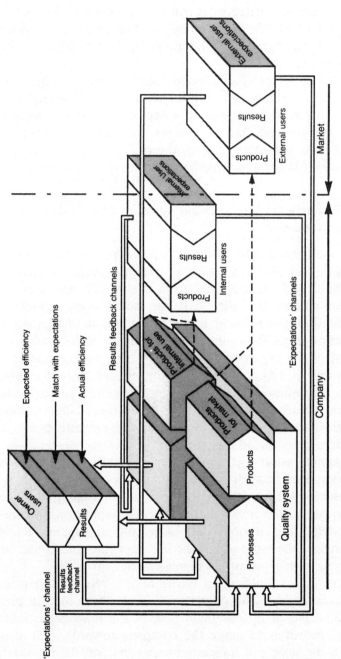

Fig. 2.6 Internal users and their 'expectations' as regards quality and efficiency.

The owner user category is considered here only in relation to the benefits accruing to the company through process efficiency, an aspect highlighted in the mission. Other aspects will be discussed later.

The second factor, continuous improvement, is already included in the quality system (and concerns nearly every component of it: **role of management**, **values and culture**, **management of human resources**, **infrastructures**, **technical resources**). However, it is so important that for the practical purposes of use of the model it is certainly worth emphasising.

2.2.6 The primary improvement mover and the brakes on improvement

The model must give visibility to the **primary improvement mover**, the organisation principle that ensures that improvement is planned and implemented from a strategic perspective and becomes a securely rooted dynamic factor in the organisation. By definition, the **primary mover** is the source of movement: it receives no input from other drivers, but transmits movement to the rest of the organisation, which in turn must create its own drivers instead of being passively kept in motion by the primary mover. If continuous improvement is to become a securely rooted dynamic factor in the organisation, decentralised drivers must be created. Once operational, they must independently power their respective parts of the organisation.

Metaphors aside, top management is clearly the indispensable primary mover: it must create a quality system that enables the company to perform its quality mission. In 'creating' the quality system, top management is the system's 'supplier'; in managing the system, it is itself a user. The role of supplier tends to predominate the more senior the manager; the role of user tends to prevail moving down the management ranks.

Figure 2.7, simplified to illustrate the role of the primary mover, exemplifies the points that will be examined in greater depth in Chapter 3. The main task of top management as the primary mover is to guide the company towards total quality, through the long and difficult changes that will be required. In

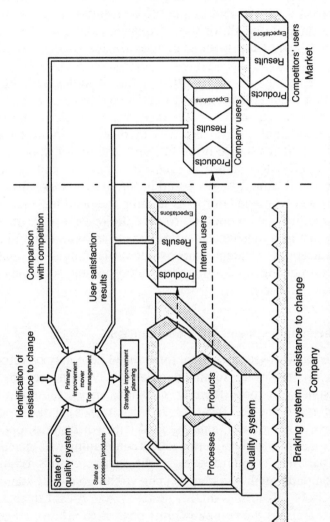

Fig. 2.7 The primary mover of improvement and the brakes on improvement.

performing this task, top management's primary role is to act as the **chief planner and builder** of the organisation – the company system – in preparation for the competitive challenge.

Strategic improvement planning, supported by assessments of the company's results and competitors' results, of the state of processes and, above all, of the adequacy of the quality system, is the chief task of top management as the leader of the quality mission.

The base of Fig. 2.7 shows a factor that is undesirable but to some extent inevitable in any organisation: resistance to change. In this case, resistance to the changes required along the road towards total quality. The changes involve such radical trans-formations that resistance often becomes the major impediment to total quality. Resistance is such an important and complex question that it cannot be discussed in full in this book, although reference will be made later in examining the need for education on total quality. The model has to take the resistance factor into account, just as a mechanical system has to take inertia and fric-tion into account. Strategic improvement planning must analyse resistance to change in depth and develop suitable strategies and tactics to minimise it.

2.2.7 The quality system: not a new concept

Since the quality system concept introduced here may be difficult to grasp at first, prior to the detailed analysis in section 2.3, comparisons with more familiar situations may be useful. The frame of reference for the ISO 9000 standards is the product quality assurance model, and the goal is to verify the supplier's ability to generate and deliver products conforming with specifica-tions. The 9004 standard defines the characteristics required by the company quality system to achieve this goal. The standard uses precisely this term – quality system – and uses it to refer to all the capabilities the company must possess to achieve its goal.

The same meaning, of 'necessary capabilities', is assumed here for the quality system, but the context is entirely different. The focus is no longer conformity to specifications, but the ability to interpret the market, to compete in satisfying the expectations (both explicit and latent) of users who, for the most part, will not be individually known, to do so with minimum use of resources, to continuously improve this performance over time, etc. It is obvious that:

1. the set of capabilities needed to fulfil the total quality mission will be far more complex than that needed to ensure conformity to specifications;
2. verification of capabilities is by definition the objective of standards conformity certification.

The objective of total quality is far broader and no capability assessment could claim to judge the state of the company in relation to the quality mission (particularly if it is an external assessment!). The thesis of this book is that, in the modern context of total quality, the 'voice of the users' (results) and the 'voice of the processes' – and the correlation between the two – must be added to the capability assessments. The quality system concept can also be considered in relation to another assessment scheme, in this case a total quality scheme, the US Malcolm Baldrige Award. Analysis of the individual items in the award's seven categories shows that some of these items (only a small number, unfortunately) come under this book's 'results' heading (user satisfaction); other items relate to process assessments and process-product measurements; the remaining and by far the largest group of items refers to the elements of the company system of significance to **total quality management**, in other words, the elements that form the quality system. This book's objection is that the Malcolm Baldrige Award does not make a conceptual distinction between the three classes: **capabilities** (quality system), **external results** (customer satisfaction) and **internal results** (processes-products), and that it gives excessive weight to the assessment of capabilities (a carry-over from standards-based assessments).

2.2.8 The elementary model: conclusions

The model includes the following factors of critical importance to the total quality mission:

77

- user **expectations**: an external factor and point of reference for the company's activities and quality assessments;
- **results**: assessments, in terms of customer satisfaction, of the company's ability to respond adequately to user expectations;
- **processes**: the specific activity streams through which the company interprets user expectations, transforms them into goals and from there into products;
- the **quality system** (more precisely, the quality subsystem of the organisation system): the set of characteristics required by the organisation system in order to fulfil its quality mission.

Within the quality system, a primary critical factor – shown separately in the model – is top management's role as an **improvement mover**, that is, as a structural dynamic factor, the only possible guarantor that the system is moving along the road to continuous improvement. **Strategic improvement planning** is the typical activity of this mover. The braking action of **resistance to change**, and the consequent need to identify and neutralise resistance, has also been shown in the model.

In the model, expectations are an **external reference**, which the company cannot influence. They are the touchstone, outside the company system, against which results are assessed.

Results, **processes** and the **quality system**, on the other hand, are all elements of the company. They can be assessed, planned and modified. They are the three fundamental components of the **total quality management** model for the company setting out to accomplish its quality mission.

The examples in Table 2.1 illustrate the relationship between the three basic components of the model. The table analyses the positive consequences for 'processes' (second column) and 'results' (third column) of a series of positive characteristics (**capabilities**) of the quality system (first column).

2.2.9 Assessing the three components of the model

For a better understanding of the model, a few preliminary observations can be introduced regarding the assessment of the model's components in relation to the mission. This topic will be

Table 2.1 Relationship between the three components of the model

Positive characteristics of the quality system	. . . lead to properly functioning 'processes'	. . . and therefore to quality 'results' for users
The company has good vertical alignment (good hierarchical communication, systematic involvement of lower levels in decision-making processes)	Identification of improvement goals and their diffusion in the company is correct and effective	Improvement goals that best match user expectations Reduction of differences between results and goals
Deep-rooted customer culture	Identification of user requirements is effective Wide use of methodologies like quality function deployment to increase ability to interpret the market The internal process chains are managed with the supplier-customer logic	The company's results are more competitive because the quality of goals improves (positive quality rises) Costs and execution times are decreased (internal user satisfaction)
Good horizontal integration	Goal planning and horizontal deployment processes function correctly, as does supervision	Benefits for external customer and internal user satisfaction (optimisation of global costs and execution times)
Adequate training system	All processes are managed professionally	Better results throughout, externally and internally
Information is viewed as the vital 'sap' of the organisation and the pivot of decision-making processes	Processes have the necessary indicators for management, control and supervision Simple, streamlined information systems enable information and data to circulate rapidly to the right users	Gradual move away from management by opinion towards management by facts, with significant benefits for external and internal users

covered in full in Chapters 3 and 7, but a brief preview will help illustrate the nature of the three basic components.

Certain difficulties arise as regards the **measurability** of results (first line in Table 2.2), since assessments are concerned with users and are often conducted by third parties. The method adopted must avoid distorting users' judgements and must be applied with precision. Processes and products are easier to measure. Measuring the quality system is extremely difficult. Apart from conventional audits, which can be applied only to the more tangible elements of the system, little progress has been made with either assessment methods or indicators.

As far as the **reliability** of the assessments is concerned (second line of Table 2.2), results by definition are the most reliable (assuming that assessments have been correctly performed), because the assessment is direct and final, and not subject to interpretation or extrapolation. The reliability of process assessments depends entirely on the state of control of the process: for processes with no control, reliability is very low, whereas it is very high for processes that have been controlled, improved and periodically aligned with user results over a long period of time. The reliability of the quality system assessment may be very low, especially if intangibles (for example, characteristics of the role of management, of the human and social corporate environment) are assessed by external parties and/or by non-experts. It will

Table 2.2 Relationship between the three components of the model

Aspects of assessment/measurement	Components of the model		
	Results	Processes	Quality Systems
Measurability	++	+++	--
Reliability	+++	+ → +++	-- → ++
Significance of assessments in relation to current situation	+++	++ → +++	+
Significance of assessments in relation to potential for improvement	+	++	+++

80

rise if the assessment penetrates the heart of the company, examining it from various viewpoints, including that of the experts and above all that of the system users (Chapter 3).

As far as the **significance** of the assessments in relation to the current situation of the company is concerned (third line of Table 2.2), results are the most meaningful of the three components. Process assessments are potentially significant if processes are carefully controlled and aligned with the field. In that case, they will be of greater importance to management than results, because they are available in real time and enable corrective action to be taken to prevent negative results in the field. Finally, as regards the **significance** of the assessments in relation to the potential for improvement (fourth line of Table 2.2), results will do no more than indicate historical trends.

Processes are fairly significant, since a thorough audit of a process enables the company to assess the current state of that process, the difference as compared with the optimal process and the action planned or being taken to close the gap. But it is the assessment of the quality system that highlights the company's true improvement potential. As has been seen, this assessment is difficult and intrinsically unreliable; but if the company management really wants to lay a solid foundation for improvement, it must know the position of the entire organisation in relation to its quality mission.

The model's three components are examined in the following section, which provides the depth of detail needed for their assessment. In view of the difficulties involved in assessing the quality system (Table 2.2), which plays such a fundamental role in improvement, guidance is offered for assessing the state of the quality system, the potential for improvement, and the weaknesses to be corrected.

2.3 A CLOSER LOOK AT THE MODEL

2.3.1 The company's links with the market

The basic model described the fundamental links between the company and the market: the input-output channel through which user expectations are interpreted and acquired, the output products channel, and the input results feedback channel. These channels will now be examined in greater detail, together with all the company-market links of relevance to the 'quality mission'.

2.3.2 The company's 'partners'

Of all the external parties with which the company deals, two in particular are of crucial importance to the quality mission:

- intermediate users as compared with the end customers;
- suppliers.

Intermediate users may be distributors, sole agents, authorised dealers and value-added resellers: they are known as **indirect channels**. The relative processes follow on from the company processes, they are the terminal segments between the company and its customers.

Suppliers may provide the company with parts and materials and be located at the beginning of the company's production chain; or they may supply services and consultancy and be located at any point along the company processes. The relative processes therefore often intersect with the company processes.

A model for excellence and continuous improvement must necessarily cater for suppliers on one hand and distributors/dealers on the other. The aim is to form partnerships that ensure that the quality mission is shared by these parties.

Considering the problem from the point of view of process management, it is evident that if management is already critical at the level of interfunctional processes (section 1.4), it is even more critical when activities directly controlled by the company interconnect with activities controlled by other, juridically separate parties with their own business goals. This situation is typical of the networked company, whose partnership agreements are precisely geared to the goals of the **leader company**, the party that answers to the end customer. The leader company must have control over the entire stream of processes across the network, with guaranteed visibility on the results, processes and

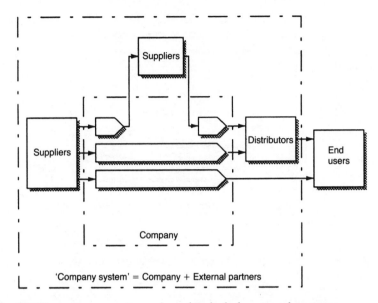

'Company system' = Company + External partners

Fig. 2.8 The company system enlarged to include external partners.

quality system of each partner, and be able to intervene on any factor that influences quality, costs and execution time.

The company and its partners form a system, which must be considered in its entirety for the purposes of the quality mission. In this case, reference can be made to a company system and to a quality system extended to the company system.

Figure 2.8 illustrates the relationship between the company, its suppliers and its distributors (the term distributor is used to signify any intermediary between the company and the end customer). From now on, external partners will be specified only where necessary; otherwise they will be treated as an integral part of the company system.

2.3.3 External users in the extended sense

Besides end customers and intermediate users, the model must also consider external users in the extended sense. We will begin by examining the **outgoing flows** from the company to the

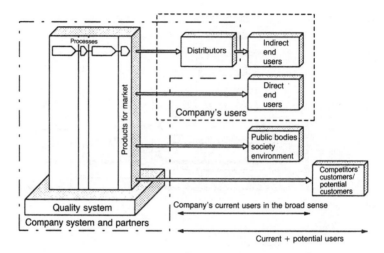

Fig. 2.9 The external users of the company in the extended sense.

market, enlarging the field of observation to include all recipients of 'products' generated by the company (see Fig. 2.9, where the processes-products component has been further simplified). In Fig. 2.9, the company's customers in the strict sense are:

- the end users of the company's products;
- the intermediate users (distributors), who, as seen, are also partners and thus form part of the company system.

At the broader level, the company's users are people, communities, environments that in some way are – or could be – adversely affected by the company's activities or expect a positive return from the company's presence or activities. The importance of these users depends on many factors, primarily cultural and political: the greater a society's awareness of human and social rights/duties and the need to improve the quality of life, the greater the need to take these users' expectations into consideration (this user category is shown as public bodies, society, environment in Fig. 2.9).

The other important recipients of the company's 'products' are the customers of competitors and, more generally, everyone who is not yet a customer of the company but could become so. This group 'uses' products whose quality is critically important to the success of the company: information, special offers, advertising, the global image of the company, which in turn is affected by the quality of all the other 'products' flowing from the company to the market. In particular, the satisfaction of the company's current customers has a ripple effect among its potential customers.

Now the incoming flows from users in the extended sense can be considered (Figs 2.10, 2.11, 2.12). The interpretation/ acquisition of user expectations channel is the conduit for the requirements/expectations of all external users (Fig. 2.10). It helps the company identify requirements prior to the definition of the goals of new 'products for the market'. Input at this stage must come from all target users (the company's own users and those of its competitors, intermediate and end users, users in the strict sense and users in the extended sense); to the extent that the company manages to learn what its competitors are doing to interpret and respond to the market's requirements, input may also come from reference competitors (competitor information channel).

The customer perception surveys channel provides the results of the periodical market surveys conducted by the company in order to draw up a user expectation menu for a particular market sector and adjust its customer satisfaction tree accordingly. This information, together with customer satisfaction results, provides important input for the strategic improvement planning process.

In the basic model in Fig. 2.1, the results feedback channel referred to the satisfaction of the company's customers. In Fig. 2.11, it is extended to include surveys of reference competitors' customers and opinion/image surveys conducted among public bodies and the general public.

Figure 2.11 also shows other types of survey and assessment that help the company ascertain its current position on the road to excellence, in relation to the companies it has chosen as points of reference. These references can be the company's main competitors, in which case customer satisfaction surveys must be flanked by product and, where possible, process and quality-system benchmark tests; non-competitors that are leaders in

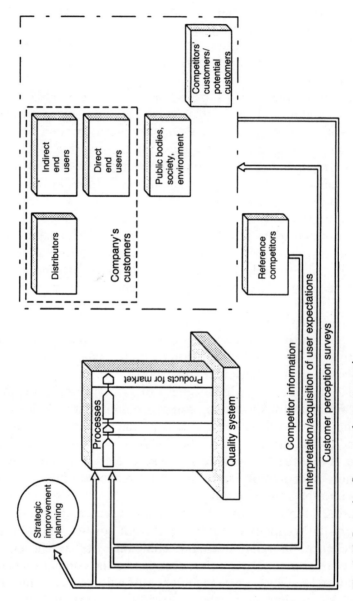

Fig. 2.10 Incoming flows: market expectations.

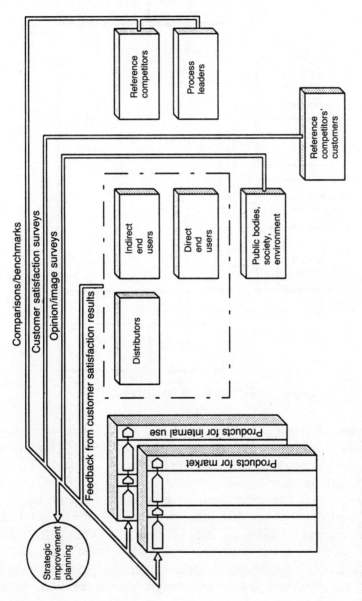

Fig. 2.11 Feedback from results.

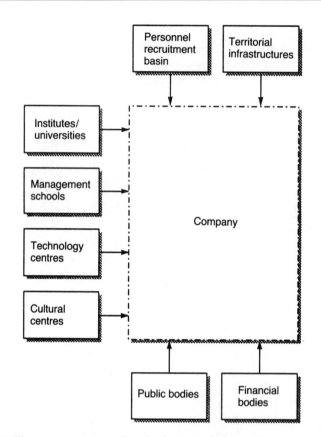

Fig. 2.12 The company's 'suppliers in the extended sense'.

processes of interest to the company, and against which the company's own processes can be usefully compared (for example, distribution/delivery), or, more generally, leaders in the quality system area.

The results of the customer satisfaction surveys mainly provide input for the processes that generate the goals of new products for the market or input for improvements to existing products. When they cover the entire customer satisfaction spectrum or segments of the spectrum, they provide **current quality profiles**, which planning will match with **target quality profiles**. Comparisons and benchmarks provide input both for processes that generate products for the market and for processes that generate 'products' for the company's internal use. Strictly speaking, customer satisfaction surveys can provide input for the latter type of process, too; however, this input is obtained through the interpretative medium of internal assessments and process audits or quality system surveys, and is not direct.

2.3.4 Suppliers in the extended sense

This section examines the **incoming flows** from all those bodies of which the company is in some way a user. The most important flows as far as the quality mission is concerned are from suppliers in the strict sense, who, as seen, should be 'partners' of the company and an integral part of its quality system. But, as with users, the picture is not complete unless 'suppliers' in the extended sense are considered (Fig. 2.12). Some of these suppliers coincide with users in the extended sense, the reason being that they are users because they are suppliers: for example, it is in the company's interest to furnish assistance and support for the environment from which it recruits its personnel, especially schools, which provide a basic culture and education. Even though these suppliers in the extended sense do not take a direct part in the company's activities and generally have no contractual ties with it, an organisation whose objective is excellence cannot afford to consider them simply as sources of materials whose quality and efficiency is somebody else's responsibility.

Strategic improvement planning must include a section laying out long- and short-term goals, strategies and priorities in relation to these suppliers, in order both to obtain specific benefits and to help improve the quality of the environment in which the company itself operates.

The part of the strategic plan dealing with suppliers in the broad sense and users in the broad sense should be the specific responsibility of top management.

2.3.5 Internal users and suppliers

Figure 2.13 illustrates the formal network of internal supplier/user relationships of relevance to the model. Here, the most important processes are those that generate 'products for the company' (management services-support-information). These processes have specific internal users, subdivided into two categories in Fig. 2.13:

1. top management (recipients of the most condensed reports);
2. other users.

For both categories, results must be assessed in terms of customer satisfaction.

Top management plays various customer and supplier roles. Most notably, it is the supplier of the quality system and the resources needed to manage processes (block 3 in Fig. 2.13). Its role as supplier and guarantor of the company quality system is particularly critical, but little understood in today's managerial culture: without an adequate 'system', operations managers will never manage to optimise the **Times-Quality-Costs** triad.

If correct, this apparently small detail justifies one of the theories of a new approach to company assessments presented by the author when the European Quality Award was being set up (Conti, 1991c), a theory sustained in this book: namely, that if top management is the supplier and the company's employees are the users (block 4 in Fig. 2.13), assessment of the quality system should be based chiefly on the users' opinions (interviews, questionnaires), not on reports drawn up by a group of managers delegated by top management, which is what happens with some of the major awards. These reports will always be optimistic and sometimes a long way from the real situation as experienced by those who work daily with quality system tools.

Returning to Fig. 2.13, top management's role as a user of business-financial results should also be considered (block 5). Having built a quality system for the company and played a propelling role in improvement (the **improvement mover** in Fig. 2.7), top management expects to see certain results on the market: increased market shares and better margins. Apart from the difficulty of quantifying these results (see below), the model must make the supplier-customer role clear, so that appropriate indicators and analysis techniques can be developed. Top management also expects results in terms of process ef-

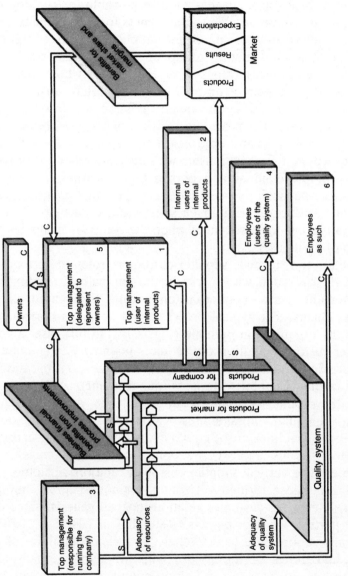

Fig. 2.13 Internal supplier (S) and customer (C) roles.

ficiency, again achieved through quality initiatives: this is the second input in block 5.

Finally, since top management is responsible for running the company and is accountable to the owners for the company's net worth, it plays another important supplier role, as the global manager of a fundamental group of 'internal customers': the company's employees (block 6 of Fig. 2.13), whose relationship with the company is optimal when maximum satisfaction is achieved on both sides. The quality mission requires that employees generate the maximum satisfaction of all external customers. It follows that employees themselves must be satisfied, in other words, their relationship with the company must provide them with professional and personal gratification, a pleasant workplace, particularly as regards interpersonal relations, and financial satisfaction. Employee satisfaction is one of the most important areas for assessment when the company evaluates the results of all its users.

Besides the formal supplier-customer roles described in Fig. 2.13, everyone who works in the company, including top management, plays supplier-customer roles throughout all the process chains. The typical process chain develops horizontally across the organisation pyramid (Fig. 2.14); in this case, a good supplier-customer relationship requires teamwork, alignment of all processes in the chain with the end customer, optimisation of global results (Chapter 4, Process Management).

But the supplier-customer relationship can – and for the purposes of the quality mission must – also develop vertically, down the hierarchical lines of the company, with the superior acting in some ways as his employee's supplier and in some ways as his customer. The vertical supplier-customer relationships obviously differ from those formed horizontally, among peers. They are obviously supplier-customer relationships **sui generis**, since one of the parties, whether he acts as supplier or customer, is hierarchically subordinate to the other. So a clear definition of the rights and duties of the parties will not help rationalise the relationship, nor is such a definition one of the goals of quality.

Nevertheless, a clear definition of the expectations of the 'customer' – when the superior is the customer and when the

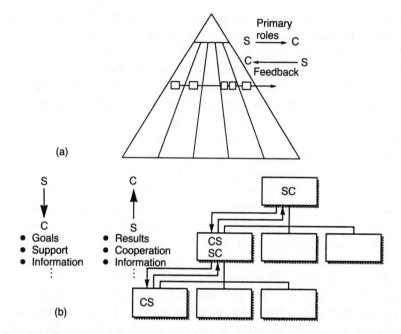

Fig. 2.14 Supplier-customer roles: (a) by horizontal lines (processes); (b) by vertical lines (hierarchy).

subordinate is the customer – and the duties of the 'supplier' is useful for a correct understanding of each role. Then the customer-supplier relationship will prove beneficial if it is geared to partnership and cooperation, if it helps eliminate bureaucratic, authoritarian attitudes on one hand and obsequiousness or lack of interest on the other, if it fosters leadership, participation, synergy, efficacy and efficiency.

Most people agree that total quality requires greater leadership by management. But leadership means motivating one's staff, dedicating the necessary time, attention and commitment. In other words, the manager must expand his 'supplier' role in relation to his staff and necessarily reduce it in relation to his own superior. A simple but sure criterion for assessing the progress made by a company adopting the total quality approach is to see how much time managers dedicate to their superiors (providing reports, letters or even just time) and how much they dedicate to their own staff, in short, how much time managers spend 'looking upwards' and how much 'looking downwards'. The management style of companies that make the most progress in quality is usually based on extensive delegation, problem prevention, careful collection and distribution of information, decision processes that involve operating staff. This means managers spend more time 'in the field', providing guidance for staff or simply setting an example. On the other hand, better information and fewer problems mean that time spent with the superior is used more efficiently, so in the end each manager has more time to dedicate to processes and improvement.

Conversely, in companies that make least progress in quality, top management is generally busy dealing with crises or trying to placate the anxiety caused by uncertainty, which in turn stems from a lack of reliable information and/or the unpredictability of results. This 'requisitions' a significant portion of the time that should be spent guiding staff. In extreme cases, top managers are required to be physically grouped together (in large corporate headquarters), although this proximity does not necessarily inspire a team spirit. Indeed, it often achieves the opposite result, and at the same time keeps managers away from their staff.

2.3.6 Analysis of the results component

Since results have been defined as the measurement of the satisfaction of the company's various users and the appreciation of potential users, this section will simply summarise the previous remarks on external and internal users and describe assessment criteria.

Merging Figs 2.9–2.13 to provide a graphic summary would be an unnecessary complication; these figures are to be used separately, when the model is adopted for specific analyses. The tree chart in Fig. 2.15 provides the best graphic summary. The chart includes a block for the **customers of reference competitors**, as a reminder that assessments of the company's own customers are not absolute: at times, objective difficulties may make it impossible to satisfy customer expectations fully (for example,

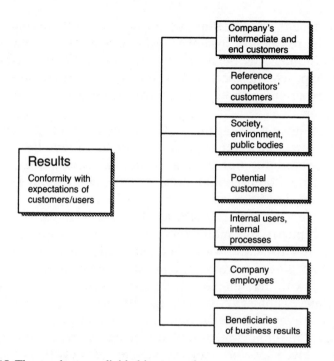

Fig. 2.15 The results tree, divided by type of user.

when technology is immature, as was the case in software for many years), so the position of all competitors is low; or all companies are competing to provide the customer with added value, so that customer expectations continue to rise. Measurement of customer satisfaction is therefore relative: the company must choose its reference competitors carefully and always compare their situation with its own. The criteria for assessing 'results' vary according to the class of user (Fig. 2.15).

Results for the **intermediate and end customers** of the company and its competitors can be obtained through customer satisfaction surveys (Chapter 3) or vendor ratings. It is important to use assessment criteria and methods that keep distortions of customers' perceptions to a minimum. For **users in the extended sense** (public bodies, the community, environment), results can be obtained through opinion and image surveys.

The results of **potential customers**, obtained through image surveys, are valuable in showing whether and to what degree the company image as perceived by current customers extends to this group, whether potential customers are conditioned by previous experiences, how effective the company's advertising is, and so on.

In a company geared to quality, assessment of the results of **internal users of internal processes** should already be an established procedure. For certain critical indicators, these results may be monitored continuously; in the majority of cases, they are obtained at intervals through questionnaires.

Regular surveys of **company employees** will indicate the degree of involvement and motivation, the sense of belonging to the company, satisfaction with work, financial remuneration, career paths, etc. These surveys are equivalent to customer satisfaction surveys, with the employee viewed as a customer – a very important customer. A substantial difference exists between this type of survey and the second type of employee survey, which examines the fitness-for-use of the quality system and considers the employee as a user of the system. Fitness-for-use surveys will be discussed under a separate heading.

Moving to the primary **beneficiaries of financial-business results** – the company's owners and its top management, whose performance is closely linked with these results – assessments conducted by financial experts are prejudicial, because inevitably they focus solely on an analysis of the company's financial statements. Financial and business results are influenced by a wide range of exogenous and endogenous variables. Separating the effects of initiatives designed for the purposes of the quality mission from everything else is a difficult task, which requires a thorough command of process and result indicators and a complete understanding of the correlation between these indicators and business management indicators. Moreover, the results of important quality initiatives tend to appear on the bottom line over the long rather than immediate term, as market share increases, cost reductions (especially structural costs) and decreases in fixed assets and working capital (Chapter 6).

Nevertheless, an assessment of the business and financial

benefits arising from quality is necessary – although very difficult – but it must be performed by an interfunctional team of experts led by top management.

2.3.7 Analysis of the processes component

Figure 2.4 illustrates the general pattern of the company chain of processes from user expectations to the deliverable product (Fig. 2.4(a)) or to the service performed in full or in part on the user's premises (Fig. 2.4(b)). This section deals with peculiarities that may emerge in processes depending on the product generated and the type of user (external or internal).

The first and most general type of process has already been examined in Fig. 2.4 and so will be discussed only briefly here. The other two types of process (products for internal users) will be discussed in greater detail, before examining assessment criteria.

(a) Processes that generate 'products' for users outside the company

In Fig. 2.4(a) (referring to hardware or software products or other 'deliverable' products), the process-product chain is subdivided into a series of blocks. The first block represents processes that begin with identification of market expectations and move to product goals – or **functional specifications** (second block). The specifications are the 'product' of the first chain of processes. The third block comprises the various execution processes, including product development (from functional specifications to technical specifications and project documentation) and production. The output of these processes is the 'product' (fourth block), which reaches the customer through the delivery processes (fifth block).

In the variation shown in Fig. 2.4(b), which refers to **service products**, a first group of execution processes takes place within the company and is therefore supported by the entire company quality system (back-end processes). The last part of the chain takes place in the **user environment** and is a decisive factor in

97

customer satisfaction (any error or imperfection is immediately perceived by the customer).

These **front-end** processes-products are supported by the components of the company quality system that relate to the individual, his skills, his relational abilities, his resourcefulness. In these cases, the excellence of the result depends on the qualities of the individual (the company quality system must cover job descriptions and personnel recruitment criteria), but also on the system's ability to educate, guide, motivate, support and reward the solitary bearers of the corporate image who come into contact with the customer in a thousand different circumstances. This is the **high touch** principle, to which growing attention has rightly been dedicated over the last few years as sensitivity to the quality of service has risen (Desatnick, 1987; Block *et al.*, 1986; D'Egidio, 1989; Carlzon, 1990).

Processes (a) and (b) are the two extremes of a whole range of process-product situations referring to external users. As users express growing interest in the service component associated with the product acquired and in the service content guaranteed by the product, and as suppliers enhance service value in order to boost competitiveness, so case (a) in its purest form becomes increasingly rare, and a mixed situation tending towards case (b) becomes more common.

(b) Processes that generate products for the company's internal use: processes that generate support 'products' (usually services and information) for other processes (Fig. 2.16)

These processes typically support the company's core business, in other words, they support the operating processes that generate products for the market. Examples of support processes include information management, administration, personnel management and development, maintenance, etc. With these processes, close coordination between supplier and customer is possible during both planning and assessment. It is also vital to the quality of results and must be actively pursued.

In particular, the managers of the supplier process (support process) and the user process must together define the needs of

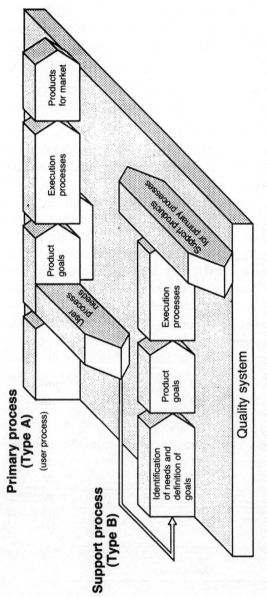

Fig. 2.16 Support process (type B) which generates products for use by primary processes (type A).

the latter ('user process needs' in Fig. 2.16) and organise any initiatives that may be needed to improve the capabilities or goals of the supplier process. Comparison of results with user requirements must be based on both supplier assessments (of conformity with goals) and fitness-for-use evaluations by the user, based on agreed criteria and frequent correlation of results.

(c) Processes that generate products for the company's internal use: processes whose goal is improvement of the quality system

While processes (a) and (b) are usually permanent, processes whose purpose is to modify the company system, in particular the quality system, are associated with specific initiatives and end once the goal has been reached (Fig. 2.17).

The quality system consists of different elements, any of which may need to be modified through improvement initiatives designed to achieve specific goals. In fact, during the formative phase of the quality system, the company's improvement plans will be concerned chiefly with initiatives and processes of this type, because adjustments to the quality system are vital to improve processes and products and consequently results. Assessing the match between the product and the goals is straightforward (the product is the intended improvement), but assessing results in terms of customer satisfaction is more difficult. The problem lies in defining the customer, or more precisely, the user of the quality system. Does a system have a user?

Without doubt, the company's employees are users of the quality system (as blocks 3 and 4 of Fig. 2.13 show); not users of the results of the company's activities – like the external/internal

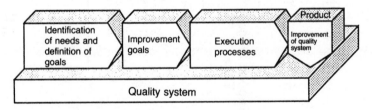

Fig. 2.17 Process aimed at improvement of the quality system (type C).

users of the company's products, or employees themselves in terms of their expectations of personal gratification – but operators and therefore users of the company machine that produces these results. So the assessment of the system's fitness-for-use must come, through the appropriate channels, from the company's employees, each of whom will evaluate the system in relation to his or her individual role.

The quality system can be likened to a large workshop, which has to be equipped so that each worker can perform his job as required. It has to provide the right environment, training, guidance, machinery, tools, etc.

The people employed in the workshop, at their different levels and each in relation to his particular role, are the people best qualified to judge the fitness of the resources available to help them achieve their goals. They are the users of these resources, and the higher their level of responsibility, the wider the range of use. But as their level of responsibility rises, the role of supplier emerges together with that of user. The workshop's foreman has the greatest responsibility as supplier: it is his job to ensure the workshop is fit for the mission to be accomplished. In consultation with the users, the foreman must decide what resources the workshop should provide for its users/workers. At a lower level, his staff share responsibility for 'creating' an adequate system, but at the same time they are also users of part of the system. Moving down the hierarchy, the role of supplier gradually diminishes and eventually disappears, while the role of user gradually becomes more specialised.

Returning to the quality system, the company's CEO has the chief responsibility for the system; he is the supplier of the system (Fig. 2.13) and must ensure that it is fit for use at all levels, for the purposes of the quality mission.

It is therefore the duty of management – and of top management in particular – to guarantee that the result of every improvement initiative is always assessed by the users (type (c) processes). In addition, top management must ensure that the state of the quality system in relation to the mission is periodically assessed.

This type of assessment will be examined later; the intention here is simply to show that assessment of the quality system is possible and that the chief assessment tool is the user survey, which investigates users' perceptions and opinions.

In practice, the **system audit** is the most frequently used tool today. This is an assessment conducted by experts and/or management of the sector concerned. Audits vary from those specified by the ISO 9000 model, which cover the part of the company quality system concerned with product quality assurance, to audits of the global company quality system based on the Malcolm Baldrige Award or the European Quality Award.

In the author's view, the audit is useful only to assess the state of control of the more tangible processes and components of the quality system, whereas the opinions of significant samples of employees at the different levels of the company are more significant for assessments of the more critical and less tangible parts of the system. These opinions can be collected through individual and group interviews and questionnaires, ensuring that information is treated confidentially.

This issue will be dealt with in greater detail in Chapters 3 and 7.

2.3.8 Process measurements

This section examines briefly the criteria for current measurement and periodic assessment of processes: measurability/assessability is the necessary condition for every element in the model. This topic will be examined in greater depth in analysing process management (Chapter 4) and assessments conducted for strategic improvement planning (Chapter 3). The reference here is case 2.4(a), the deliverable finished product: the variations for the other cases can be easily extrapolated.

Figure 2.18 shows the current process and product measurements adopted by the company to ensure that its subsequent user results coincide as closely as possible with – or exceed – expectations.

The figure refers to all processes:

• processes that begin from user expectations and lead to product goals;

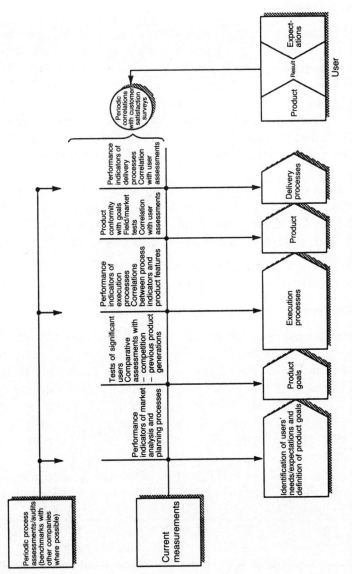

Fig. 2.18 Current process measurements, periodic assessments and correlations with customer satisfaction results.

- processes that begin from product goals and lead to deliverable products;
- delivery processes.

Current measurements guarantee results only if all the processes involved are under control and the right indicators are used. Periodic **assessments/audits** must be conducted to monitor the state of control and the degree of excellence (Chapter 3). The upper part of Fig. 2.18 refers to these audits.

Periodic correlation of current process measurements (especially execution process measurements) and current end product measurements with the results of customer satisfaction surveys is also essential.

This analysis of the processes component can be concluded with a simplified representation of the relevant part of the model (Fig. 2.19). The figure shows the three types of process considered and reiterates the results, processes, quality system tripartition.

2.3.9 Analysis of the quality system component

The quality system is by far the most difficult component to describe in the model. It has been defined as the company subsystem incorporating all the elements that contribute to the accomplishment of the quality mission; that is, all the structural, technical, managerial, human and social elements of the organisation together with all the elements of the system of values that play a significant part as far as the excellence of results and continuous improvement are concerned.

Distinguishing all the variables that affect the quality mission, and identifying the relationships and hierarchy that exist between these variables, clearly comprise a formidable undertaking, given the still highly immature stage of development of total quality management. Any description of the quality system today is necessarily a working hypothesis involving subjective choices. Analysis of the assessment criteria used by the **Deming Application Prize** and the **Malcolm Baldridge Award** shows that significant differences still exist among the characteristics con-

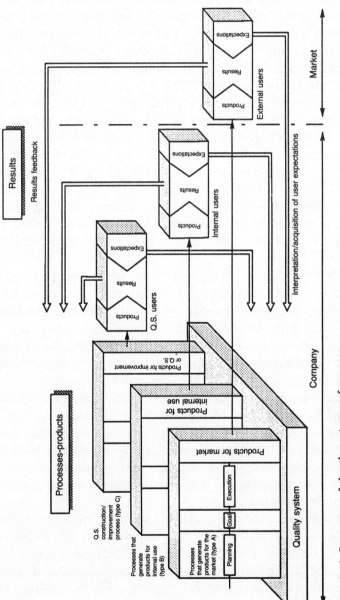

Fig. 2.19 Summary of the three types of process.

sidered fundamental to excellence. But these two awards are not based on a quality mission model of the company such as that presented in this book: their models stem from the assessment criteria chosen, not vice versa. The lack of a frame of reference means that criteria are jumbled together (Chapter 7 has a more detailed discussion of the awards, including the European Quality Award, in relation to the TQM model issue). The Malcolm Baldrige 'results' category, for example, includes the results of the company's product and process assessments, but not customer satisfaction results. Customer satisfaction results, which are restricted to external customers, are included in the customer satisfaction category, but this category also includes items covered by the processes and quality system categories in the model proposed here. A search for internal user satisfaction results in the Malcolm Baldrige Award yields a limited item related to employees only in the human resources utilisation category.

Readers may or may not agree with the model presented in this book (which has largely been adopted as the model for the European Quality Award), with its fundamental subdivision into results, processes and quality system. But it is undeniable that the lack of a reference model makes selection of assessment criteria extremely arbitrary and leads to a proliferation of approaches.

In the comparison which follows of the approach presented here with the criteria of the Malcolm Baldrige Award, the Deming Application Prize or other schemes, it should be remembered that the quality system described in this book corresponds conceptually with the Malcolm Baldrige (or Deming) list minus user results and processes, which here are considered as separate categories.

It is assumed that the reader is familiar with the Malcolm Baldrige Award and the Deming Application Prize (Malcolm Baldrige National Quality Award, 1991; Deming Prize Committee, 1989). The first-level criteria, or categories, of the two awards are listed in Table 2.3, side by side to facilitate comparison. (A fuller comparison including the European Quality Award is made in Chapter 7.)

Table 2.3 First level criteria of awards

Malcolm Baldrige Award	Deming Application Prize
1. Leadership	1. Policy
2. Information and Analysis	2. Organisation and its
3. Strategic Quality Planning	management
4. Human Resources Utilisation	3. Education and dissemination
5. Quality Assurance of Products	4. Collection, dissemination and
and Services	use of information on Quality
6. Quality Results	5. Analysis
7. Customer Satisfaction	6. Standardisation
	7. Control
	8. Quality Assurance
	9. Results
	10. Planning for the future

These two lists of what ought to be the main criteria for judging total quality differ considerably. If the analysis were extended to include the total quality system menus used by companies, consultants and researchers, further differences would emerge over a broad spectrum of similar or related but by no means identical criteria. These include:

customer orientation;
total involvement;
process management/horizontal integration;
vertical alignment;
continuous improvement;
role of management;
supplier involvement;
communication;
measurement.

In view of this dispersion – and the fact that each new entrant has his own list of **first-level categories** – it is legitimate to wonder whether it will ever be possible to draw up a rational homogeneous set of criteria for describing – and consequently assessing – the elements of the organisation system that concern the quality mission. One answer could be that total quality is not yet a mature discipline and that more time is needed to develop a rational homogeneous set of criteria. This is true, but in the meantime the differences will tend to increase and become established. So the possibility of a more rational approach ought to be considered now.

An explanation for the differences can be found. In today's highly fluid environment, the problems encountered by companies experimenting with total quality management are similar, but not identical: they depend on the cultural context, geographic location, the features of the individual company and the internal level of quality development. This has inevitably led to differences and priorities. A short list of first-level criteria drawn up by a fairly mixed group of people from different backgrounds would be unlikely to contain less than 20–30 categories.

Since the general tendency is to have less than ten first-level criteria or categories, it is obvious that a unified list is impossible. Moreover, while unification of self-assessment criteria is a logical goal, there is certainly no need to unify the criteria on which the awards are based; indeed, there is a comprehensible tendency towards differentiation.

The cause of total quality, however, is not served by maintaining apparently random differences: it would be much better to reach agreement on a general type of model that allows for differentiation and customisation. The root of the problem seems to be that, as seen, everyone wants to assign first-level status to the criteria they consider of greatest importance for total quality, even if this means giving top ranking to a criterion that in a corporate organisation hierarchy should be placed at a lower level. Take the example of **training**: this could be considered a first-level criterion for total quality, but in hierarchical terms it would certainly be more logical to include it in the human resources management category; similarly, leadership is fundamental, but it is obviously a sub-category of the role of management.

With the criteria used to date, it has become common to adopt a partial term at the first level to indicate an entire concept. For example, when the term 'leadership' is used at first level, it actually covers a much broader concept, and the second-level criteria refer to the more general concept of the role of management rather than to leadership alone. This 'licence' to use a part at first level to indicate the whole means that the differences between the various schemes may – and in fact do – diminish at the second level (in the Malcolm Baldrige Award, the second level is the level of 'items', while the first level is the level of 'categories'). But since there is also a certain amount of pressure to reduce the number of second-level criteria (the Malcolm Baldrige Award items have been cut from 66 to 32 in four years), the consequences of the subjective choices made at first level are inevitably reflected at the more analytical levels – and this leads to unjustifiably large differences in assessment criteria.

A number of approaches can be taken to define the quality system:

- a **purely inductive approach** of the kind generally adopted to date, based on experience (this means that a reasonably limited number of first-level categories has to be selected, on an inevitably subjective basis, from the criteria considered significant);
- a **deductive approach**, which uses a general model of the organisation system to identify the elements that form the quality subsystem;
- a **mixed approach**, which combines organisation models with the elements experience has so far shown to be of relevance to quality.

Here the third approach is adopted. This involves a 'non-ideological' deployment of the characteristics of the quality subsystem, in other words, the elements in the quality subsystem are not pre-established choices and all the elements considered important are included. The choices will be made when the assessment criteria are defined, by allocating suitable weights to the different characteristics.

The mixed approach requires an organisation model that can be matched with the requirements of the quality mission.

The organisation system model used here (Fig. 2.20) is an interpretation of state-of-the-art organisation and management theories (Kast and Rosenzweig, 1985), which gives convincing

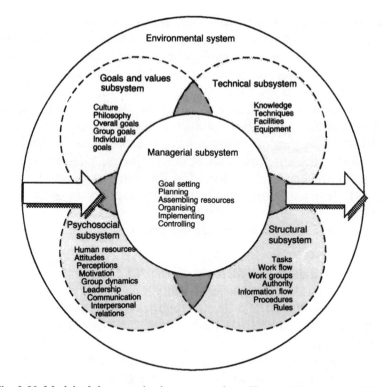

Fig. 2.20 Model of the organisation system, from Kast and Rosenzweig (1985, p. 114), reproduced with permission of McGraw-Hill.

results. But what really counts is the methodological approach: it seems to be applicable to any structured model of the organisation system, for example the **seven S** McKinsey model, which, given its origins, is certainly suited to the purpose (Peters and Waterman, 1982).

The organisation model used here has five subsystems (Fig. 2.20):

- the **managerial subsystem**, which is responsible for setting goals and strategies, planning, resource location, organisation, implementation and control;
- the **values subsystem**: the company's culture, values, missions;
- the **psycho-social subsystem**: human resources, individual and group attitudes, communication, informal organisation, etc.;

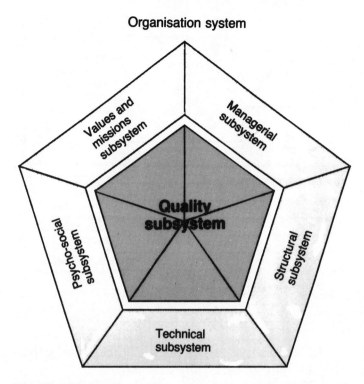

Fig. 2.21 The relationship between the quality subsystem and the components of the organisation system.

- the **structural subsystem**: infrastructures, process management organisation, procedures, etc.;
- the **technical subsystem**: covers skills, technologies, tools, etc.

Figure 2.21 shows how the quality system hooks on to the organisation system of Fig. 2.20. The larger of the two pentagons represents the organisation system, whose five subsystems are represented by the five triangles. The smaller internal pentagon represents the quality subsystem (always referred to here as the quality system).

Figure 2.22 illustrates the first-level subdivision of the quality system. Each first-level criterion is a set of elements of relevance to the quality mission (the wording already indicates a match

111

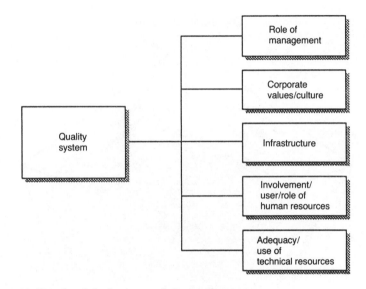

Fig. 2.22 First-level deployment of the quality system.

between the five subsystems of Fig. 2.20 and what experience suggests is relevant to the quality mission).

Figure 2.23 illustrates the second deployment phase, from the first-level to the second-level criteria. Here, the inductive 'match' with knowledge based on experience in the field of total quality widens, and the choice of criteria becomes accordingly more subjective.

General agreement on a group of not more than 50 criteria is not impossible. Fifty should not be considered an alarmingly large number: the model is **not** a prescriptive tool, but a descriptive guide, which can be lightened by the allocation of weights.

Weights allocation is fundamental to the quality system model proposed here. The tree charts in Figs 2.22 and 2.23 list the full menu of organisation system elements that may be of relevance to the quality mission. This is an open, general-purpose model.

When the quality mission is related to a specific class of companies and/or market sectors, then some criteria may become irrelevant; these criteria are allocated a **zero weight** and the model is simplified. Other criteria may be so heavily weighted

Role of management
- Leadership
- Definition/dissemination quality policies
- Creation/management of the quality system
- Definition goals/strategies and strategic planning
- System audits
- Creation of values
- Management team unity
- Responsibility versus public bodies/society/environment

Corporate values/culture
- Customer orientation
- Excellence and continuous improvement
- Team spirit/matrix mentality
- Management by facts
- Respect for the individual
- Participatory management

Infrastructures
- Management by goals and means. Vertical alignment
- Process management/horizontal integration
- Information/data collection/analysis/transmission/uses
- Customer satisfaction measurement/improvement organisation
- Strategic/operational improvement planning operation
- Improvement organisation/teams
- Assessments/audits
- Involvement external partners
- Standardisation
- Benchmarking organisation
- Product/service quality assurance

Involvement/use/role of human resources
- Motivation/involvement
- Communication
- Team work
- Internal supplier-customer relations
- Attitude to improvement
- Interpersonal relationships
- Empowerment/participatory management/decision-making processes
- Policies/standards/procedures
- Job rotation
- Education and training
- Reward system

Adequacy/use technical resources
- Diffusion/application statistical knowhow
- Process management methodologies/tools
- Problem-solving methodologies/tools
- Policy deployment diffusion/use
- Quality function deployment diffusion/use
- Information technology diffusion/use
- Standardisation methodologies/tools (SDCA)

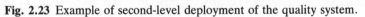

Fig. 2.23 Example of second-level deployment of the quality system.

113

that they virtually become first-level criteria (or categories for the Malcolm Baldrige Award). In short, the allocation of weights can turn an open, general-purpose model into any specific model, including the models of the Malcolm Baldrige Award, the Deming Application Prize and the European Quality Award (if necessary, extending deployment to a third level). Weights can effectively eliminate a criterion – a point worth repeating – or they can turn a third-level criterion into a virtual first-level criterion.

The general model can be regarded as a **guide for the construction of specific models** and a **reminder** as regards the **rational allocation of each criterion within an organisation model**.

Weights are particularly important for quality award assessments. Indeed, the specific nature of the award is reflected in its allocation of weights. Weight allocation highlights the award's underlying 'ideological' position and, more generally, the criteria adopted and the differences between one award and another.

Use of a widely accepted general-purpose menu and the allocation of weights can also make a significant contribution to the definition of specific quality system models for companies operating in related sectors. The general model can provide a basis for intercompany studies and experimentation: cooperation among companies, even competitor companies, should be possible in this field.

The quality system model described here was first presented in the document, mentioned earlier, used as a conceptual basis for the European Quality Award (Conti, 1991c). But, to repeat a point made above, the approach proposed is not dependent on the model in Figs 2.20–2.23. The main objective is to form a general-purpose non-prescriptive model to act as a matrix and guide for the construction of specific models, and thus avoid arbitrary, subjective methods of selection of the kind that have created as many total quality system assessment models as there are awards (indeed, as there are consultants and companies!).

2.3.10 Assessing the fitness-for-use of the quality system

The clear distinction made here between quality system, results and processes/products certainly simplifies assessment compared with models that mix these categories together. Nevertheless, assessing the fitness-for-use of the quality system in relation to the mission is a difficult task, since it is intrinsically more critical than assessing results and measuring products/processes. (Chapters 3 and 7 have a more detailed discussion of the assessment issue.) It was seen earlier that the traditional approach, whereby the quality system is assessed by or on behalf of the company's management, leads inevitably to bias, particularly when the assessment is conducted for external purposes. Management, and top management in particular, is the supplier of and responsible for the company's quality system, and as such will tend to make a positive assessment of its work.

A more reliable assessment can be made by users; and the users of the quality system are the people who work in the company, at every level.

Assessments of the fitness-for-use of the quality system in relation to the accomplishment of the quality mission must therefore be based largely on sample surveys at every level of the workforce, with a guarantee of anonymity to ensure full cooperation. The surveys will normally be based on questionnaires, which can usefully be supplemented with direct interviews, as long as the interviewer (preferably someone from outside the company) is capable of soliciting the maximum frankness and sincerity from the interviewee. The questionnaires and the interviews must be designed to obtain precise opinions on every item in the quality system model used by the company, that is, on every branch of the quality system tree.

This kind of survey provides the most valuable information on the fitness-for-use of the quality system, particularly as regards elements such as management leadership, company values, management style, participation, decision processes, teamwork and communication.

The quality system also includes a series of more tangible elements, particularly in the **infrastructure** and **technical and methodological resources** categories, for which conventional system audits can be highly significant. So the assessment of the quality system must also include this type of audit. Audits will be of even greater value for the system's most tangible elements, because they give greater specific detail than the opinions ex-

115

pressed in sample surveys. The reverse is true for the least tangible characteristics.

The two types of assessment are complementary and both can be usefully compared with the reports drawn up by management as the supplier of the quality system, which describe the system as it 'should be' (the aim of surveys and audits is to describe the system as it is or as it is perceived by its users).

The quality system is the most significant component when assessing the company's improvement potential (especially in the self-assessments conducted for the purposes of annual improvement planning, see Chapter 3). So it is important that the company make systematic use of internal surveys and audits in order to refine its skill in handling these intrinsically difficult quality system assessment tools.

A final point, to repeat the observation made in discussing results: employee surveys designed to monitor opinions on the fitness-for-use of the quality system are conceptually distinct from customer satisfaction surveys. The two types of survey will be dealt with in section 3.2 on self-assessment.

The model at work: improvement planning

3.1 THE NEED FOR STRATEGIC – AND HIGH QUALITY – PLANNING TO KEEP ON COURSE FOR TOTAL QUALITY

This chapter begins by recalling the observations made in Chapter 1 as regards the strategic importance of the term 'improvement' in the context of total quality. With **positive quality** competition, improvement moves beyond the static concept of a simple reduction in the difference between performance and goals, into the sphere of continuous change. Here, goals move forward all the time and performance must be improved continuously to keep up. Improvement planning is the subject of this chapter. It is the first fundamental issue for companies translating a total quality mission into goals, strategies and priorities.

Planning in the context of the quality mission is necessarily strategic. The company must draw up hypothetical competitive scenarios, which evolve over time, and identify its dynamic position within these scenarios for the coming years.

Modern quality theories place great emphasis on goal definition processes and important methodologies and tools have been developed to help planning processes establish high-quality goals: quality function deployment, policy deployment, and the seven managerial tools.

The reason for this emphasis was explained in section 1.1

(Fig. 1.2), which can be recalled briefly here. Competitive results can only be achieved through:

- quality of goals;
- quality of execution.

Traditional quality theories focused mainly on the right-hand pillar, the quality of execution processes. Modern thinking certainly confirms (indeed elevates) the importance of execution quality, but its particular focus is the left-hand pillar, the quality of goals, the quality of specifications: 'doing the right things', minimising the global costs of non-quality (which arise from doing the wrong things as well as from not doing them right first time) and missed revenue opportunities.

First, the company must aim high, then it must hit centre. This is a competitive quality vision, focused chiefly on goals and the degree to which goals match user expectations, both expressed or perceived expectations and latent expectations (which are often brought to light only by the company that succeeds in combining technological knowhow with attention to the market).

If modern quality theories attach such importance to goal definition processes (and consequently provide methodologies and tools to help optimise these processes and plan new products, new services, etc.), there would appear to be no reason why the strategic improvement planning process itself – which identifies the areas in which the company system should be improved – should not be subject to the rules of total quality. And yet this is frequently the case in companies that have formally declared their adherence to continuous improvement.

Two typical examples demonstrate the point: the more frequent case is the company that continues to separate improvement planning from corporate strategic planning. Inevitably, this means goals are defined at the inappropriate level of operating staff, who are naturally conditioned by their own visibility on problems and their own capacity for intervention, and set goals accordingly. The second type of company has already promoted improvement planning to the level of strategic planning, but instead of applying the new total quality approach to its strategic planning process, it does the opposite and applies the traditional company-centric approach. Planning therefore tends to be **driven** by management and the official interpreters of market requirements and the state of the company, instead of being **led** by the market itself and the real company.

In the first example, the results of the improvement planning process are mere drops in the ocean: the company's major problems are not considered, plans are geared to local improvement issues, improvement barely manages to scratch the surface of the company; at best, it penetrates only the manufacturing sectors, which by tradition are more sensitive to quality. Important goals are more likely to be defined in the second case, but there is no guarantee that the basis for planning is complete, that full checks will be made of the means needed to achieve goals, or that macro-goals will be distributed appropriately within the company and translated into clear goals for each individual process (policy/goal deployment). In short, the necessary propulsory force exists, but the company may not move in the right direction.

3.1.1 Strategic planning and micro-planning

The frequency of strategic improvement planning, which defines or reviews the company's mid/long-term goals and strategies, will be dictated by the speed with which the reference scenario evolves. However, it must coincide with general business planning. The expression 'mid/long-term' is entirely relative to the speed of change in the reference scenario; but, given the costs of the assessments required for correct planning processes, an annual cycle is advisable for 'major' strategic planning. Within the annual cycle, the company will proceed with **continuous micro-planning**, that is, all the local plans (made at all levels) for specific improvement initiatives, which constitute the essence of total quality.

In the total quality approach, in fact, the macro-improvement goals set by strategic planning will be achieved not only through a number of quantum leaps (exceptional improvements, usually attained through macro-innovation), but also – and above all –

through a wide range of often small initiatives, based on wide-spread creativity and innovation (incremental improvement: Fig. 1.6). Widespread innovation must be the main product of the total quality culture, although it must be carefully disciplined or chaos will ensue. This means improvement must be planned and tested so as not to interfere with existing processes, using PDCA methodologies (and SDCA methodologies for consolidation and maintenance).

The combination of annual strategic planning and distributed micro-planning will enable the company to keep on course towards total quality. But if planning processes are to be of high quality, the company must possess the ability to assess its current situation (general or local, according to the level of planning) and historical and current improvement trends.

3.2 GETTING STARTED: ASSESSMENT OF THE CURRENT SITUATION AND OF IMPROVEMENT TRENDS (SELF-ASSESSMENT)

The first step in the planning process is to assess the company's **current** situation with regard to the quality mission.

The term 'self-assessment' is used to define this activity, indicating that the assessment of the company is performed at the wish not of a customer or any other external party, but of the company itself, led by its top management. A word of warning, however: self-assessment **does not signify** that the assessment reflects the opinions of management, expressed directly or through the company staff: the task of management is to get others to speak – users in particular – and to listen to them. Nor does it mean that external parties are excluded from the process. On the contrary, external parties are usually in the best position to monitor the voice of the users without influencing them and to perform specialist assessments; but they are working for the company, operating as experts in a company process.

The model described in the previous chapter suggests the input for the self-assessment process. In Fig. 3.1(a), input 1

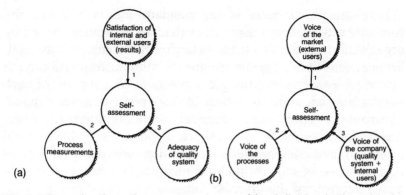

Fig. 3.1 Input for the self-assessment process: (a) subdivision in line with the model; (b) internal users are moved from 1 to 3. Input 1 becomes 'the voice of the market' and input 3 'the voice of the company'.

represents the results of customer satisfaction surveys of all user classes; input 2 represents the results of current measurements and periodic audits of the company's main processes; input 3 represents the results of the audits and fitness-for-use surveys on the quality system.

The groups in Fig. 3.1(b), are slightly different: internal-user satisfaction results are moved from input 1 to input 3, so that input 1 becomes 'the voice of the market' (the company's customers plus external users in the extended sense), and input 3 becomes 'the voice of the company' (internal-user satisfaction plus the results of fitness-for-use assessments of the quality system – audits and quality-system user surveys: section 2.3). Input 2 is unchanged; for consistency, it can be called 'the voice of the processes'.

Figure 3.1(b) is interesting because it offers a convincing description of the **three voices** that must constantly guide management as it steers a course towards total quality, planning macro- and micro-improvement initiatives (Conti, 1991b).

The **voice of the market** must certainly be a guide for the company competing at the level of customer satisfaction. Careful monitoring and interpretation of the market will enable the company to detect the first signs of change and to be a protagonist of change.

121

Listening to the **voice of the company** means believing the company is a vital organism rather than an inert mass shaped by organisation charts. It means believing the company has intelligence, sensitivity, experience and distributed responsibility. It means an awareness of the great potential contribution of each person and each group, which all too often is never tapped. Horizontal, vertical and diagonal communication (in other words, communication by the shortest route, not by hierarchical channels) and 'deregulated' information are the vital sap of decision-making and essential if continuous learning is to become a characteristic of the organisation.

Finally, companies that listen to the **voice of the processes** appreciate the importance of skill, the need to quantify and measure phenomena, to base management on facts, not on opinions (whose weight is often proportional to hierarchical ranking rather than to competence).

The **ideal company** listens to these voices continuously. With reference to Fig. 2.10, it defines its product/service offers according to the match between its continuous readings of the market and the possibilities offered by technology; with reference to Fig. 2.11, it continuously 'adjusts its sights' and improves its performance in line with the feedback from results, which it monitors carefully: product quality/reliability data, service quality indicators, surveys on the reasons for missed sales, customer complaints, customer satisfaction and customer defection surveys, etc.

As far as the voice of the company is concerned, the ideal company tends to gear its culture to the networked approach rather than the hierarchical approach. It views organisation in terms of **relationships** rather than **blocks**. Decision processes are based on information from the people who know and the people who operate, vertical and horizontal relationships stress the importance of participation and cooperation (Fig. 2.14).

Finally, the ideal company bases process management on quantitative indicators, related on one hand to user results and on the other to wider-ranging, higher-level indicators needed by top management to run the company correctly.

But the ideal company is an abstraction. The **real company** cannot take for granted that the communication channels described above will function properly, nor can it assess distortions in the channels through use of those channels; in other words, it needs an external criterion on which to assess the system. The ability of the company channels to transmit the voices can be assessed by temporarily short-cutting these institutional channels and creating direct links between a top management 'listening centre' and customers, employees and processes.

This is the subject of the first part of this chapter: a strategic improvement planning approach that short-cuts institutional channels to listen directly to the voices of the market, the company and the processes.

Figure 3.1(b) has been discussed at length, because it illustrates the concept particularly well. Figure 3.1(a) does not differ greatly from Fig. 3.1(b), but it has the advantage of greater consistency with the model and therefore maintains the continuity of the analysis. With reference to Fig. 3.1(a), each of the three inputs in the assessment process can now be examined, beginning with results.

3.3 ASSESSING RESULTS: SATISFACTION OF ALL USERS

References to the model are provided by Figs 2.11, 2.13 and above all Fig. 2.15.

Results, the degree to which the company meets user expectations, are assessed chiefly through direct surveys, which short-cut institutional channels and apply directly to users. But the assessment must also take account of all the information routinely provided by institutional channels, partly because this information will certainly be complementary in some ways (for example, consolidated data on customer complaints or customer defections), and partly because it is vital to check how far the information corresponds with direct customer surveys (the distortion of the channels). Having made this distinction, this section focuses on **specific** surveys that short-cut the usual channels. Satisfaction surveys of the company's own customers and those of its reference competitors (first and second blocks in

Fig. 2.15) provide by far the most revealing information on the current situation and trends, so these are examined first.

3.3.1 External user surveys

Customer satisfaction is the result of the user's comparison between the product and his expectations (Fig. 2.1), where 'product' signifies every company response to an element or group of elements in the user expectation menu (Fig. 2.2). Section 2.2 showed that tree charts are a useful way of representing the expectation menu or the customer satisfaction menu of a certain class of user in relation to a particular offer (for example, young users in relation to CD players, or corporate users in relation to information technology). The customer satisfaction tree shows everything that a particular class of users regards as the quality attributes of a particular offer. So the company setting out to measure the satisfaction of a certain group of users cannot build the tree on the basis of its own knowledge or opinions, it must have the tree built by the users themselves.

(a) Building the customer satisfaction tree

Section 2.3 defined surveys whose aim is to obtain a customer-built tree as customer perception surveys (quality as perceived by users). These surveys must be conducted among significant users: not just the company's own customers, but those of its competitors, who are meaningful solely as reference users. It is always best to commission the survey from a specialist company, which possesses the necessary specific experience and lacks bias. Generally speaking, the first stage will consist of detailed direct interviews with a limited sample of reference users, from which a preliminary tree will be plotted. Then the survey will be extended to a numerically significant sample to fine-tune the tree and assign weights to each branch.

Figure 3.2 is an example of a tree for medium-large users of information technology systems. It shows the first two levels of branches, with weights assigned to the first-level branches.

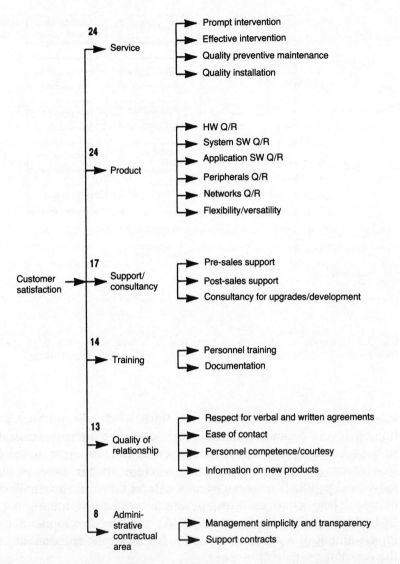

Fig. 3.2 Example of customer satisfaction tree for medium-large users of information technology systems, with weighted first-level branches (source Olivetti).

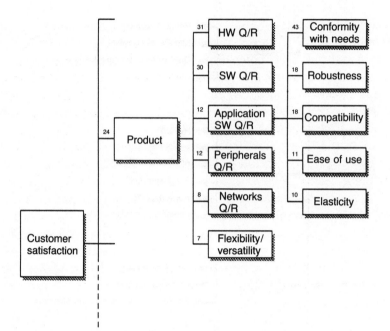

Fig. 3.3 Example of extension of branches, with weights, to the third level (medium-large users of information technology systems) (source Olivetti).

Figure 3.3 extends the tree to the third level. The number of branch levels depends on the purpose of the survey: general surveys covering the entire customer satisfaction tree usually stop at the second or third level, whereas specific surveys on individual products or services may extend down to the smallest details. The second case usually applies when the intention is to build a quality deployment matrix for the development or improvement of a product or service (or a specific component of the customer satisfaction tree).

To date, very few merchandise sectors have widely accepted customer satisfaction trees (the term 'standard' is avoided because it would be a contradiction in terms: elements as variable as users' expectations and perceptions of quality cannot be confined within standard models). Nevertheless, it is not unreasonable to suggest that a customer satisfaction tree offering an accurate picture of user perceptions and expectations could be built at a given time for a specific class of user in a specific market and for a specific offer, and that it could be used as a reference by all suppliers. This is much easier for manufactured goods (such as automobiles), but becomes gradually more difficult as the offer widens to include service, support and the quality of the relationship.

Hopefully, users and suppliers will reach the conclusion that working together to build a customer satisfaction tree (or trees) for their sector offers mutual advantages: it would promote discussion of the elements to be included, stimulate independent surveys (for example, by the trade press), prepare the way for less controversial quality awards and reduce costs for companies by eliminating the need for individual customer perception surveys (in fact, only companies that realise the need for this type of survey and can sustain the relevant costs actually conduct customer perception surveys).

(b) Assessing the satisfaction of the company's own customers and those of reference competitors

Once the company is equipped with the tool (the customer satisfaction tree with its weighted branches), it can begin conducting customer satisfaction surveys among its own customers (intermediate and end users) and sample groups of reference-competitor customers (Fig. 2.15, first branch and sub-branch).

The surveys usually take the form of questionnaires, with each question relating to a particular branch of the tree. Customers are frequently asked to use a scale of 1 to 5 for their answers:

1. utterly dissatisfied;
2. dissatisfied;
3. neutral judgement (motives for satisfaction and dissatisfaction balance out);
4. satisfied;
5. extremely satisfied.

The survey can be conducted by a specialist firm or directly by the company itself. The company conducts the survey itself

127

when it wants to demonstrate its concern for its customer and its firm intention of improving satisfaction on the basis of the indications provided. In this case, the chief officer of the supplier company should send the questionnaire to his opposite number in the customer organisation, with a letter explaining the survey, stressing the value of the answers given and asking the recipient to ensure that the answers are a true reflection of the customer company's opinion. This approach is essential when the supplier-customer relationship is personal and direct (OEM or contractual relationships, relationships with large customers or distributors); vendor ratings are often used in these cases, with suppliers frequently involved in setting criteria and informed of the results (Fig. 3.4 is an example of a vendor rating for electronic component suppliers). Direct delivery of the questionnaire is also useful in targeted surveys designed to assess customer satisfaction in particular areas (for example, delivery/installation) and/or to extract **diagnostic indications** on areas presumed to be unsatisfactory. In this case, it is important to be sure the questionnaire is received by the person or people in the customer company who will provide the information required.

Generally speaking, however, in the case of a large and varied user group, the most objective way of obtaining reliable information across the entire customer satisfaction tree is through a specialised third party. The specialist organisation must be given a complete list of the supplier's customers wherever possible (direct customers and dealers/resellers), so that it can identify the samples to be interviewed.

If users are not known individually (mass consumer products, indirect users), the research specialist will adopt the customary techniques to form the samples. Interviews may be conducted face-to-face or over the telephone, depending on requirements, size of the sample and related costs.

The supplier company must provide the interviewers with precise specifications, for example, on user classes and the significance of the samples, to ensure the reliability of results. It is particularly important to specify precisely the company functions that should be covered by the interviewees.

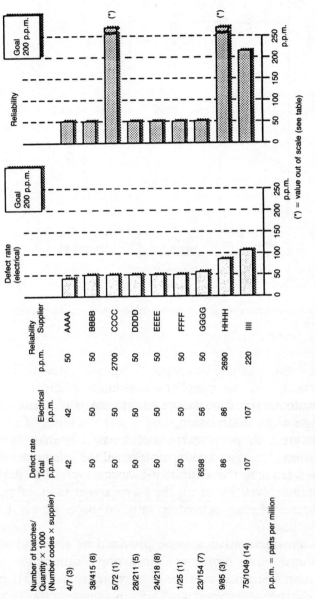

Number of batches/ Quantity × 1000 (Number codes × supplier)	Defect rate Total p.p.m.	Electrical p.p.m.	Reliability p.p.m.	Supplier
4/7 (3)	42	42	50	AAAA
38/415 (8)	50	50	50	BBBB
5/72 (1)	50	50	2700	CCCC
28/211 (5)	50	50	50	DDDD
24/218 (8)	50	50	50	EEEE
1/25 (1)	50	50	50	FFFF
23/154 (7)	6598	56	50	GGGG
9/85 (3)	86	86	2690	HHHH
75/1049 (14)	107	107	220	IIII

p.p.m. = parts per million

Fig. 3.4 Vendor rating for suppliers of integrated memory circuits (DRAMs), first half of 1990 (source Olivetti).

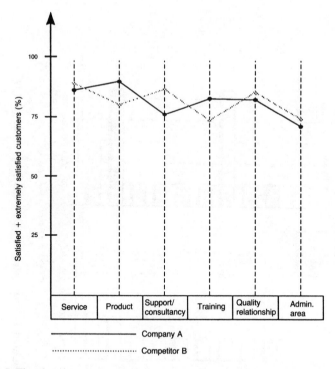

Fig. 3.5 First-level customer satisfaction profiles (medium-sized users of computer systems).

The results of the surveys can be processed in various ways, depending on the information sought and the types of category being analysed. A particularly useful graph is that shown in Figs 3.5 and 3.6: the x-axis represents the elements of the customer satisfaction tree at first-branch level (Fig. 3.5) and second-branch level (Fig. 3.6); the y-axis shows the total percentage of 'satisfied' plus 'extremely satisfied' users (levels 4 and 5 of the 1–5 scale).

Useful information can also be provided by a second type of graph, whose y-axis represents the average satisfaction values for each item (weighted average of answers from 1 to 5), and by 'five-bar charts', which compare shifts in values on the 1–5 scale

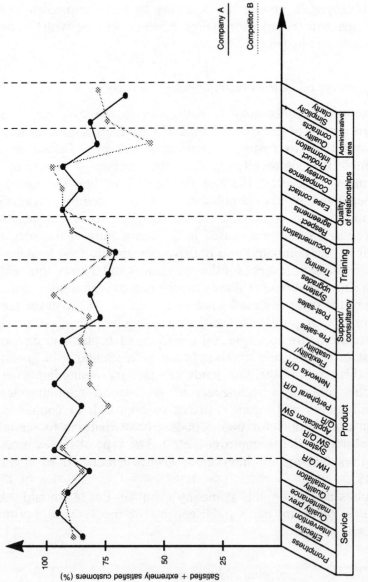

Fig. 3.6 Second-level customer satisfaction profiles (medium-sized users of computer systems).

over time. Nevertheless, at global level the most significant graphs are those shown in Figs 3.5 and 3.6.

These graphs enable the company to make immediate comparisons with competitors (Figs 3.5 and 3.6) or with its own previous results (Fig. 3.7).

(c) Surveys of customers in the extended sense

Surveys on the company's customers in the extended sense (third branch of the tree in Fig. 2.15) are more similar to image surveys than to customer satisfaction surveys. Taking as an example the community in which the company – or one of its factories – is located, the best way to find out how the company is perceived by the population is to commission a specialist organisation to conduct a survey designed to reveal negative perceptions (the harm caused to the community or the environment by the company) and positive perceptions (the benefits of the company's presence for the community and the environment).

In short, this type of survey monitors the community's perception of the company's influence on the quality of life in the area.

Surveys of public authorities usually give the most precise information, for example, on questions of health and environment protection and on compliance with standards in general. But this type of user, too, tends to attach increasing importance to the company's willingness to go beyond minimum legal requirements and adopt a proactive approach of cooperation with and support for public bodies (contributions to schools, social initiatives for employees, etc.). This type of survey usually requires face-to-face interviews, always conducted by a third party.

Assessments of the company's public image should also include important items published by the media, with a critical analysis of sources.

(d) Surveys of potential customers

Surveys of potential customers (fourth branch of the tree in Fig. 2.15) check this group's perception of the company and

132

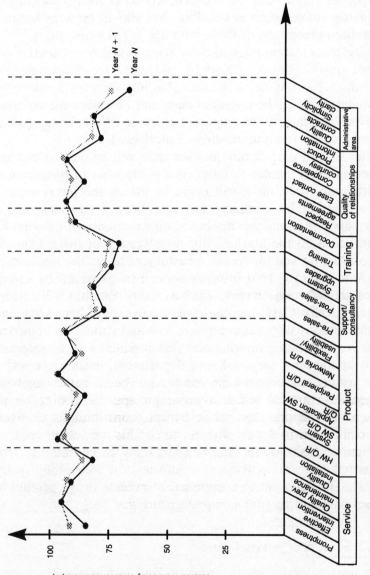

Fig. 3.7 Development of customer satisfaction over time. Comparison between two consecutive years.

provide vital information on the possibility of boosting market share. These are complex surveys, which deal not only with image but often with the 'dissatisfaction' of former customers; the latter information is valuable, but should be kept separate from the perceptions of those who are not yet customers.

Like the customer satisfaction questionnaires, potential customer questionnaires should be addressed to the people who influence purchasing decisions. An introductory section will examine the way the potential customer perceives the company and also attempt to investigate the source of this image (advertising, market reputation, direct experience).

The second part of the questionnaire will be more analytical, covering items similar to those on the branches of the customer satisfaction tree, but it will begin by asking the interviewee to state whether his company has ever been a customer and to specify whether answers are based on experience or on what has been heard on the market. But investigation of the reasons for dissatisfaction and the loss of a customer are not the main object of these surveys. That information can be provided by specific **customer defection surveys**, which a quality company will perform systematically. Customer defection surveys are designed to identify the reasons why customers are lost and should be compared with corresponding internal analyses conducted on a systematic basis by the sales and marketing department, in the same way as the production department conducts regular defect analyses. During the annual self-assessment process, depending on the amount of information available through institutional channels, the company will decide whether to conduct *ad hoc* surveys.

Figure 3.8 shows the type of chart that can be obtained from potential-customer surveys (for information technology system users). The surveys can also be used to create image profiles for target competitors (one competitor in Fig. 3.8).

3.3.2 Surveys of internal users

The next category on the tree in Fig. 2.15 is customer satisfaction results for internal users: the fifth branch of the tree refers to **internal users of internal processes**, the sixth branch to

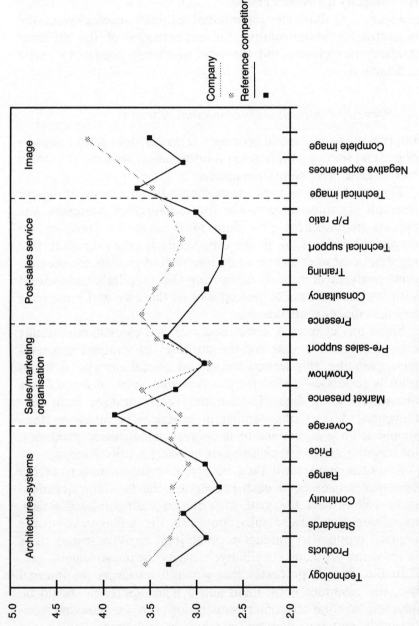

Fig. 3.8 Image survey profiles of non-customers of the company.

company employees, and the seventh branch to **beneficiaries of the company's business results**.

Figure 2.13 illustrates the internal supplier-customer roles and is useful for understanding the expectations of the different internal user classes and the type of survey needed to assess satisfaction.

(a) Surveys of internal users of internal processes

Internal users of internal processes (Figs 2.15 and 2.16) are users of general services, management information systems, personnel recruitment processes, training, etc.

The satisfaction of these users should be monitored at regular intervals by those responsible for the supplier processes: the process management procedure must allow for feedback, to ensure that results are fit for use. Similarly, the procedure that regulates customer-supplier relations should provide for periodic joint analyses of results, comparing the supplier's assessments with the assessments or perceptions of the user and remedying any differences immediately.

Since this chapter is concerned with the assessments usually conducted once a year for the purposes of strategic improvement planning, this section focuses on annual surveys. A list of priority processes is vital for this type of survey, to avoid being overwhelmed by data. The list may grow or vary from year to year, but a specific number of processes is advisable (they should include a number of high-level management processes, for example, strategic planning or monthly results reviews).

A questionnaire will then be given to the managers of the customer processes of each process on the list. The questionnaire will retrace the year in terms of customer satisfaction, examining not only results, but also the willingness of the internal supplier to conduct periodic joint analyses, promptness in resolving problems, flexibility, capacity for improvement, etc.

In the case of processes that generate products for internal use, the customer is on hand and a team approach should be adopted so that customer satisfaction can be assessed continuously and remedial action taken in real time. The annual self-assessment performed as the basis for improvement planning will show the extent to which the company operates as it should – and the corresponding results.

(b) Employee satisfaction surveys

The company's employees form the most general and important category of internal users. They are the most significant component of the company's assets (the second being its customers and the third the assets normally found in the balance sheet). Their sense of belonging, of self-fulfilment, their motivation, their satisfaction with the present and confidence regarding the future are fundamental to the success of the company. The company will therefore verify the level of employee satisfaction and changes that occur in time and space (in the various company sites) with questionnaires covering all significant aspects of the relationship between the company and the individual employee: motivation, sense of achievement, and remuneration, career.

The obvious danger for this type of survey is people's natural tendency to complain about the situation and to feel the company is in their debt. This is inevitable and must be expected to emerge to a certain extent in the surveys. The significance of results can be improved, however, by explaining to employees during training how the results of the surveys are used: when people realise their answers are anonymous and will bring no individual benefits, and that put together they provide the company with information to improve human resources management, then they are more likely to view the questionnaire as an opportunity for making a constructive contribution to self-assessment rather than as a chance to air personal grievances.

(c) Assessing the effects of quality on the company's business results

The beneficiaries of the company's business results are a very particular user group. Strictly speaking, they are the company's owners (and therefore often widely dispersed, as in the case of shareholders); broadly speaking, they include everyone who benefits from the prosperity of the company: its employees first of all, then its suppliers, the social environment, etc.

Since this is such a large and varied group and since – as will be seen shortly – subjective assessments are of little value, assessments by experts are more reliable than user surveys. Before examining this point further, it should be made clear what type of business results are to be assessed.

The business results in question are those arising from quality. Benefits for the income statement can be summarised as follows (Fig. 2.13):

- benefits arising from increased customer satisfaction: higher market share, the possibility of applying premium prices;
- cost reductions arising from process quality improvements (not just reduction of non-conformity, but elimination of activities with no corresponding value: section 1.4 and Fig. 1.12);
- lower interest expense as a result of a reduction in working capital through greater efficiency in process times;
- other benefits that are even more difficult to calculate, such as those arising from reductions in time-to-market.

Other possible benefits – not visible in Fig. 2.13 – affect the company's assets, even if they are reflected only in part in the balance sheet:

- lower utilisation of capital at equal revenue levels;
- a stronger customer base;
- improvement and consolidation of the quality system.

As noted above, in this user category, significant customer satisfaction results cannot be obtained from surveys: first, because any benefits arising from improvements in customer satisfaction and processes are so closely intermeshed with the effects of other endogenous and exogenous variables that neither shareholders nor financial analysts can isolate them; second, because beneficiaries are sensitive to short-term results, while the majority of benefits arising from improvement emerge over the mid/long term. Business results must therefore be assessed with extreme caution by specialists capable of distinguishing benefits arising from improvement. Leaving aside the merits of the skills available today for this type of assessment (section 6.3) to concentrate solely on **who** should assess business results, estimates should be drawn up by an interdisciplinary team of experts led by the administration/financial function, acting on behalf of top management.

3.4 ASSESSING THE STATE OF PROCESSES

An assessment of the state of the main company processes is the second basic input for the company's self-assessment (input 2 in Fig. 3.1).

What are the company's main processes? Obviously, the answer will vary from one company to another, but in all cases it will be useful to limit the number of processes to be assessed. Once again, assessing too many can be counter-productive, particularly at the beginning.

Processes that generate products for the market are considered first. Two guidelines should be used in choosing the processes to be assessed. The first is the importance of the product generated in terms of business (revenues, or margins). The second is its importance – or critical relevance – in relation to customer satisfaction. With reference, for example, to Fig. 3.2, the assessment might include the branches of the customer satisfaction tree to which users assign the greatest weight, for a total, say, of 70% of overall weight.

After identifying 'products' on the basis of the two criteria mentioned above, the processes that generate these products will be given priority. In all cases, a 'map' of significant company processes should always be close at hand, so that the situation can be constantly monitored and new processes included in the self-assessment as required each year. As far as processes that generate products for internal use are concerned, management, as the user, will make the choice.

Once the list has been drawn up, the state of each chosen process will be assessed in accordance with the procedure illustrated in Fig. 2.18. The assessment will be based on:

- current measurements of the process, the product and delivery of the product;
- a correlation of these measurements with customer satisfaction surveys;
- previous audits.

During the self-assessment, each process will be carefully audited: all the results of the current measurements taken during the year and summaries of the previous year will be considered and process/product results will be compared with customer satisfaction results.

The audit will give the process a score, following a classification of the type illustrated in Table 3.1. Since processes will normally be interfunctional, the assessment will be based on the criteria described in Chapter 4 (process management).

Finally, it should be noted that the procedure suggested here is unlikely to be applied to top-level strategic processes directed by senior management, at least until the total quality culture has

Table 3.1 Audit scores

Score	State of the process
0	Process not in a state of control
1	Process in a state of control (state of statistical control for production processes). Indicators are active and effective, the process capabilities are known, corrective feedback loops function correctly.
2	As 1, plus: 1. process performance matches product goals, i.e. the process naturally produces the product within the established defectiveness limits; 2. good correlation between process indicators and product quality indicators.
3	As 2, plus: 1. correlation with customer satisfaction results.
4	As 3, plus: 1. process performance matches customer satisfaction goals; 2. adequate correlation between process results/product/customer satisfaction.
5	As 4, plus: 1. current planning and execution of consistent, aligned improvements for customer satisfaction, product and process.

naturally extended this type of quantitative assessment method to these processes. In the mean time, the principle of submitting the main company processes to a critical inspection should be maintained. It is suggested that top-level strategic processes be analysed by the company's first line at self-assessment meetings, with the assistance of a senior external consultant skilled in the application of total quality techniques to this kind of process.

3.5 ASSESSING THE STATE OF THE QUALITY SYSTEM

As noted earlier, assessment of the quality system is the most difficult but also the most important assessment for the purposes of improvement, because the quality system is the base that supports the company processes, which in turn generate results (Fig. 2.5).

This is the third input for the assessment process (Fig. 3.1(a)). The trees in Figs 2.22 and 2.23, adjusted where appropriate to meet the requirements of the individual company, or the assessment models of the Malcolm Baldrige Award, the Deming Application Prize and the European Quality Award, can be used as reference models for the quality system assessment, excluding elements related to internal and external results.

The tool conventionally used for assessing the quality system is the system audit. This type of audit is described in many publications and was recently adopted by the ISO standards (Standard 10.011).

The aim of normal system audits (see introduction to the standard mentioned above) '. . . is to ascertain whether the various elements of the system are suitable for achieving pre-established quality goals'. Total quality, however, is not concerned with pre-established quality goals but with the moving, competitive target of customer satisfaction and continuous improvement: this already indicates that audits are not suitable for assessing the quality system when the company's mission is total quality. Since the total quality mission involves above all the company's intangible characteristics, audits should be flanked by surveys of the users of the quality system – the company employees – on the fitness-for-use of the quality system itself. These surveys are more effective than audits in assessing the intangible characteristics which are so important to success in the area of total quality. Quality system assessments will therefore use the following two tools:

- employee surveys/enquiries, designed to assess the degree to which, in the interviewee's opinion, the various components of the quality system support the contribution the company expects from him or her in achieving its mission (this is an assessment of the quality system from the users' point of view);
- audits at various levels in the company, designed to extract more precise quantitative information on the state of the more tangible elements of the system.

3.5.1 Employee surveys as a tool for assessing the quality system

Employee surveys will use a questionnaire based on the chosen quality system model, for example, the menu in Fig. 2.23 (adapted to the individual company). The questionnaire will focus in particular on:

- the role of management;
- the company's values;
- the human/social system: involvement, utilisation and roles.

Questions should not reproduce the brief conceptual definitions of the quality system model (for example, Fig. 2.23). They should be enlivened (and formulated in positive as well as negative terms) to facilitate comprehension. The examples in Table 3.2 are based on a survey conducted in Olivetti in 1989, with the assistance of ODI (Organizational Dynamics Inc.).

Again, the answers to these questions can be ranked on a scale of 1 to 5, as in Table 3.3. The significance of the survey must be clearly explained at meetings between superiors and their staff, from the top of the company to the lowest levels, adopting the **cascade** approach.

The survey must be clearly explained in terms of **what it is**

Table 3.2 Survey questions

Item on the tree (Fig. 2.23)	*Questions*
Attitude to improvement	• I am stimulated to offer suggestions to improve the environment, processes, results. • An ability to anticipate problems is typical of the people who work in the company. • We continue to make the same mistakes. • The employees support the company's efforts to improve quality. • We try to improve our work even when we consider the result achieved to be satisfactory.
Leadership	• Management is consistent in pursuing improvement and provides an example and lead. • Management is clearly improving the quality of its own work. • In this company, bosses are the first to practise what they preach. • We spend more time with our bosses than with our staff.
Definition and dissemination of policies and goals	• Management has clearly defined a quality policy and strategy. • I know what my company's goals are. • I know how my work helps to reach these goals.
Recognition	• A commitment to improvement is a significant element in career development. • Those who resolve a problem receive greater recognition than those who prevent it or suggest how to avoid it.
Training	• I receive the training I need to work with colleagues on improvement initiatives. • My boss ensures that his staff have enough time for training.

not: it is not an employee satisfaction survey, it is not targeted at the employee as a person (specific surveys exist for this purpose, as was seen earlier). Then it must be explained in terms of **what it is**: a survey concerned with the **role** of the employee and his **professional skills**. The employee must be urged to consider the questions objectively in relation to his own role and using his own skills as his criterion for assessment.

The employee must help the company understand the degree

Table 3.3

Question	I agree
1	Not at all
2	No
3	Don't know
4	Yes
5	Completely

to which the quality system meets the needs of its users in accomplishing the quality mission. His position is similar to that of the worker who keeps machinery running correctly, when he is asked if he has all the tools and assistance he needs to do his work properly.

3.5.2 System audits as a tool for assessing the quality system

System audits mainly involve management, or those responsible for operations, and should be based on checklists. Checklists are similar to questionnaires, but are expressed in specialised terms and designed to build up an objective, quantitative picture of the situation. Audits deal with the most quantifiable categories of Fig. 2.23, in particular:

- infrastructures;
- technical and methodological resources.

They will also examine the most quantifiable items within other categories. For example, in the human/social subsystem category, items such as:

- teamwork;
- policies, standards, procedures;
- job rotation;
- training; and
- reward system

Fig. 3.9 Type of graph used to represent answers to quality system assessment questionnaires.

can be assessed objectively by management. However, these assessments often reflect a view of the situation 'as it ought to be'. The results of the surveys, which give a view of the situation 'as perceived by the user' will provide the necessary complementary information.

Audits conclude with brief reports, accompanied by data – preferably in the form of graphs – including comparisons with results of previous audits. They usually also make recommendations for improvement, which provide useful input for strategic planning as an indication of the steps the sector itself already considers necessary.

Surveys/enquiries conclude with graphs of the type shown in Fig. 3.9, one or more for each question in the questionnaire, according to the level of analysis required. These graphs will be analysed one by one, and possibly converted into scores for the different branches of the tree in Fig. 2.23.

The example shown in Fig. 3.9 reveals a breakdown in vertical communication, in particular as regards the goal deployment system.

145

3.6 COMPARATIVE ANALYSIS OF SELF-ASSESSMENT RESULTS. GAPS WITH PREVIOUS GOALS AND WITH COMPETITORS. IDENTIFICATION OF STRENGTHS AND WEAKNESSES

The large mass of data produced by the three assessments must undergo any kind of analysis that will provide useful information: it is best therefore to store the files on magnetic media, and to develop special processing applications to run on personal computers.

In addition to the data of the three *ad hoc* assessments, the company will collect the annual summaries of institutional data on customers, employees, processes, and non-quality costs, as well as all available historical data, in particular data from the previous year's self-assessment. The first step is to condense the data and prepare the material on which top management will be working during the strategic planning process. Although this is the first step in conceptual terms, the company should not wait until strategic planning has been completed before beginning detailed analysis; correct planning requires interaction among the various hierarchical levels, so that the lower levels analyse the same data in parallel with higher levels, but in greater detail. The top management summary should identify weaknesses or critical elements in relation to user satisfaction (customers and the other classes of user), processes and the quality system (Fig. 3.10). It should also identify the company's strengths, to better exploit their commercial potential.

As far as critical areas are concerned, it is important during this preparatory phase to conduct sensitivity analyses with the operating managers, or even just brainstorming sessions if analyses are not possible, to assess the possible margins for improvement over the short and long term.

The report submitted to top management will be concerned only with the main weaknesses – a maximum of 20, possibly not more than 10 – and will group together user satisfaction, processes and quality system. Clearly some of these weaknesses will be related to one another, typically processes and results.

For each weak area, the report will give a 1–2 page summary

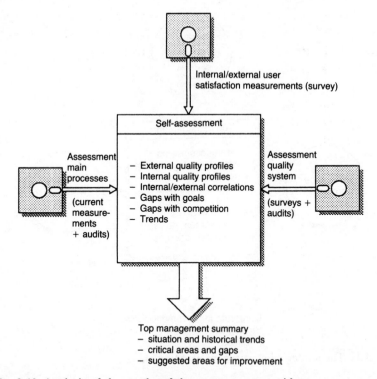

Internal/external user
satisfaction measurements (survey)

Self-assessment

Assessment main processes

(current measurements + audits)

- External quality profiles
- Internal quality profiles
- Internal/external correlations
- Gaps with goals
- Gaps with competition
- Trends

Assessment quality system

(surveys + audits)

Top management summary
- situation and historical trends
- critical areas and gaps
- suggested areas for improvement

Fig. 3.10 Analysis of the results of the assessments provides top management with an overall picture of the situation.

(possibly with graphs, but these should be kept to a minimum, too) of the situation emerging from the assessments, historical trends, gaps compared with competitors, and elasticity as regards improvement. In addition to this brief report, the intermediate documents drawn up at the various levels of detail will also be available (even if only in personal computer files), to permit top management to examine any points in detail in real time.

3.7 STRATEGIC PLANNING: PRELIMINARY DEFINITION OF GOALS, STRATEGIES AND PRIORITIES

At this point, the work of the company's top management (the chief officer and his first line) begins: it is a task that cannot be

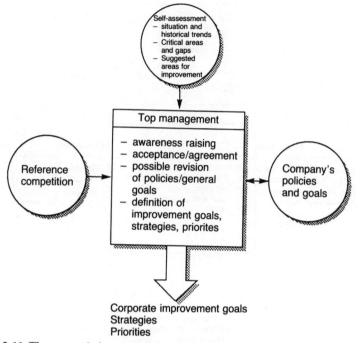

Fig. 3.11 The strategic improvement planning phase.

delegated. In other words, the **primary improvement mover** shown in Fig. 2.7 comes into play.

It was seen earlier that top management plays absolutely the most critical role in the quality system. Top management is the **unmoved mover**: if it lacks the will-power and the strength to play its strategic role, everything will come to a halt. Self-assessment is always the first fundamental step: if top management consents to a self-assessment of the kind described, which highlights weaknesses (including weaknesses in top management's leadership in the area of quality), then the unmoved mover is more likely to be set in motion, even if it may not continue to play its propulsory role later on. When the mover stops, however, everything else not only stops but regresses.

Top management must be provided with (Fig. 3.11):

148

- the results of the self-assessment – current situation and trends – in as condensed a form as possible, but clearly reflecting the real situation, and comparisons with the results of the previous year's self-assessment;
- the results and information available on reference competitors;
- the company's policies and goals as regards its quality mission. This is the reference framework for 'the company as it would like to be'.

Top management must also be told how the summary was prepared and how the critical areas were selected. It will then decide whether to accept the summary or to add/remove certain areas.

Once top management has approved the list of priority areas for improvement, the summary will be used as the guide for the planning process. For each critical area, the top management team will draw up a brief description/definition of the situation as reflected in the self-assessment: this description will probably not introduce any new elements, but it represents the **explicit acceptance and agreement** of the company's senior management team.

The team's next step, for each critical area, is to analyse the company's and its competitors' results, historical trends, shortfalls between the previous years' goals and the results achieved, as a basis for drafting new improvement goals. The goals are drafted – over a long-term timescale, with annual subdivisions – and execution strategies are simultaneously defined (Fig. 3.11). These goals are not final, because they still have to be validated through the deployment process (see following section), but they indicate what top management believes the company should do to fulfil its missions and remain competitive. In view of the limitations that will emerge during deployment, the team will also list the goals in order of priority (Fig. 3.11).

Together, Figs 3.10 and 3.11 offer another, more detailed illustration of the **primary improvement mover** in Fig. 2.7 of the model, which is the fundamental role of top management. It is important at this stage that top management set the company's improvement goals from the user perspective, with clear, direct reference to the end results the company intends to achieve (**final goals**). The goals will not be translated into business terminology, into 'means' and processes, until later.

At the end of this stage, top management may also decide to modify the company's policies and goals (the two-way arrow in Fig. 3.11).

Some of the improvement goals set by top management will be functional – concerned with just one company function – while others, usually the majority, will be interfunctional. This difference is important in the **goal deployment stage**.

3.8 GOAL DEPLOYMENT

Policy deployment is the term generally used to refer to the process by which goals are conveyed to the company, although goal deployment would be more appropriate; the process is also known by the hybrid Anglo-Japanese term **hoshin planning**. Other people prefer the term **vertical deployment** or **vertical alignment**, since the main object of the exercise is to align goals from the top of the company down to the lowest levels: but in fact, as will be seen, goal deployment is achieved through an intersection between vertical deployment and horizontal deployment along the process stream (**quality function deployment**).

Two extreme cases help to clarify the concept. First, an 'authoritarian' company, where improvement planning is the exclusive domain of top management and where all sectors and levels are required to align themselves accordingly: here, goals and strategies are deployed in a one-way process, from top to bottom (Fig. 3.12(a)). This is management by objectives practised in an authoritarian fashion: everyone knows what his objectives are – and may also understand their connection with the company's goals – but there is no guarantee that these objectives can be reached or that they will help optimise the global result. Furthermore, the connection at the various levels between these objectives and customer requirements is not clear.

Now take the case of a company with no top-level strategic improvement planning; each function/level is required to draw

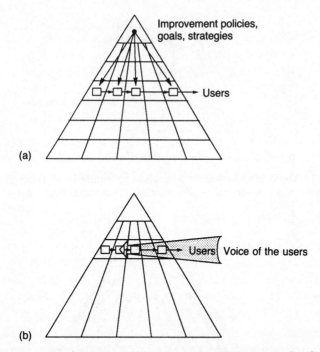

Fig. 3.12 Formation of improvement goals at operating process level. Both cases are extreme and inadequate: (a) extreme example of one-way vertical deployment (authoritarian); (b) extreme example in which improvement goals are defined solely through horizontal deployment (QFD).

up its own improvement plans, and may indeed begin correctly by identifying shortfalls between customer expectations and results and developing consistent process improvement goals. Figure 3.12(b) illustrates this situation: the function adopts the horizontal process of quality function deployment, which begins with the customer and moves back through the company processes to the source.

Neither of the two companies adopts a correct approach to the goal planning/deployment process. Correct goal planning/ deployment must combine horizontal deployment (which refers market needs to company processes) with vertical deployment (which refers corporate strategy to the different sectors of the company), as shown in Fig. 3.13. The figure also shows vertical deployment as a two-way process: vertical deployment must

151

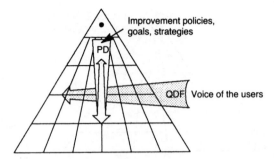

Fig. 3.13 The correct formation of goals at operating levels is achieved through the intersection of vertical deployment with horizontal deployment.

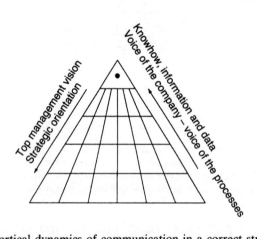

Fig. 3.14 The vertical dynamics of communication in a correct strategic planning process.

be an interactive high-low/low-high process, so that the thrust, vision and strategic orientation of top management can be combined correctly with the knowhow, information and data possessed at the lower levels (Fig. 3.14).

Interactive vertical deployment must maximise the contribution of the entire company to the planning process, as shown in Fig. 3.15. Before passing goals down to the next level, each level will check goals – means compatibility together with the lower level. Since the means for achieving goals on one level will become the goals of the lower level, this compatibility check is

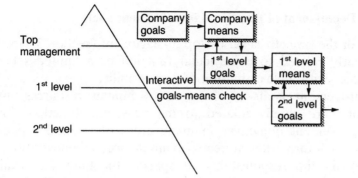

Fig. 3.15 Before passing goals down to the next level, each level checks goals/means compatibility with the lower level.

essential to avoid the risk of unrealistic goals being passed to the lower level.

Figure 3.15 illustrates an important change compared with the usual management by objectives approach: it moves from management by objectives to management by objectives and means; the supervisor is responsible for checking together with his staff that suitable means exist before finalising goals; 'bottlenecks', where existing means are not sufficient to permit goals to be reached, are therefore identified beforehand and specific action can be taken to avoid them, or objectives can be modified. Goals are more credible, and the supervisor/staff relationship functions on a more correct basis.

According to K. Sasaoka, chairman of Yokagawa Hewlett Packard (YHP), a certain period is needed to set this collective approach to goal definition and deployment in motion, but once it has been established it leads to considerable improvements in the quality of actual goals and facilitates acceptance by all concerned. At YHP, for example, in the first year top management's requirements were accepted in full; a few years later, only 60% were accepted, while the remaining 40% underwent modifications and substitutions during lower-level interaction (King, 1989).

The following sections examine deployment of functional goals and deployment of interfunctional goals.

153

3.8.1 Deployment of functional improvement goals

Some of the objectives set by top management (section 3.7) will be clearly related to a particular function or a limited set of functions, with a clear division of responsibility.

Improvement goals in the area of human resources, for example, are chiefly related to the personnel function, just as improvement objectives in many areas of internal support services – information systems, maintenance, administration – are chiefly the responsibility of specific functions (a certain degree of interfunctionality almost always exists, but when a goal is predominantly the responsibility of one particular function, interfunctionality can be disregarded). Goal deployment in these cases proceeds as shown in Fig. 3.16. The chief officer and the first line begin a systematic analysis of goals, to identify the best means for achieving each one. At this level (the top corporate level), means are sometimes known as **critical success factors** (CSFs). The CSFs for a specific goal are all those means considered necessary and sufficient to the attainment of that goal.

The joint analysis of goals by top management and heads of function concludes with the assignment of goals to each function, as shown in Fig. 3.16. As soon as the interactive 'catch-ball' process between top management and the first line generates hypotheses regarding the means to be used, the first line sets off a similar catch-ball process with the second line. The process is then repeated between the second and the third lines, and so on down to the junior management levels (Fig. 3.17).

Improvement goals may concern the quality system, in which case the sub-goals are usually assigned to specific managers within the relevant function, or the processes that generate 'products' for the market or for the company's internal use.

The integrated process management level is usually reached after one or two vertical deployment steps. But it is difficult to generalise: in complex, highly bureaucratic organisations, it may be necessary to come down through a number of levels before reaching the process managers. When vertical deployment reaches processes, it begins to intersect – indeed, it must

154

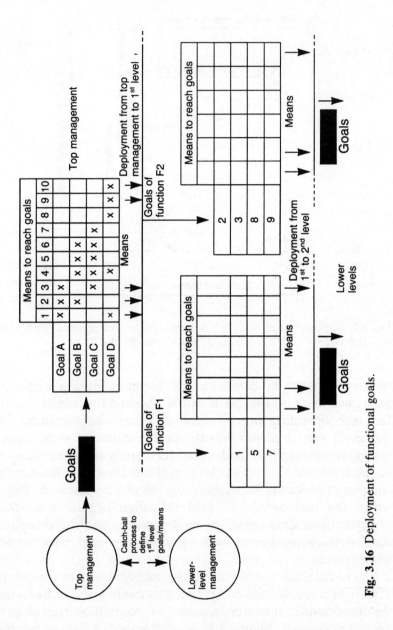

Fig. 3.16 Deployment of functional goals.

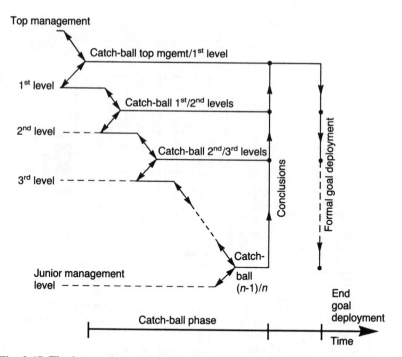

Fig. 3.17 The interactive catch-ball process from one management level to the next is necessary for correct planning and alignment of goals.

intersect – with the horizontal deployment process beginning from customers, so that goals can be checked for consistency. In fact, the operating process level is where the consistency of the goals set from above with specific customer expectations (external or internal) and customer satisfaction data can be verified. Above all, it is the level at which the capabilities of the company's processes in relation to goals can be assessed. This is where the real process of goal validation begins, and where important elements regarding final decisions and the consolidation of goals, strategies and priorities are sent back to top management.

Figure 3.18 illustrates the intersecting deployment process by which goals are defined and assessed at every level, in particular the transition from company goals to function/department goals and process goals. Figure 3.19 is a 'close-up' of the intersection

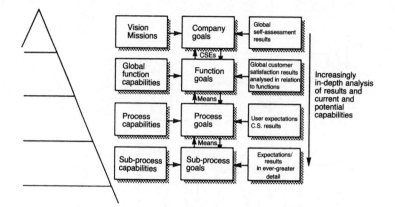

Fig. 3.18 The intersection of vertical deployment with horizontal deployment and verification of actual and potential capabilities at each level.

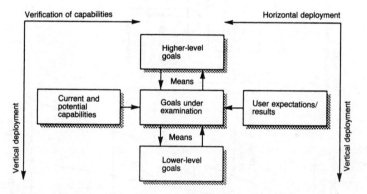

Fig. 3.19 A close-up on the vertical/horizontal deployment intersection + capabilities check.

between vertical deployment and horizontal deployment, with verification of actual and potential capabilities.

To give an example (Fig. 3.20), self-assessment might have highlighted the need to improve satisfaction/motivation among human resources: top management sets this as a goal, possibly with quantitative targets based on the satisfaction levels revealed by internal surveys. The chief officer and his first line begin the

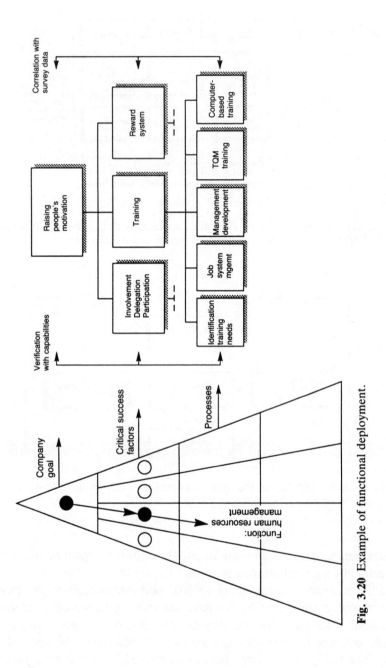

Fig. 3.20 Example of functional deployment.

interactive vertical deployment process, 'intersecting' horizontally with data from internal employee surveys. The following CSFs are identified:

1. involvement/participation/delegation;
2. training more closely geared to user needs/expectations;
3. reward system.

During the next deployment step, for example for training, a number of specific areas for improvement are identified:

1. identification of training needs/requirements;
2. job system management;
3. management development programmes;
4. TQM training;
5. computer-based training (CBT).

In this case, deployment leads to the start-up of type C processes, as defined in section 2.3 (Fig. 2.17), that is, processes designed to improve the company quality system. The concrete improvement goals for the processes concerned will be set by the management in line with the findings of the intersecting analyses of goals set from above, current situation and current and potential capabilities.

3.8.2 Deployment of interfunctional improvement goals

Many of the goals set by top management (section 3.7) will be interfunctional, in other words, they will depend to a large extent on contributions from a series of functions, and on the cooperation and alignment of these functions. Indeed, the most important company results (and frequently therefore the main improvement objectives) are related to strongly interfunctional processes, which cut across many company functions: results such as improvements in quality, in costs, and in product delivery. Goal deployment in these cases covers not one function but a group of functions, which may not be easy to identify at first: the chief officer and his first line will work together to identify the functions involved and establish the CSFs.

The CSFs for a particular company goal can be identified by

analysing, on one hand, the 'user results' for that goal as shown in the self-assessment and, on the other, the company's current and potential capabilities as shown in the processes and quality system sections of the self-assessment (Figs 3.21(a) and 3.21(b)). The CSFs should not be subdivided among the functions, even if at first sight some of them may seem to belong to a particular function; the CSFs are common to all the functions associated with the particular interfunctional goal under consideration, and must be treated as such in the subsequent vertical deployment step or steps, until the managers of the processes of the interfunctional chains are reached.

If, for example, the second level is the level of the interfunctional processes (that is, the managers of the **functional segments** of the interfunctional process chains are second-line managers), then the first line, together with the managers of the second-level processes presumably involved, will start to build the CSFs/processes matrix. As the matrix is formed, it will become clear which processes are in fact involved, so that some process managers may join the team and others may leave it (the reason for the use of the term 'presumably').

Having identified the interfunctional processes with the greatest impact on the CSFs – and therefore on the goal defined by top management – the team will set goals for each interfunctional process. Put together, the goals set for the interfunctional processes will be the equivalent of the specific corporate goal, that is, they will be a translation in **corporate language** (process language) of the goal set by top management in **user language** (as noted earlier, this is the language in which top management should express the company's goals).

Who is to be made responsible for the interfunctional process goals? The question is pertinent, because in conventional functional organisations no one is responsible for these processes (section 1.4). The post must therefore be created. For the time being, operating responsibility will be considered; a 'political' problem of responsibility also comes into play, which will be examined later.

To ensure unified management of the interfunctional process, a process management team must be created, composed of the

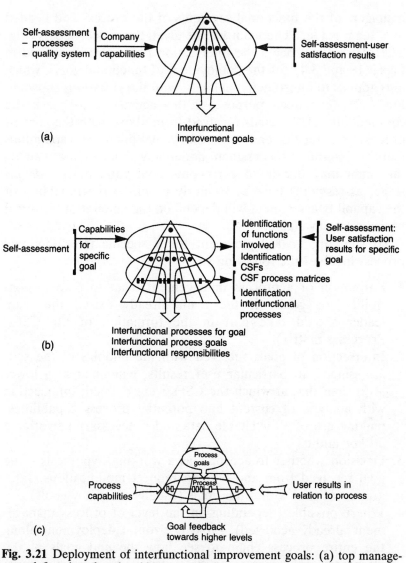

(a)

(b)

(c)

Fig. 3.21 Deployment of interfunctional improvement goals: (a) top management defines interfunctional improvement goals; (b) **for each goal**, top management identifies the functions involved and the critical success factors; the first and second lines identify the interfunctional processes. Top management allocates interfunctional responsibilities; (c) the goals of **each interfunctional process** are checked at the intersection between vertical/horizontal deployment + capabilities.

161

managers of the functional segments of the process and headed by a team leader. The team will be given the process goals (Fig. 3.21(c)) and will begin the intersection procedure illustrated in Figs 3.18 and 3.19 for the deployment of functional goals, which also applies to interfunctional goals, with the variations shown in Fig. 3.21. The main purpose of this activity is to check the compatibility of the goals received from above with the current process-user results and with the actual/potential capabilities identified in the self-assessment and in any supplementary audits the team may decide to carry out (goal validation). At this stage, assessments have to be fairly rapid, so the reliability of the capability assessment will depend on the amount of historical process data available.

To sum up, goal deployment for a specific interfunctional process involves the following steps:

1. Formation of a process management team to take responsibility for goals (if the team already exists, the team leader should take part in the formation of the CSFs/ Processes matrix).
2. Intersection of goals received with the findings of the self-assessment, in particular user results, examined at a lower level than that at which the CSFs were defined; intersection with analysis of current and potential process capabilities, making use of all available data and if necessary performing *ad hoc* audits.
3. Decision whether to accept – as a working hypothesis – the goal received from above or to request modifications. Integration of goal with other goals (usually efficiency goals).
4. Where possible (depending on the level of process management already achieved), rapid horizontal deployment along the entire process chain to see how the end goals of the interfunctional process can be distributed among the functional segments of the process stream.

A thorough deployment procedure would continue, moving down from each functional process segment to the sub-processes below. In turn, these sub-processes would check the compatibility at their level between the goals received from above and the horizontal deployment + capabilities assessment. The goal deployment process is not complete, in fact, until goals–means compatibility checks have been performed at the lowest managerial levels and the findings have returned back up to top management (as shown in Fig. 3.17).

In practice, only an experienced company can conduct this exhaustive type of deployment in a reasonable timescale: the procedure requires expert management teams, processes under control, and familiarity with horizontal deployment.

So it is more reasonable here to consider deployment from the point of view of a company still at the learning stage. In this case, the vertical/horizontal intersections will provide approximate indications for goal planning; real horizontal goal deployment among processes will take place during the implementation phase, which will be discussed in the next chapter.

Goal deployment can be illustrated by taking as an example the deployment of a customer satisfaction goal, in the area of product support services.

The goal is to improve customer satisfaction for this item (or for this branch of the tree, or for this point in the customer satisfaction profile) by a specific number of percentage points, within two years: for example, to raise the number of customers who consider themselves 'satisfied' or 'very satisfied' from 90 to 95%. This is a final goal according to the definition given earlier, that is, it concerns user satisfaction; it is therefore consistent with the recommendation made concerning goals set by top management at company level.

Figure 3.22 provides a guide for the deployment of this goal. Since improvement is concerned with customer satisfaction, the basis of reference for horizontal deployment at the various organisational levels is the customer satisfaction tree with its various branch levels.

The chief officer and the first line examine customer satisfaction results for product support services. Taking account of the company's missions and its general strategic goals, they set the long and short-term goals for this area and, together with the relevant heads of function, identify the critical success factors (Fig. 3.23).

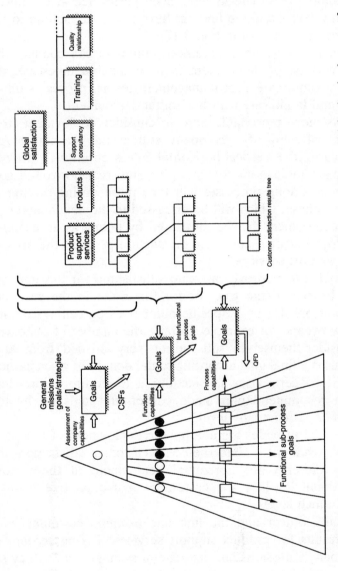

Fig. 3.22 Example of interfunctional deployment: improvement of customer satisfaction in the area of product support services.

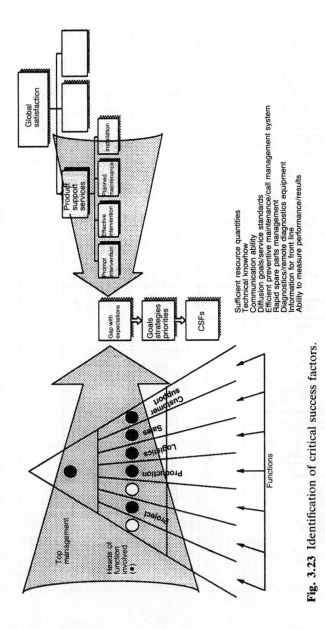

Fig. 3.23 Identification of critical success factors.

Global satisfaction

Product support services

Prompt intervention

Effective intervention

Planned maintenance

Installation

Gap with expectations

Goals strategies priorities

CSFs

Sufficient resource quantities
Technical knowhow
Communication ability
Diffusion goals/service standards
Efficient preventive maintenance/call management system
Rapid spare parts management
Diagnostics/remote diagnostics equipment
Information for front line
Ability to measure performance/results

Top management

Heads of function involved (●)

Project

Production

Logistics

Sales

Customer support

Functions

Fig. **3.24** The transition from critical success factors (CSFs) to processes.

CSFs \ Processes	Personnel selection	Education and training	Definition/up-date service STDs	Activity/resource planning	Call management information system	Spare parts information/logistics system	Development diagnostics HW/SW	Preparation procedures, documentation, manuals etc	Hot-line anomaly solving	Telephone interface management	Measurements of service quality indicators	Personnel management, assessment, reward	Weight (1–5) 5 = max.	Assessment current situation (1–5) 5 = excellent
Sufficient resource quantities				●							●			
Technical knowhow	●	●									●	●		
Communication ability	●	●								●	●	●		
Diffusion service quality STD targets	●	●	●								●	●		
Efficient preventive maintenance/call management system				●	●					●	●			
Rapid spare parts management				●		●					●			
Diagnostics/remote diagnostics equipment				●			●	●			●			
Full information for front line									●		●			
Ability to measure performance/results		●	●		●	●			●	●	●	●		
Assessment of current state of process (1–5) 5-excellent														
Improvement goals														

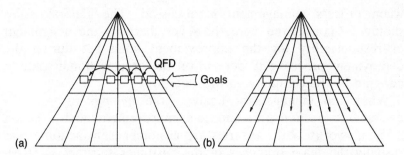

Fig. 3.25 (a) Horizontal deployment of goals of process and (b) vertical deployment of functional goals to sub-processes.

At the next deployment stage, the first and second line analyse the CSFs to identify the processes involved (Fig. 3.24); once the processes have been identified, the team of function and process managers checks capabilities against customer satisfaction results and CSFs and sets global goals for both functional and interfunctional processes.

At this point, if time permits, the team of interfunctional process managers will begin horizontal quality function deployment (QFD) from the 'mouth' of the process stream back towards the source, so that consistent goals can be assigned to each functional process segment (Fig. 3.25(a)). The next vertical deployment phase is purely functional (Fig. 3.25(b)).

When the improvement goal is related not to external customer results but, for example, to the quality system, the customer satisfaction tree can be replaced with a similar tree (the quality system tree, Fig. 2.23), where, in relation to the company pyramid, top management would correspond to the main trunk of the quality system tree and the lower managerial levels to the different branch levels (Fig. 3.20 illustrates this type of situation, in relation to functional deployment.)

3.9 RESPONSIBILITY FOR INTERFUNCTIONAL IMPROVEMENT GOALS

The question of responsibility for interfunctional processes was introduced in section 1.4 and will be examined in Chapter 4 when process management is discussed. The general issues should be considered here, however, because the assignment of responsibility for the improvement goals set during the deployment process will depend on the organisational solution adopted by the company on this point.

When top management analyses the findings of the self-assessment (section 3.6) and sets improvement goals (section 3.7), it works with a series of customer satisfaction areas (usually the main branches of the customer satisfaction tree). For example, for external customers these areas could be **product, product support services, support and consultancy, administrative relationship**, etc. (Fig. 3.2). Posts with overall responsibility for each of these areas rarely exist in the functionally organised company. Someone may have overall responsibility for the product, but even here responsibility is often split between design and production. Responsibility for the other areas apparently exists, and is assumed to be the last link in the chain. For example, product support services are responsible for only some of the factors that contribute to customer satisfaction in this area: product serviceability, spare parts availability, and modifications management are factors that have a strong impact on customer satisfaction, but they are usually outside the control of the service manager.

Another crucial area for customer satisfaction for which clear responsibility often does not exist is product delivery: delivery speed, punctuality, conformity of the products delivered with those ordered, and functionality on installation usually involve a wide range of responsibility. In setting global improvement goals linked to end results, top management faces the problem that no post with overall responsibility exists to assign the goal to.

Two solutions are possible:

- The company can create posts responsible for specific customer satisfaction areas, operating from level (a) of Fig. 3.21, that is, when interfunctional improvement goals are identified.
- The deployment phase involving identification of interfunctional processes is carried out (Fig. 3.21(b)) and responsibility for the goals is assigned to the relevant **process owners**.

Although companies today tend to choose the second solution, the first is a more faithful interpretation of the quality mission spirit, and is more useful in helping companies 'read the situation from right to left'. The company that chooses the first solution creates posts for the **supervision** and **safekeeping** of related customer satisfaction areas; these are interfunctional posts, **within which** interfunctional processes and possibly also (but not necessarily) the process owners are located.

The process owners play a 'political' role as the guarantors of the interfunctional processes, that is, they guarantee that these processes can pursue their goals (goals set and/or approved by the company) without undue interference from the functions. The task of the process owners, therefore, is to **counterbalance vertical power**. The operating role is guaranteed by the **process management team** and its leader.

When a company chooses the first solution, the managers made responsible for the various customer satisfaction areas must have sufficient political power within the company to act as guarantors for the interfunctional processes within their areas, thus eliminating the need for process owners. Reference is made to managers responsible for customer satisfaction areas, because these are generally the most significant areas in an improvement plan, but the principle applies to internal **improvement areas** as well, for example, the management information system area and the time-to-market area. In all cases, top management goals and the corresponding improvement responsibilities should be expressed from the perspective and in the language of the user.

Whichever organisational solution is chosen (area manager or process owner), the people appointed to the posts must be senior company officers. Various solutions are possible:

- The new role can be assigned as an additional responsibility to first-line managers who already have function responsibilities.
- The new role can be assigned as the sole responsibility, but always to a first-line manager with the necessary authority.

The first solution has the advantage of what could be called a **do ut des** logic, since many if not all the function managers would simultaneously have an interfunctional responsibility; each manager would require the cooperation of his colleagues as far as his interfunctional duties were concerned, and would in turn cooperate with them as regards his functional duties.

The second solution could lead to the manager becoming an 'outsider' in companies lacking a strong team spirit among the first line and a strongly felt presence of the chief officer.

In either case, the interfunctional level must be a step above the functional responsibility level in the company's value hierarchy. In fact, the organisational solutions described here compensate in part but not entirely for the limitations of verticalisation. **Interfunctional management** responsibility can never be delegated in full; the chief officer and his first line must therefore be responsible as a group for interfunctional matters. Visible formalisation of this responsibility with the creation of an **interfunctional committee** is highly recommended (Fig. 3.26): this committee would coincide with the existing management committee (known by different names in different companies)

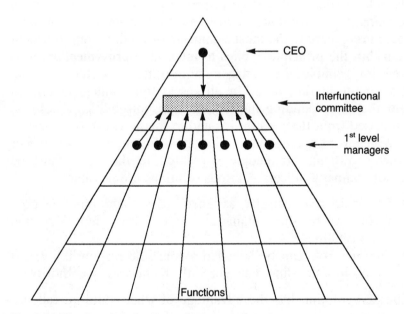

Fig. 3.26 The interfunctional committee.

and would assume the role of interfunctional committee when dealing with typically interfunctional issues such as quality, costs and times. It would monitor interfunctional plans and examine problems that interfunctional managers have been unable to resolve directly with heads of function.

The interfunctional committee, as shown in Fig. 3.26, is hierarchically superior to the functions. This is a typically Japanese view of the corporate organisation (Imai, 1986). Generally speaking, the question of attribution of interfunctional responsibilities is part of the vast area which R. Charan (1991) calls the 'corporate social architecture'. The interfunctional committee solution described here comes under the heading of what are known today as **network solutions**: groups of managers formally invested with major interfunctional responsibilities in connection with the company's strategic goals.

3.10 INCORPORATING GOALS, STRATEGIES AND PRIORITIES IN IMPROVEMENT PLANS

The interactive deployment process described above, with the gradual adjustment of corporate goals, leads, ideally, to a situation in which the company's strategic improvement goals have been circulated to the entire organisation and gradually transformed, at the various levels, into function goals and, for the processes that cut horizontally across the company, into interfunctional goals.

The consistency between goals at different levels depends on the precision of and degree of participation in the catch-ball process, but also on the speed with which the horizontal intersections provide elements for assessment. This will depend on the state of control of the processes (and therefore on the availability of data provided by significant indicators) and on familiarity with process capabilities. Keeping the goal deployment process within a reasonable timescale only permits rapid horizontal deployment (QFD) and swift capability checks: real horizontal deployment and real checks on capability improvement potential are not possible until the improvement plan is implemented, during process management.

An obvious point can be made: improvement planning will be perfected year by year, as the quality of the company processes improves (see the 1–5 scale in section 3.4). Poorly controlled processes do not provide significant elements for assessment at the intersections of Figs 3.18 and 3.19, while well-controlled processes provide objective data for the comparison of current and potential capabilities with market requirements and top management requests.

3.10.1 Annual and longer-term improvement plans at corporate, functional and interfunctional level

The results of the planning-deployment process will be incorporated in the **operating plans at corporate level** (goals, strategies and priorities validated through deployment), at **functional level** and at **interfunctional process level**. In practice, these plans are nothing more than the consolidation of the results of the strategic planning and deployment process described above, together with information on the way goals are to be achieved (strategies, tactics and tools, particularly at organisational level), a timetable and allocation of responsibilities. The corporate plan, for example, must briefly include:

- the situation and historical trends – in particular for the previous year – as reflected in the self-assessment, to establish the starting point;
- top-level goals, strategies and priorities on completion of the verifications performed during the deployment process;
- a clear distinction between functional and interfunctional goals and, for the latter, identification of the functions involved and designation of those responsible for the improvement areas and/or of the process owners.

In short, the corporate plan covers historical data and the results of the interactive process between the chief officer and the first line. Similarly, at the other levels, the plan will cover significant historical data and self-assessment data (basis of reference), the goals, strategies and priorities received from the higher level on completion of the catch-ball process (that is, agreed objectives).

The plans drawn up at interfunctional process level and at function level are particularly important. An annual improvement plan must be drawn up for each interfunctional process, under the responsibility of the process owner or of the improvement area manager. It will include:

- a summary of historical data supplied by existing process indicators;
- the findings of the self-assessment, in particular the audit scores (section 3.4, Table 3.1);
- studies performed and to be performed on capability improvement potential;
- goals and priorities received from the higher level;
- comparison between goals and current and potential capabilities and estimates of the degree of improvement needed in the various fields; and special emphasis on the need for new indicators and new measurements;
- identification of organisational deficiencies and action planned to eliminate them (in particular, as regards the management team and any improvement teams set up by the management team);
- clear links between the improvement goals of the interfunctional process and the goals of the functions involved; deployment of the global interfunctional process goals among the functional segments (Fig. 3.25(a)) must be followed by vertical deployment within the function (Fig. 3.25(b));
- a timetable indicating verification dates (in the case of longer-term plans, clear indication of the results expected during the present year and in following years);
- **management indicators**, in other words, the basic process performance indicators in terms of both effectiveness and efficiency (these indicators will provide a basis for assessment of the results achieved);
- clear indication of responsibilities.

173

The contents of the company's function plans need not be listed here; the list will clearly differ, but it can be made up easily by following the same basic guidelines and taking account of differences.

Corporate goal deployment will assign to functions both their own functional goals (through vertical deployment) and their share of interfunctional objectives (through horizontal deployment) (see above and Fig. 3.25).

Since the function is a vertical organisational element – a piece of the company – it clearly must not only receive improvement goals from above, but also submit its own goals, **particularly as regards efficiency**. The planning process described in this chapter is a strategic and therefore essentially top-down process. For optimal results, significant bottom-up contributions are necessary. Besides participating in the planning/deployment phase, however, it is vital, during the following stage when operating plans are being drawn up, that each function should autonomously seek continuous optimisation, within the framework of global optimisation.

Improvement implementation and process management

4

4.1 CONTINUOUS MICRO-ASSESSMENT/MICRO-PLANNING AND IMPROVEMENT INITIATIVES

As seen in section 3.1, annual strategic planning sets macro-improvement goals at corporate, function and interfunctional process levels. But the real opportunities for improvement will arise, and specific initiatives will be planned, from day to day, through careful process management, judicious positioning of indicators, measurement and feedback activities, continuous analysis of results, and comparisons with competitors and other reference companies and through teamwork.

This continuous, widespread micro-planning is vital if the company is to achieve the necessary improvements to compete in quality and costs.

Figure 1.6, in section 1.1, illustrates the point, introducing the fundamental concept of continuous improvement and planning. For each improvement goal, the plan shows the company's current position and the targets it intends to achieve in specified periods; specific improvement initiatives are the steps by which these targets will gradually be reached.

In practice, the distinction between the macro-planning stage and the micro-planning and initiative implementation stage is not so clear-cut. The plan will already indicate how the company intends to achieve improvement, even if these indications are no more than general guidelines to be examined in detail later. Vice versa, the horizontal deployment of interfunctional process goals (Fig. 3.25(a)) and the consequent vertical deployment from each functional segment of the process to the sub-processes beneath (Fig. 3.25(b)) – for which there is rarely little time during macro-planning – will be perfected during the improvement implementation stage.

But widespread improvement micro-planning, typical of the company that has assimilated the dynamic principle of continuous improvement, cannot be restricted to the confines of the company's annual plans. There must be room for any improvement initiative, even those not covered by the plan.

Figure 4.1 illustrates the concept that if improvement is to be of both strategic and practical value it must be generated by two forces:

- a top-down force which begins with the company's macro-results (Chapter 3) and provides the basis for its main strategic guidelines, its macro-objectives;
- a bottom-up force generated through day-to-day work, which focuses on one hand on micro-results, to identify specific improvement **requirements**, and on the other on processes, to identify the **possibilities** for improvement.

It should be noted that **results** are the source of both forces, at high and low level respectively. This can therefore be called a **results-driven** vision of improvement. The area for micro-planning and improvement initiatives lies in the company's operating area, its activities and its processes. This is where the goals relayed from above intersect with process skills and knowhow, and are turned into specific improvement initiatives, and where the company's process skills and knowhow autonomously generate other initiatives.

In the operating area, the creative dimension of improvement has a basis in the routine dimension of management, standardisation, conformity with existing standards and procedures: this is the area of **process control**. If stable improvements are to be obtained in any result, the process that generates the result must be under control. Figure 4.1, which, on the right-hand side,

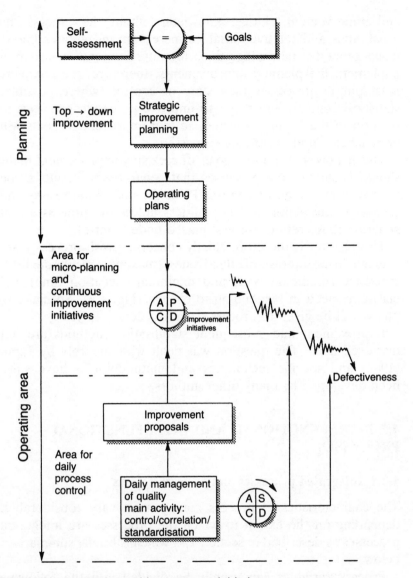

Fig. 4.1 Micro-planning and improvement initiatives.

reproduces the PDCA-SDCA staircase of Fig. 1.5, shows how each new improvement phase requires the stabilisation of the previous phase. Process management sets off a self-perpetuating cycle: through the alternation between control/stabilisation phases and improvement phases, knowledge about the process, its capabilities and relative variables increases; and greater knowledge generates new suggestions for improvement. In order to implement the planned improvements, therefore, the company must put its processes in a state of control (where possible, statistical control) and begin to improve process capabilities in relation to the results expected, so that improvement goals will be reached – and eventually surpassed.

This means that the first goals of company improvement plans should be to put the processes that generate the results to be improved in a state of control. Plans for improving results and customer satisfaction will be fruitless unless the processes that generate those results are first placed under control.

This chapter is therefore chiefly concerned with process management in the interests of effectiveness (maximum results quality), efficiency (minimum costs and minimum execution time) and elasticity/speed in responding to change (Fig. 1.4). Special emphasis will be given to process streams (section 1.4).

Improvement and subsequent stabilisation methods are not discussed here. The question was dealt with superbly by Juran (1982) and specific techniques and methodologies have since been developed by many other authors.

4.2 INTRAFUNCTIONAL AND INTERFUNCTIONAL PROCESSES

4.2.1 Integrated processes and process streams

The characteristics of process management vary considerably, depending on the extent to which the processes are integrated processes as described in section 1.4, which is briefly summarised below.

Process variables can usually be divided into the following categories: people's skills/knowhow, equipment, information/ training, procedures/documentation, conditions in the workplace. Each of these is inevitably subject to a degree of spurious variability.

The problem for process control is to keep this variability

178

within defined limits, so that the variability of the process results remains within statistically defined and therefore predictable limits. The task of the **control system**, which is an important component of the process, is to monitor variability and to activate corrective feed-back loops when the process exceeds the permitted tolerances. In particular, the control system will monitor the dominant variables, which are known beforehand to have the greatest influence on variability.

But another variable exists, which is usually not considered because the process manager is able to control it and because, as long as its possible negative effect on results is modest, it is included within the information variable: this is the **organisational integration** variable, the degree to which the people working in the process communicate and are coordinated with one another, so that information, the vital sap of the process, flows freely and work is performed in a coordinated fashion, wherever possible in parallel, keeping times to a minimum and avoiding errors.

In section 1.4, the conventional term 'technical' is used to describe the variables over which the process manager has sufficient control to keep results within statistically predictable limits. Like true technical variables, these variables can be traced back to an aleatory level where deviation is measurable. In these cases, variability can actually be measured. The conventional yardstick for variability is the distribution '6σ' (Fig. 4.2), known as **capability**: capability indicates a process's 'natural deviation', its best performance when all special causes of variation have been removed.

Experience shows that the **organisational integration/communication** variable slips easily out of the control of individual managers when the process becomes more complex. As the process extends over the boundaries among functions and sectors, communication falters and becomes distorted (Fig. 1.19), integration weakens; even if they want to, none of the managers of the organisational areas covered by the process can, by themselves, bring the management and communication variables back under control. The wider the company area covered by the process, the higher the position of the manager who can control these variables, but this manager is usually unable to exercise control via the vertical channels of the company hierarchy. The **integrated process** was defined in section 1.4 as a process in which all variables, including organisational integration – in particular, communication – can be placed in a state of control (statistical control wherever possible), so that results are statistically predictable. In other words, the integrated process is a process in which, for the purposes of control, all variables can be regarded as technical variables, according to the definition in section 1.4.

When the organisational integration variable is not under control, then the activity should be divided up according to its main organisational barriers, those that prevent control. In this way, the process is subdivided into a series of smaller units, each of which meets the requirements of the integrated process and can therefore be kept under full control by the process manager. This subdivision transforms the macro-process into a network of integrated processes. This network can be called a process stream (more precisely, an **integrated process stream**), since it indicates activities that flow, like a stream, along supplier-customer chains.

Since it is customary to refer to intrafunctional processes and interfunctional processes (and, for the latter, to functional segments of the process), the legitimate question arises whether these two types of process correspond respectively to integrated processes and integrated process streams. The answer is no. Although the boundaries between functions are organisational barriers of varying heights, along which the process can be subdivided, it cannot be assumed that barriers to integration do not also exist within a function, indicating that the process itself should be subdivided. So while the guideline for subdividing the macro-process into a process stream may initially be functional, each functional segment must then be analysed immediately to see whether it can be regarded as an integrated process or whether it must be further subdivided into units that will meet this requirement. The distinction between integrated process and process stream is fundamental to the ability to manage processes effectively – not just to improve them, but to meet current goals.

Management of the integrated process is a technical issue. It can be delegated in full to the process manager, who will work with existing tools. He will apply the Juran trilogy approach (planning-control-improvement) and the traditional process management and quality function deployment methodologies.

Management of the process stream, on the other hand, is a complex managerial question, which requires a new approach, new organisational solutions, and the direct involvement of management. The aim of process stream management is to **restore the organisational conditions that allow quality to develop at a technical level**, as in the integrated process. A clear distinction therefore exists between integrated process management, which is a 'technical question' and process stream management, which is a 'managerial question'. The following sections deal with both types of process management, giving particular emphasis to process stream management, since integrated process management has already been dealt with elsewhere and by other authors (Juran, 1982, 1988; Pall, 1990). The application of quality function deployment to the process stream in order to improve planning and goal deployment will also be examined.

In certain sections of this book, the expression 'interfunctional process' is often used as a synonym for 'process stream'. Although, strictly speaking, this is not correct (see above), the term 'interfunctional process' has entered common usage. The term 'process stream' is more general because it can also be applied to non-integrated processes within a single function, but it is offered as a suggestion; its use is not widespread (Tosalli *et al.*, 1990).

Before examining process management, the concepts of process **capability** and **state of control** should be touched on briefly, although detailed discussion of these issues is outside the sphere of this book.

Figure 4.2(a) illustrates the normal situation for a variable of a process in a state of statistical control (that is, a process in which all **special causes** of variation have been eliminated and only **common causes** remain, the aleatory causes that are intrinsic to the process). In practice, this 'normal' or 'Gaussian' frequency distribution may not be valid if individual measurements are shown on the graph, but it will always be valid if the average values of sufficiently large sub-groups of measurements are shown. With this qualification, the curve can be considered normal for the purposes of process management.

181

The distribution is established by the average value $\bar{X}$ (or $\bar{\bar{X}}$ when the graph shows the average values of subgroups of measurements) and the standard deviation σ (sigma). Conventionally, the 'capability' of the process, in relation to the characteristic considered, is taken as the range 6σ ($\pm 3\sigma$), which covers 99.73% of distribution. To assess the adequacy of the process in relation to user requirements, process capability must be compared with the tolerance range T allowed by the user (Fig. 4.2(b)). If the distribution is centred with respect to the tolerance range, and 6σ is less than the width of this range, then in at least 99.73% of cases the result will meet the user's expectations; non-conformity will be less than 0.27%. It is clear that non-conformity can be reduced to extremely low values, close to zero, when circumstances permit a reduction in deviation and 6σ, because in this case the ratio between the range of tolerance and capability, the so-called **capability ratio** C_p, increases. Naturally, the two ranges must be centred with each other (the C_{pk} ratio indicates this).

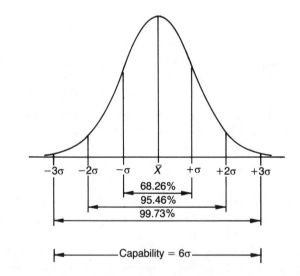

(a)

Capability = 6σ

Fig. 4.2 The concept of capability and the match between capability and tolerance. (a) Capability is often defined as $C = +3\sigma$. The normal distribution is established by the average $\bar{X}$ and the standard deviation σ. Capability is often defined as $C = \pm 3\sigma$. (b) Non-conformity (NC) emerges when capability C and estimated average $\bar{X}$ do not match tolerance (range and centring).

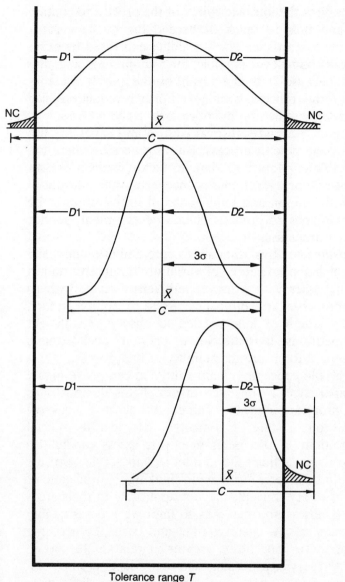

Capability C inconsistent with tolerance range: capability ratio $C_p = \dfrac{T}{6\sigma} < 1$

Capability consistent with tolerance range: capability ratio $C_{p'} = \dfrac{T}{6\sigma} > 1$
Centring of distribution adequate
$C_{pk} = \dfrac{D_{min}}{3\sigma} > 1$
(D_{min} = minimum of $D1$, $D2$)

Capability consistent with tolerance range: capability ratio $C_p = \dfrac{T}{6\sigma} > 1$
Centring of distribution inadequate
$C_{pk} = \dfrac{D_{min}}{3\sigma} < 1$

Tolerance range T

Fig. 4.2 (*cont.*)

183

Capability measures the intrinsic ability of the process to contain variability – and thus to reach or exceed the target – for a certain output characteristic. The variability expressed by capability is the minimum level possible for that process and that characteristic, because it is the result of the purely aleatory components of the process variables. Further reductions can only be obtained by structural modifications to the process.

The concepts of **state of statistical control** and capability are fundamental to any type of process. But in processes where the dominant variable is people, the human factor, or in processes with a low repetitiveness level, these concepts must be introduced and applied with caution and intelligence, if they are not to be rejected. These types of process include development, service and commercial processes.

In these instances, it is difficult to approximate the ideal situation in which special causes of variation are absent; and in the case of processes with a low repetitiveness level, such as development processes, it is difficult to assess capability. In fact, because of the length of time needed to observe a sufficient number of repetitions, it is difficult to prevent special causes from emerging and to ensure the stability of the process.

Nevertheless, the concepts remain valid and can prove highly beneficial. Experience in the most diverse fields demonstrates that use of appropriate indicators and control charts helps show the deviation from a state of control and to identify special causes of variation. It also helps managers assess capabilities and take improving action. Development and service process managers would be greatly mistaken in thinking that the state of control and capability concepts are not applicable to their areas of operation. There is no other way to improve process quality and consequently results quality, time and costs. Indeed, the importance of these concepts is greater in relation to certain development and service processes than to production processes. In software development processes, for example, the difficulties, costs and time involved in debugging the finished product make closer control of the development process and continuous improvement of capabilities inevitable.

As far as services are concerned, customer satisfaction rests entirely on process capabilities, in particular on the capability of the employees concerned, which depends on their business and behavioural training, clear definition of the service standards expected, the support they receive from the company and so on. The service process in fact delivers the product to the customer as it is generated, so there is no opportunity to correct non-quality, whereas in production processes recovery action can be taken to correct errors caused by insufficient capability.

With this digression on state of control and capability, the issue of process management can now be considered.

4.3 MANAGING THE INTEGRATED PROCESS

Management of the quality of the integrated process can be divided into three phases: planning, control and improvement. During the quality **planning** phase, the process is planned and developed so as to generate naturally (that is, as a result of its capabilities, not as a result of subsequent adjustments) the quality expected by users, with the minimum use of resources; in other words, to generate the maximum value for users at minimum cost and in the minimum time.

The sequence of planning activities can be summarised as follows:

a. Identification of the **users** of the results of the process.
b. Identification of these users' **expectations**.
c. Transformation of the users' expectations into **process goals**, expressed in **process language** (that is, as measurable goals, with relevant tolerances).
d. Definition of global **efficiency** goals (costs and time).
e. Development of the process with the capabilities needed to generate the target output (this phase must be conducted in close contact with the process 'suppliers', to establish input quality characteristics).
f. Definition of the **output** and **input quality indicators**; definition of the **process indicators** as regards both quality (correlated or correlatable with output quality) and efficiency (correlated with the cost/value and activity time/chronological time ratios).

g. Development of the control system, that is, the system (people and equipment) responsible for keeping the process in a state of control; this system includes measurement points, sensors, data entry, reduction and processing, production of indicators, and corrective feedback loops. The 'control system' may be a sophisticated automated system (in the case of highly repetitive production processes) or it may depend on the thoroughness and flexibility of the people involved (in the case of development and service processes where repetition is low or not identical). Planners must bear in mind that the control system is not only a tool for process regulation but also a **learning tool** for the process managers: through the indicators, the process should **communicate** with those who manage it, revealing in ever greater detail the links between process variables and capabilities and between process variables and end results in relation to the product, costs and execution time. Indicators therefore play a crucial role in process management. It will not always be possible to create the most efficient and 'eloquent' indicators during the planning phase; the indicators will be perfected during the subsequent control and improvement phases. But this will only be possible if the control system is planned correctly. If, as is often the case, information technology tools are used to ensure more effective, efficient control, then these tools, too, must be designed as openly as possible, allowing for later upgrades (section 4.7) and a high level of interaction. The potential for improvement depends to a large degree on the **dialogue** between the process and its managers, via a dynamic, adjustable system of measurement points, processing points and indicators, which can be experimented with easily.

h. Process start-up and testing, achievement of a state of control; monitoring of capabilities in relation to the quality indicators chosen and the tolerances allowed; comparison with hypotheses, adjustment or planning of improvement initiatives.

i. Checking of efficiency results against goals and consequent action.

j. Confirmation to process users that output goals will be met (immediately or within a specified period) or request for goals to be re-examined.

The **control** phase is the operating phase, in which it is assumed that the process will achieve its goals with the minimum deviation – in all cases within the tolerances allowed. For this purpose, the control system's feedback loops protect the process against the ever-present risk of its capabilities being undermined by special causes. It is during the control phase, or operating phase, of normal process management that active or passive attitudes to the process emerge.

If attitudes are active and the control system is adequate, interactive and flexible, then the process managers will gradually improve their knowledge of their processes and begin to consider not only correction (achieving current quality goals with the permitted non-conformity rate), but also **improvement** (reducing non-conformity rates and improving quality goals). The 'improvement–new goal stabilisation–new improvement' staircase (Fig. 1.5) is thus implemented.

Unlike planning and control, improvement is not a clearly defined phase in the process life cycle; as has been seen, **improvement initiatives** can be developed at the end of the planning phase, following the pilot tests, or at any time during the operating phase.

For improvement, the process must be in a state of control and quantitative information about the capability or capabilities to be improved must be available. Improvement may stem from the need to improve the capability ratio, that is, the ratio between tolerance (external constraint) and capability (intrinsic characteristic of the process): this is usually a requirement of the process manager, aimed at improving results and costs. Or it can stem from users, who demand a reduction in tolerance ranges or, more generally, an improvement in the fitness-for-use of the process output, without any deterioration in the capability ratio.

In the competitive stakes, a great deal depends on process improvement, because of its potential to improve the quality results and/or costs and/or execution times.

4.4 MANAGING THE PROCESS STREAM

As mentioned earlier (sections 3.9 and 4.2), the specific purpose of process stream management is to restore the organisational integrity of the flow of activities, which is undermined by the company's hierarchical-functional organisation. Organisational integrity is the *sine qua non* condition for successful 'technical' management of the quality of individual integrated processes, as described in the previous section.

Reconstructing the organisational integrity of process streams is obviously a matter for management in general, beginning with top management; in particular, it is the duty of the chief officer to involve all management in defining the corrective action to be taken within the functional organisation to make horizontal integration possible. This is a highly critical area: a solution that fails to take account of the existing corporate culture and the real distribution of power within the company risks provoking a negative reaction, which could endanger the result. All solutions tend to limit vertical powers and to require the development of a horizontal process-based culture as a preliminary to the development of a network culture (Drucker, 1988; Bartlett and Ghoshal, 1990). However, some solutions are less traumatic than others, and the company should be able to choose the most suitable formula for its own needs once management has carefully discussed and accepted the idea of horizontal integration. A constant feature of any solution should be the creation, for each important process stream, of a permanent stream management team, composed of the managers of the stream's integrated processes led by the most senior manager and/or by the manager with the greatest interest in the result. This team is an invaluable tool for integration, but its power is not usually sufficient to counter-balance the diverging pressures that may develop along the company's vertical lines of organisation; for the key company processes, it is therefore essential to appoint a team **guarantor** at the highest level, if possible at first-line level, from where the vertical organisation begins (Fig. 4.3).

Opinions differ on this point. Some people believe the guarantor should be the actual 'owner' of the process stream; but, owing to the complexity of the stream, the risk arises of a control structure being created – even in the most elementary form – which could remove responsibility from the team and its leader and consequently intensify (rather than dilute) the antithesis between

188

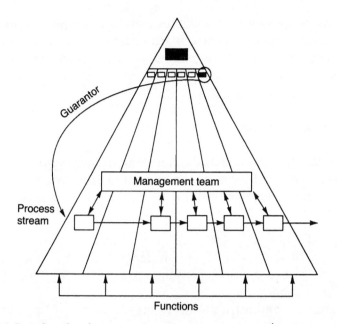

Fig. 4.3 Interfunctional process stream management requires a management team and, when necessary, a guarantor to ensure integration.

the new horizontal power and the vertical function powers (wide experience of matrix structures confirms this). Other people believe the guarantor's role must be solely that of guarantor. His main responsibility should be to ensure that the necessary organisational conditions exist to permit the management team to achieve fully its interfunctional goals, to act as an organisational 'watch-dog', in other words. According to this view, shared by the author, the guarantor must be seen by the team as an aid to overcoming organisational barriers, not as a further layer of power and control. In short, the guarantor's responsibilities are connected with the **organisational integration indicators** (see below) rather than with the process results indicators. Achieving the balance is difficult, however, and the best solution will be the one that offers the greatest possibility of achieving effective horizontal integration within the cultural context of the specific company. At methodological level, process stream management

189

consists of the same three phases as integrated process management, although their contents are different since organisational and managerial issues are being dealt with rather than technical issues.

4.4.1 Goal planning

Planning is the first and most important activity of process stream management, and requires the **maximum integration** among the managers of the processes in the stream. Planning consists of two phases:

1. identification of users' requirements/expectations and definition of the goals of the stream (similar but not identical to the corresponding planning phase in integrated process management);
2. alignment and attribution of goals to individual processes in the stream.

Two problems usually arise in the **definition of the stream's overall goals**:

- a lack of involvement of end customers (the users of the results of the stream) in the definition of requirements;
- insufficient participation of the various company functions covered by the stream, in the definition of common goals (quality, costs, times).

The end customer is particularly important in the definition of requirements for processes that generate products/services for the market, especially nowadays as companies compete increasingly at the level of positive quality, maximising value as perceived by the customer. End-customer participation must take place in a context of swift, effective interaction with the company, which involves not only the institutional functions of marketing and product planning but many corporate functions. Quality function deployment methodologies are particularly useful in disseminating customer requirements through the company to all the functions concerned. The interesting question of

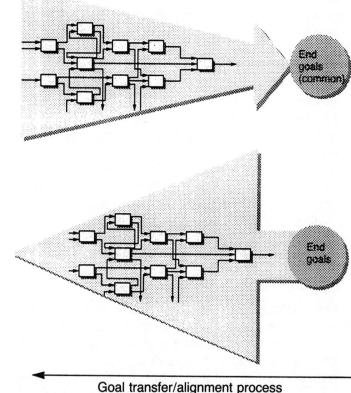

(a)

(b)

Goal transfer/alignment process
'from the mouth to the sources'

Fig. 4.4 Process stream management: goal planning and deployment phase: (a) definition of common goals; (b) transfer/alignment of goals to all processes in the stream.

quality function deployment in relation to process streams is discussed in a later section, to avoid interrupting the logical sequence of planning, control and improvement, although the reader should note that it is a logical part of both phases 1 and 2 of planning. For the time being, it is sufficient to note that this phase must be handled by a team composed of the managers in the stream, who must define all common quality, time and cost goals (Fig. 4.4(a)).

The alignment and attribution of goals to individual processes

in the stream also requires a team approach, to ensure that goals are transferred consistently, from the mouth to the source of the stream (Fig. 4.4(b)). This stage consists of alternate phases of deployment and planning, as will be seen in the discussion of quality deployment below.

The transfer of goals upstream is accompanied by the definition of suitable indicators for the interfaces between processes. These will include not only stream indicators, but **indicators enabling management to assess the level of integration/communication**. The latter will become the most significant indicators for the stream. They often take the form of brief verbal descriptions, but may also be expressed in numerical form when they are the result of surveys/questionnaires in which opinions are ranked according to a scale (see the quality system surveys described in section 3.5).

Assessments/surveys which provide horizontal integration indicators include:

- Periodic questionnaires completed by the managers of the processes in the stream in their dual role as suppliers-customers. These questionnaires ask for quantitative judgements – using, for example, the 1–5 scale described in section 3.5 – on the level of communication, on the effectiveness of team planning, on visibility throughout the stream right up to the end user, on the application of quality function deployment, on the control phase, on improvement teams and initiatives, on the difficulties created by vertical function lines and on the effectiveness of the process guarantor in overcoming these difficulties, etc. In short, the questionnaires investigate the degree to which the rules are observed and the suitability and effectiveness of these rules.
- Questionnaires distributed at lower levels, in particular to the people working at the interfaces in the stream.
- Formal reports by the management team and the improvement teams.
- Assessments by the process guarantor.
- Assessments by the function managers and, if it exists, by the interfunctional committee.

192

4.4.2 The control phase

This is the operating phase, known here as the **control phase** to maintain the analogy with integrated process management and because its purpose is organisational control of observance of the rules, criteria, and goals established previously during the planning phase. The difference with integrated process management, where the purpose of the control phase is to protect process capabilities against special causes of variability, should be noted.

During the control phase, the team's role is marginal at operating level but of primary importance at strategic level: its job is to **safeguard the stream** and enforce the rules established during planning, intervening only in exceptional cases, when unresolved interface difficulties between supplier and customer threaten to become conflicts (Fig. 4.5), or, in the more frequent and serious case, when the organisation's vertical forces threaten to re-erect barriers to the process stream.

The difficulty of resolving interface problems is sometimes due to flaws in rules, in goal planning, and to real capability problems which cannot be straightened out over the short term: problems that extend beyond the local level and may require a review of procedures, goals and indicators in part or all of the stream. The team must be ready to intervene in these cases before the problems become chronic or generate conflict.

In other cases, persisting local problems indicate poor communication or a lack of cooperation, and will be resolved by the team leader, assisted where necessary by the stream guarantor; in fact, the control phase, in which activity actually takes place, is the test bed for the hypotheses formulated during planning and for management consistency in general.

In the absence of problems, the control phase for process stream management would consist of periodic meetings of the team to examine progress, while true control activities would be performed within and at the interfaces between the integrated processes. In dealing with problems, the team should aim to bring the stream towards this ideal situation, making particular efforts to ensure that the interfaces become areas of coopera-

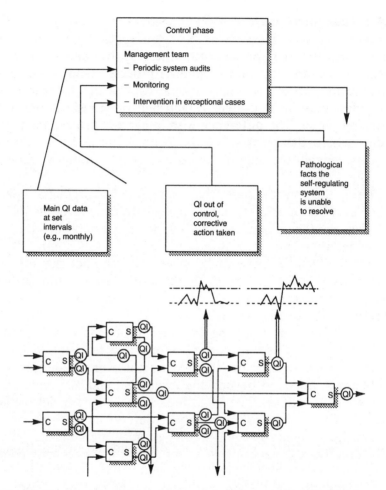

Fig. 4.5 Process stream management: control phase, tasks of the management team. QI = quality indicators/integration at process interfaces; C/S = customers/suppliers.

tion rather than trench warfare, the natural sites for preventing problems, for rapidly resolving any problems that do occur, and for joint decisions by the supplier and customer to call in the team when they are unable to handle the problem at their level.

The degree of operating autonomy of each process during the control phase will depend on the effectiveness of the joint planning phase, the smoothness of communications, the strength of the supplier-customer partnership, and the speed with which the real difficulties and problems in the stream, identified at local level, are brought to the attention of the team for correction and improvement.

4.4.3 Improvement

As has been seen, improvement of the integrated process is possible only if the process has been placed in a state of control (strictly speaking, of statistical control). A state of control is a realistic proposition for the integrated process, since all the variables involved are technical variables, which can be controlled by the process manager. In theory, the same principle applies to process streams, if improvement is defined as a structural modification which improves the stream's natural ability – its capability – to reach its goals. But reference to the capability of a process stream implies a level of control over the management and communication variables sufficient to enable the entire stream to be treated as an integrated process. This is an ideal limit, a perfect situation; for practical purposes, the possibility of improvement must be considered even if the stream is not in a fully consolidated state of control. The problems covered by improvement must, however, be **chronic** (not individual episodes, which will be dealt with by corrective action), and the organisational areas concerned must have a solid experience of control tools and techniques: approved indicators, regular measurements, regular data analyses, active feedback loops, and corrective action.

Improvement may involve the whole management team or just one or some of the processes in the stream. Apart from improvement of the individual process (see integrated process improvement), two situations are possible:

- If a limited number of contiguous processes are involved, responsibility for improvement lies with the relevant supplier-customer roles; an **improvement team** of representatives from the processes involved will be formed. The stream management

195

team will be kept informed of progress and results, and of how these results are expected to affect end results in terms of quality, costs and time.

- If the entire stream (or the majority of processes in the stream) is concerned, responsibility for improvement clearly lies with the stream management team. The improvement initiative will be nothing less than a planning operation of the sort described above; it will require data and experimentation, for which the management team can appoint an interfunctional improvement team to be disbanded as soon as it has accomplished its mission.

4.4.4 Conclusions

The problems involved in process quality management differ greatly according to the organisational complexity of the process concerned. As long as all the process variables, including the organisational variable, can be controlled by the process manager (integrated process), the concept of process capability applies and the significance of the terms planning, control and improvement is that conventionally assumed in the quality field. When the organisational variable is dominant – as in the case of chains of interfunctional processes – the significance of planning, control and improvement changes considerably and the main goal is to reconstruct and maintain the organisational integrity of the stream.

Placing corporate process streams under a state of control and working systematically and continuously to improve them requires the active contribution of top management to:

- ensure that process stream management guarantees the maximum organisational integrity, by neutralising the disruptive pressures that may come from the vertical organisation;
- encourage horizontal communication and interfunctional teamwork;
- ensure that a company process chart is kept identifying the process streams under control (those managed with the criteria described) and that every year company strategic planning

covers new process streams to be placed under control as well as those already under control, for which improvements are planned;

- promote process management training;
- perform independent audits to check the state of the major company processes, in particular the state of the process streams which should already be managed;
- maintain absolute consistency between the criteria of the company's reward system and the strategic goals of company process management.

4.5 QUALITY FUNCTION DEPLOYMENT METHODOLOGIES APPLIED TO PROCESS STREAMS

The effectiveness of quality function deployment methodologies (product QD, service QD, Q function D) in transferring market requirements to the company's products and processes is widely recognised. The thesis submitted here is that if these methodologies are applied at the level of integrated process streams, their potential is heightened and optimum results are achieved.

Quality deployment (this expression, abbreviated to QD, will be used from this point to indicate quality planning and deployment methodologies as a whole) can be effectively applied to the integrated process without requiring any modification. In Fig. 4.6, the letters A and C are used to indicate the QD matrix tables for, respectively, user requirements/expectations (expressed in user language) and their **substitute quality characteristics** (expressed in the supplier's language and measured by the supplier). Technical problems may arise in the A → C conversion, but problems of language uniformity or uniformity of internal quality measurements will not arise, because the process is integrated.

Quality deployment is not so easily applied to the interfunctional process, owing both to the dimensions of the process and to the fact that the various functions frequently perceive and assess quality in accordance with their own missions and goals (for example, the language and quality assessment methods of

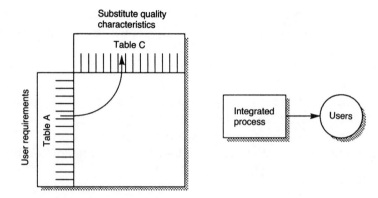

Fig. 4.6 Quality function deployment methodologies can easily be applied to the integrated process.

sales functions are closer to those of the user than those of the design or production functions). These differences are necessary, and QD should not remove them: its purpose is to translate and align languages and assessment methods into a consistent structure. Nevertheless, catering for different languages/methods would make application of QD to the entire process a laborious and complex business (and also create a chart of unmanageable proportions). Quality deployment can be applied by segmenting the interfunctional process into a stream of integrated processes, so that a simple, orderly sequence of charts can be created, instead of one large chart.

The subdivision into a stream of integrated processes linked by clear supplier-customer relationships helps management to build matrices based on uniform criteria and a uniform language, and to transfer and align goals; furthermore, the unitary approach adopted during the joint planning phase and the supervision provided by the team during the deployment phase (see previous sections) will help increase integration among the processes in the stream.

Figure 4.7 illustrates the concept: QD is applied first to the last process in the stream, to transform user requirements into goals for that process, and then, moving backwards up the stream towards its source, to the other processes, one by one.

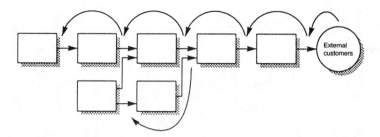

Fig. 4.7 Application of QD to an integrated process stream: goals are transferred upstream, process by process, to ensure alignment with end goals.

At each interface between two integrated processes, QD is applied in the same way as at the interface with the end customer: the requirements of the downstream process (customer), expressed in the customer's language, are entered in Table A, while the translation of these requirements into the language and in accordance with the assessment criteria of the upstream process (supplier) is entered in Table C.

An extremely simple process stream can be used to illustrate the application of QD in greater detail (Fig. 4.8), with reference to line drawings for full clarification. Since the object is to illustrate the specific features of the QD approach, the line drawings show only Tables A and C and omit the other tables that usually form QD matrices (customer assessments, goals from the market perspective, supplier assessments, and goals of the substitute quality characteristics) (Akao, 1990).

The first matrix to be created concerns the final process P1, which covers overall requirements, in particular the requirements of external customers (Fig. 4.8). It may be useful to imagine the matrix as a large desk, where the customers sit on one side (side A) and the managers of the integrated processes in the process stream sit on the other (side C). In practice, although the physical presence of a panel of significant customers on side A is desirable, external customers are usually represented by internal spokesmen, who present the results of customer surveys and interviews designed to identify customer requirements.

In the traditional QD approach, the various company functions

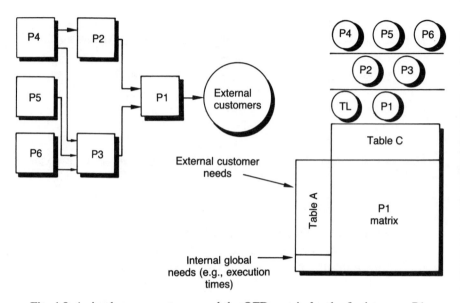

Fig. 4.8 A simple process stream and the QFD matrix for the final process P1.

involved would sit on side C of the desk. For each requirement expressed by side A, each manager on side C whose function would be involved in satisfying this requirement would create a C column with the relevant substitute quality characteristics. Obviously, the C table would rapidly become confused and unwieldy.

When QD is applied to processes, the representatives of the various company functions still sit on side C, but their roles are hierarchically ordered. First of all, they are identified as the **stream management team** and their responsibilities are assigned accordingly. The entire team participates in the validation of the A table (and in related activities not considered here, such as the identification of weights from a market perspective, comparative assessments of competitors, and identification of sales points) and in the completion of the C table, but only the managers of the relevant processes can create C columns, in their own language and with their own assessment criteria. Finally, the entire team takes part in completing the A−C correlation matrix. Figure 4.8 illustrates this: the P1 manager sits on side C of the desk, with the P2 and P3 managers behind him and the P4, P5 and P6 managers in the third row; all the managers take part, but only P1 can create columns. The team leader also sits in the front row, but his role is that of a moderator and guarantor of the correct application of the methodology.

This joint planning phase ends with an A table which has been validated by the team (complete with market assessments, comparisons with competitors, priority goals) and a C table of substitute quality characteristics, also validated, expressed in the language of process P1 (complete with measurements and quantitative goals).

The next phase is the P1 goal deployment phase (Fig. 4.9). The first part of the deployment phase concerns the P1 process alone, and covers the goals that P1 can meet **in toto**, without

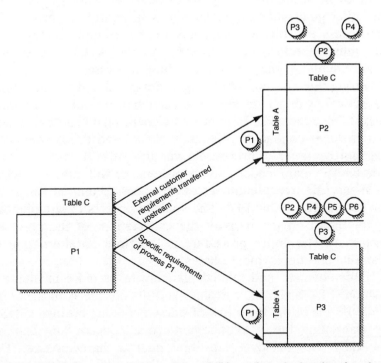

Fig. 4.9 Deployment from P1 to P2 and P3, and goal planning for these processes.

involving upstream processes (for example, the customer relation component of sales or customer support processes, which is almost entirely encompassed by these processes). A second group of goals falls entirely within the jurisdiction of individual upstream processes (for example, product reliability or manufacturing quality goals), and will be transferred in full to P1's inputs. A third group are goals covered by P1 activities fed by input from upstream processes; for these goals, the P1 manager will have to decide what input he needs to generate the required output, and submit this input as his own requirement to the upstream processes. The final part of the deployment phase concerns the specific requirements of process P1 which, though not directly linked with the needs of the end customer, are necessary to generate the planned added value (expectations of people, equipment-related requirements).

Apart from the first group – goals covered wholly by P1 – all the other goals generate expectations in relation to process P2 or process P3 (the two suppliers in the example in Fig. 4.9) and must therefore be transferred to the A table (customer requirements) of the matrices for these processes.

During this assignment of goals, 'desks' P2 and P3 must both be active, with P1 sitting as a customer on side A of both desks. Once the goals have been assigned, planning-deployment activities are conducted separately for P2 and P3. At desk P2, the representative of process P2 will now sit in the front row on side C. The team leader may be present, or will intervene when necessary; the representatives of processes P3 and P4 will sit in the second row behind P2. The goals of process P2 are planned at this point on the basis of the expectations of the process's customer. The entire procedure is therefore an alternation of planning and deployment phases.

P3 deployment and related planning takes place in identical fashion: P1 is again the customer and sits on side A of the desk, while P3 sits in the front row of side C, creating his own C table by translating the A requirements that concern him and responding with his own substitute quality characteristics. The representatives of processes P2, P4, P5 and P6 sit in the second row behind P3.

The description of QD application can be concluded here. It will already be clear that P4, for example, will have two matrices to complete, in other words, the P4 representative will sit as a supplier on the C side of two desks: his customer on the A side will be P2 at the first desk, P3 at the second. Each customer will bring to the desk the sum of the requirements transferred from the end customer, from customer P1 and his own requirements.

4.6 ANALYSING AND AUDITING PROCESS STREAMS

The first problem that arises in process stream management is to identify and describe the actual stream. This section provides a concise description of the analysis technique to be used to identify the stream and the integrated processes within it, the boundaries and links between the processes and the corresponding customer-supplier roles. It concludes with a brief mention of the stream audit, which is designed to assess the state of integration among processes and the levels of process quality achieved.

Strictly speaking, the preliminary analysis should begin at the mouth of the stream, that is, the last part of the stream, and move upstream towards its sources. The mouth, value for the user, is the meaningful element for all activities performed along the stream (the company should acquire the habit of reading situations 'from right to left', in other words, beginning with users and results and moving back through the company chains). In practice, it is more customary to analyse streams in the opposite direction, from source to mouth. This approach can be accepted the first time the stream is analysed, because an initial basis of reference is always useful; it would be difficult, in any case, to proceed otherwise, since the activity streams are already operational and the company is not an unexplored territory. So the company may as well begin by describing the process as seen by its managers, which is certainly a more rapid procedure than building the model from scratch.

But this is just the first step. Once the stream has been identified according to the views of the managers of the main processes involved, the second stage, critical analysis and validation, begins.

The following phases reproduce the quality deployment phases described in the previous section. In fact, a deployment procedure is involved here, too, although it is limited to drawing up a chart of the process stream, without considering either its contents or the end product; it is therefore a simplified deployment procedure.

4.6.1 Definition of outgoing 'products'

All the products to be generated by the stream should be identified (not the characteristics of these products). Meetings with both the users of the stream and the managers of the end processes are indispensable. So it is vital to identify all users, including secondary users.

4.6.2 Definition of the stream

The definition procedure moves backwards through the customer-supplier chains, initially from one functional process segment to another (the integrated processes in the stream have not yet been identified). Each process manager is asked to identify all his own suppliers and to give each one a weight (for example, on a 1–3 scale: important – of average importance – of little importance); the weight will appear next to the flow line linking the supplier process with the customer process. This means the stream can be simplified at any time adopting Pareto's principle, showing for example only the major links (weight 1), or the major and medium links (weights 1 and 2), or all links.

The definition phase ends at the source of the stream, where the activities begin and/or where input is provided by suppliers outside the company. It should be concluded with an accurate chart of the complete stream, showing boundaries and input/output from and to the outside; at this stage, the internal subdivision into processes is still incomplete, or has yet to be validated.

4.6.3 Subdivision of the stream into integrated processes and preliminary evaluation of the functionality of communication channels

The indications that emerge when the stream is matched against the company's organisation chart will provide initial guidance as regards the subdivision of the stream. The comparison will highlight organisational distances (Fig. 1.18) and thus provide a pointer as to the probable height of organisational barriers.

Interviews should then be conducted with the process managers and those members of their staff who act as interfaces, so that the functionality of communication channels can be assessed. These interviews are very similar to those conducted for stream management and audit activities (section 4.4), with the difference that, in this case, the interviews are preliminary procedures for the purpose of describing the stream, while the interviews for stream management and audit activities go into greater detail on a numerical basis.

At this point, the stream chart can be completed with graphic symbols indicating the level of functionality of interprocess and intraprocess communication channels. This will help management make further subdivisions in the functional process segments where necessary, so that all the processes in the final chart will qualify as integrated processes; and the completed chart showing the effectiveness of communication among the integrated processes will be useful during improvement planning.

With the appropriate adjustments, the analysis procedure used to draw up a preliminary description of the process stream can also be applied to analyses conducted for specific improvement initiatives and to periodic audits conducted, for example, for annual improvement planning. In these two cases, the analyses will refer to a stream that has already been described and validated and will tend to assess the level of organisational integration in greater numerical detail. The assessment/measurement criteria are those described in sections 3.4 and 4.4.

4.7 INFORMATION, INFORMATION SYSTEMS AND PROCESS MANAGEMENT

No company process can be improved unless the information on which decisions and subsequent initiatives are based is accurate, complete and up to date. Information is a **conditio sine qua non** for process quality, and therefore for the quality of results and the reduction of costs and execution times. Owing to its critical role, information is the first product whose quality should be ensured.

Information is not usually an independent product or an end in itself; it serves all the other products and processes. The information processes which support the company processes can be subdivided into two categories:

1. The first category comprises information processes linked with the management of operating processes, that is, the information processes needed to keep the process in a **state of control** (where possible, in a **state of statistical control**) and to enable managers to improve process capabilities. The data handled by these information systems is supplied by the process sensors, by the people concerned with control, by the process inputs and by the feedbacks from the output users. The corrective feedback loops are the nerve centres of these information processes, which together form the process control system (Fig. 4.10).

2. The second category comprises information processes that extract global data from the above-mentioned control systems for processing, comparison and possible integration with data from other processes, with external references, and with targets, etc., to form **management indicators**. These processes form the company's **management information system** and the products they generate are particularly critical: information on the state/trend and the capabilities of the company's processes in relation to goals and to the information on which decision-making processes are based (Fig. 4.10).

Although the quality of the information generated by the processes in the second group clearly depends entirely on the quality

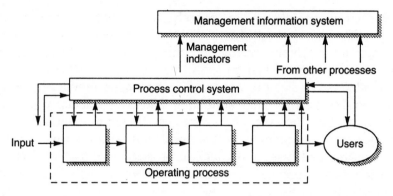

Fig. 4.10 The process control system and the management information system.

of the processes in the first group, many companies invest in management information systems without first placing processes in an acceptable state of control. The expression 'garbage-in, garbage-out' could not be more apt: under these circumstances, information systems are bound to be defective. The company thus falls back on purely administrative management procedures for the process input and output items that can easily be counted and expressed in monetary terms. Information on trends and cause-effect relationships vanishes. The company loses faith in information systems. It tries to compensate for shortcomings in quality with quantity, overloading the system with a mass of useless data, which simply aggravates the situation.

4.7.1 Process management first, information technology second

Information technology (IT) is an indispensable tool for handling management information today, and is increasingly useful for the management of many processes. But high-quality information systems can only be created from manageable and managed processes.

While it is true that the development of effective process management systems with rapid feedbacks is usually impossible without the support of computers, and that IT can help translate the data provided by process indicators into useful management information rapidly and effectively, the quality of the result depends primarily on the quality of the indicators and the process management system, and only secondly on the quality of the actual computer system.

Inadequate indicators and an inefficient management organisation are often the main stumbling blocks, particularly in the cases of interfunctional processes and/or non-manufacturing processes. They stem from technical and organisational problems in the first case, and a lack of process management experience in the second case (for example, commercial processes or development processes).

The introduction of IT in process management should therefore be preceded by a careful analysis of the process and a suitable test period, while the IT solution chosen should be easy to use and sufficiently flexible to permit modifications. The computer system should help operators understand the process better and test 'what-if' hypotheses, so that the best possible solution can gradually be implemented. In practice, no permanent optimal solution exists for processes: the changing requirements of output users or the expediency of improving process effectiveness or efficiency to satisfy existing requirements mean that process capabilities may need to be improved at any time, and so a new optimal solution will have to be found.

All too frequently, the IT solutions adopted lack flexibility or are difficult to use. The responsibility for this lies with the people who draw up the specifications for the computer system, not with those who develop it, and reflects a general lack of sensitivity to and understanding of process management. Process management training is the starting point to avoid disappointments in the use of information technology. In recent years, enthusiasm for factory automation led many companies to bypass the necessary (even if sometimes long and costly) improvements in process quality, with the result that, once the automation system had been installed, the underlying problems emerged with even greater force (someone who has to drive every day along a road full of holes will not arrive sooner and safely by increasing his speed, but by repairing the holes).

Today, companies risk making the same mistake in automating

white-collar activities. Poor information is worse than no information, so the maximum attention must be paid to the state of the process and to its ability to provide significant, correct data, before introducing a computer system, which, for its part, must guarantee maximum usability and flexibility.

4.7.2 The quality of the 'information' product

Many information products are of poor quality simply because they are the wrong products. The principle used for products intended for the market applies to this important internal product, too: the first condition for quality is to understand users' often unspoken requirements (quality of goals). The difference between products for the market and internal products lies in the consequences of error: in the first case, sales will be impaired (end of profit), in the second, company efficiency will diminish (emerging damage). In the case of the information product, users often suffer from a surfeit of data and a lack of useful information, but are not sure how to improve the situation. This is a typical case in which a **maieutical** approach is required to clarify expectations, based on an understanding of the role of processes and the importance of process management.

The traditional kind of information system, which reproduces the functional organisation and gives precedence to functions' internal **vertical** flows, cannot fail to generate the wrong product. The right product – significant information – stems from activities and processes, in other words, it is developed within a context of horizontal integration.

A management information system whose principal input is supplied by process indicators can provide the indicators required at the various company levels. The higher the position of the user in the company hierarchy, the less technical and more business-oriented the indicators will be, until, at the very highest level, macro-indicators on costs, revenues, added value, quantities and time (Fig. 4.11) will be reached.

It follows from the above observations that the quality of the information product depends, like the quality of any other product (Fig. 1.2), but more so, on the **quality of goals**. The

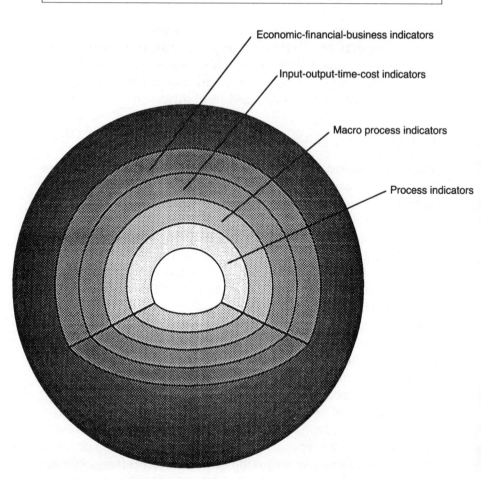

Economic-financial-business indicators

Input-output-time-cost indicators

Macro process indicators

Process indicators

Fig. 4.11 The company indicator layers.

other fundamental condition for product quality, quality of execution, is secondary, but it should not be neglected. The rest of this section looks briefly at execution quality, in the case of information processes supported by IT tools.

Figure 4.12 represents the information process, which transforms data into useful information. Quality may deteriorate at any point in the process, for two main reasons: loss of information or introduction of errors in data or information. The loss of

210

Fig. 4.12 The information process.

useful information is particularly critical: it generally stems from the necessary reduction of the volume of data and therefore reflects an incorrect evaluation of the reductions to be made for data entry, processing, analysis and output generation.

The following general steps should be followed to ensure the quality of the information process (for simplicity, reference is made here to the management information system for a process stream) (Godfrey, 1991):

(a) Identification of the information users

The process manager should supply the information system developer with a descriptive list of the information users, but it is vital that the system developer carefully re-examine the list with each process manager in the process stream concerned, particularly if the stream covers organisationally distant sectors.

(b) Identification of requirements

This step is connected with step (a). The information system developer must be sure he understands clearly the needs/expectations of each user, many of which will not appear in the list of formal specifications. This will be important above all for correct data reduction.

(c) Definition of information quality indicators

Once the users and their requirements have been identified, the next step is to define the information quality indicators, assign weights, draw up a defect classification, and identify possible sources of error in the process and the risks involved in reducing data. The users will be involved in this task.

(d) Definition of measurement points

Using the flow chart of the information process as a basis and taking account of the output quality indicators and the possible sources of error, the information system developer can establish control points, process indicators and corresponding measurements.

(e) Process control

Once steps (a) to (d) have been completed, the information process can be kept under control and correlations can be established among process indicators, output indicators and user results.

(f) Improving the process

Once the information process is in a state of control, it is eligible for continuous improvement action based on annual improvement plans and specific initiatives. Improvement teams will usually include user representatives.

4.8 THE NEW-PRODUCT DEVELOPMENT PROCESS: AN EXAMPLE OF MANAGEMENT INDICATORS

The new-product development/introduction process provides a significant example of the type of process indicator of interest to top management.

New-product development is one of the most critical processes, particularly for companies already competing at the level of time-to-market. In the most dynamic product-market sectors, such as those based on rapidly changing technology, where products' useful life can today be as short as 12 months, all competitors aim to develop new products within this tight time-scale. Few succeed.

All the players have access to the same technology (the new integrated circuits, for example), but most are handicapped by chronic delays in their schedules caused by changes in specifications, problems with hardware or software, unforeseen difficulties, incorrect evaluations, etc. Competition on time-to-market highlights, sometimes dramatically, the company's intrinsic weaknesses in process management, whether these are due to a lack of integration among functions or to problems in preventing and controlling variability. It is impossible to compete on time-to-market unless the functional segments of the development processes work as a team, running operations in parallel as far as possible and continually checking goal alignment; unless goals have been previously carefully defined and are constantly updated using quality function deployment criteria; unless processes are in a state of control and their variability is therefore limited and in all cases predictable.

Meeting all these requirements is far from easy, particularly in the product development environment. A failure to comprehend fully the importance of the issues involved lies at the root of the extreme difficulties experienced by Western companies in competing on time-to-market. Some companies do not fully understand the nature of all the requirements or appreciate how much time is needed to meet them.

A company may successfully integrate design, production, marketing, purchasing and other functions in the development process in a short space of time; it may also manage to spread the quality function deployment mentality equally quickly. But acquiring the ability to control variability in environments such as product design, which often lack a process management culture, takes time.

Competition on time-to-market, when companies operate from a more or less equal technological footing, depends chiefly on the quality of the people-processes binomial. In particular, processes must be carefully managed to keep variability to a minimum and avoid cycle repetition.

The top management of a company that intends to compete on time-to-market must achieve major changes in the new-product development sectors. These changes will be structural (parallel engineering, management teams, guarantors or process owners) and methodological (quality function deployment and accurate process control).

Naturally, major changes of this kind will not be implemented simply because top management has issued a decree. Top management control is essential and depends entirely on the availability of high-level macro-indicators extracted from the development process – more precisely, from the indicators used to manage the process. The macro-indicators may be numbers, significant graphs, or reports by lower-level managers at certain previously defined points in the development process.

The example given below, which refers to the development of an information technology product consisting of hardware and software, is fairly typical.

4.8.1 The product development and marketing cycle and checks

Figure 4.13 illustrates the product development and marketing cycle for a new product, with a series of key checks on the closely connected variables of quality, costs and time. These checks must provide top management with certain fundamental information about the product:

- its positioning in relation to competitor products in terms of price and performance (value for money, from the user perspective);
- when it will be available, with the planned quality, costs and volumes (availability conditioned by problems of cost, quality or quantity is usually the equivalent of non-availability – occurring when the greatest benefits could be reaped in terms of price).

The first check (Check 1) can be made when the product's functional specifications are drawn up, the second check (Check 2) when the project is complete, but before the main investments in hardware production have been made (if development time is short and operations are performed in parallel, the second check will not constitute such a sharp division among activities, but it will still be an important intermediate check). The third check (Check 3) takes place at the scheduled launch of marketing activities. The fourth and final check (Check 4) is performed once the transition to full production has been made, but soon

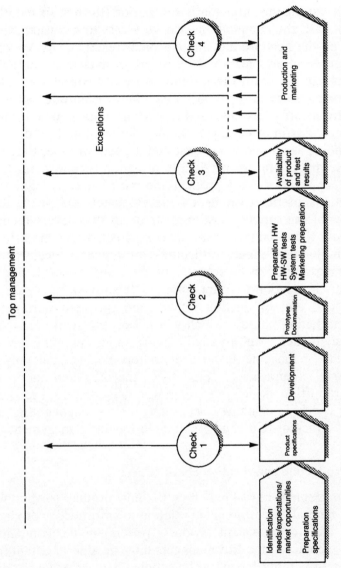

Fig. 4.13 The product development and marketing cycle for a new product with top management checks.

enough to provide useful operating and assessment feedback and above all to provide information of value for the development of subsequent products.

In fact, during the initial marketing period (the first six months, for example), the company must have access to a constant flow of data on the new product and customer reactions. Many companies are severely hampered by a lack of data from the field. The problem is almost always caused by a sectorial approach. The product sales and support functions concentrate on their respective priority missions, and regard the collection and transmission of data/information to the development and production departments as an additional cost and a waste of time; they fail to realise that, as far as this data/information is concerned, they are the **suppliers** of a key product and must meet the legitimate expectations of the **customers** – development and production (the flow of the supplier-customer stream is thus reversed compared with the usual flow from the company towards the field, a situation that can create difficulties for functions accustomed to acting as suppliers in relation to the outside world, but as customers in relation to other company functions).

The field and production information provided during the initial marketing phase – which will permit the swift correction of any anomalies – will usually be made up into monthly reports for middle management and sent to top management only in exceptional circumstances (Fig. 4.13), that is, when anomalies reach proportions which put volumes, quality and costs at risk.

Each check is examined separately below, highlighting the types of indicator that can be extracted for top management.

4.8.2 Production specification check (Check 1)

Top management must know how the new product (or the new offer in general) is positioned in relation to any previous products (offers) and to equivalent products (offers) of the company's reference competitors. But managers must be able to obtain this information without having to be product experts or learn technical jargon. Since the opinion of the user is the conclusive criterion, top management should be given the opportunity to assess specifications – the company's response to user expectations – from the user/market perspective and in accordance with user/market assessment criteria.

This first essential assessment of specifications must therefore be based on quality profiles similar to user expectation menus (section 2.2) and to customer satisfaction profiles. The best solution at this stage is to provide top management with a brief report including:

- the customer satisfaction profile (opinion of users) for the company's current offer;
- similar profiles for reference competitors;
- the **target profile** for the new offer.

Figure 4.14 provides an example of these profiles. Clearly, management may not feel happy with a quality profile for which customer confirmation will not be available for a number of years (allowing for the entire time-to-market cycle, an adequate

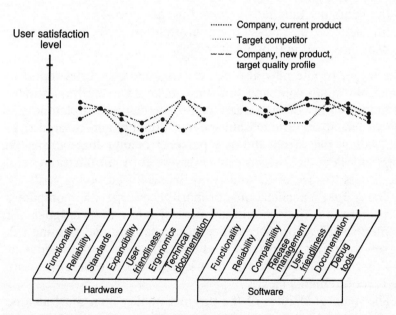

Fig. 4.14 Current customer satisfaction profiles – for the company and for a target competitor – and target profile for the new product.

period of use, and the time needed to conduct surveys), unless other information is provided to substantiate the credibility of the target profile. It is therefore useful to supplement the profile with an assessment by the function manager based on a **quality indicator for the specification generation process**.

This is a typical top management indicator, in which the function manager makes a global judgement according to a suitable quantitative scale. Top management is not looking for an analysis of merit, which would require a depth of technical knowledge not called for at top management level, but for an overall assessment by the manager who has visibility on the details; nevertheless, to avoid the risk of a wholly subjective judgement, top management will supply the criteria with which the assessment should be made. These criteria chiefly concern the quality of the **requirement-identification and product-goal-definition process** (Fig. 2.4(a)), in particular:

- how the process has been developed, if and how the quality function deployment methodology has been used;
- the company functions involved in the process;
- the sources of market data/information, which users have been involved and by what means.

The target profile may also be accompanied by a brief report in which the main company functions make an overall assessment of the feasibility of the target profile, the clarity/completeness of the specifications, the effectiveness of the deployment process in translating goals from the user perspective into comprehensible company language which can be assessed by all functions; and the fitness-for-use of the means available for achieving goals.

The target specifications primarily concern the company's customers, but they should not neglect internal users: goals for elements such as produceability, supportability and training will be set, adopting the criteria used for customers, with the advantage that the users form part of the team and can therefore state their requirements clearly.

The main guidelines of the product quality plan must also be supplied together with the specifications. In this case, the top management indicator will simply be the answer to the question of whether the full plan is available, and if not, when it will be available.

The target profile will be the main basis of reference for all subsequent checks, ending with the market/customer check. The target profile is naturally a dynamic profile, which will be modified when necessary, but a systematic change procedure will be adopted, taking account of the enormous significance of the profile for the company.

4.8.3 Pre-marketing check (Check 3)

For the sake of brevity, the intermediate Check 2 is not examined in detail; most of the observations on the final check in the development process (Check 3) apply to Check 2. The target profile (drawn up in much greater detail for operating personnel than for top management) is the main basis of reference during and at the end of development. Top management should be provided with a document of the type shown in Fig. 4.15, which

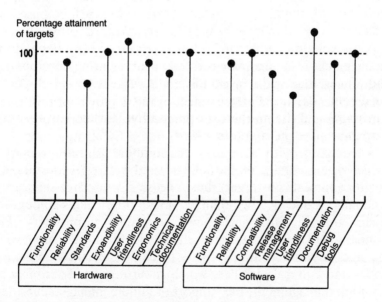

Fig. 4.15 Attainment of goals in relation to the target profile.

gives a percentage assessment of target attainment for every element in the target profile of Fig. 4.14. For some items/elements, this percentage will have a precise quantitative value (based on an actual measurement), for others it will represent the average estimate of a number of reference users, while for a third group it will represent the opinion of an internal group of managers based on tests, benchmarks and extrapolations. In all cases, the graph should reflect the final opinion of the senior product manager (function/division manager), who will be accountable to top management for the opinion expressed. A brief comment will be made on each item whose value is not close to 100%, stating if, how and when the company expects to attain the target, or, if the target is not expected to be achieved, explaining the implications of non-attainment in competitive terms.

Although top management should not be involved in specific technical questions, it may be helpful to provide a summary of the results of the main tests/checks in the form shown in Fig. 4.16. These are **standardised** results, which take as their yard-stick **completeness of tests**, in percentages, and **degree of target attainment**, also in percentages (specific technical knowledge is therefore not required). This information, too, will be based on judgements by the managers, particularly as regards completeness.

A fundamental indicator for both operating personnel and top management is the **anomaly correction curve** during development and its continuation as a **modifications curve** after development documentation has been handed over to production (for the hardware) and the marketing organisation (for the software), in particular after the marketing start-up.

A company with a serious commitment to time-to-market (which means coming to market early and well, with consolidated quality and costs on target) must necessarily improve this curve, gradually reducing the changes made after consignment of documentation, with each new generation of products. The company will only be able to achieve significant adjustments in the anomaly/modifications curve through substantial organisa-tional and cultural changes, which require great determination from top management, the support of middle management and a great deal of time.

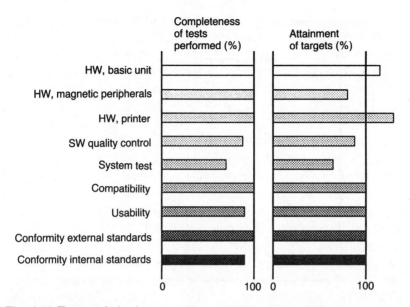

Fig. 4.16 Tests and checks on quality, reliability and usability in relation to standards. Percentages indicating completeness of the tests performed and degree to which specification goals have been achieved.

Figure 4.17 illustrates the type of curves that can be presented to management during marketing checks, as indicators of product stabilisation. Forecasts on future modification trends will also be provided (often based on special statistical models).

A standard form should also be drawn up describing and showing the availability of user documentation and documentation for the support organisation, training for sales and support personnel, support plan, supplies, etc. This information is vital in its own right, but it is essential for the purposes of customer satisfaction. The pre-marketing check should also include a **field check plan** designed to ensure the swift return of information on product quality and reliability and on any problem that may emerge at user level. A summary of the plan will be presented to top management, whose main concern, as before, is to verify the existence, completeness and suitability of the plan rather than its contents.

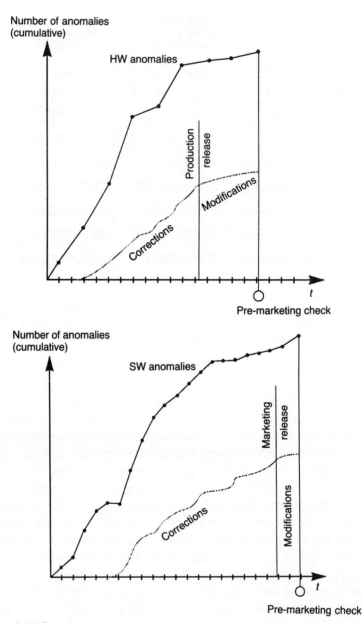

Fig. 4.17 Cumulative curves of anomalies found during the development process and corrections/modifications made, for hardware and software.

Finally, the function/division manager should make an overall assessment of the reliability of the marketing programme. The most effective approach is to prepare three charts showing the product volumes that would be issued to sales channels in three different scenarios – worst, most likely, best hypotheses – taking all the risk factors identified during the check into account.

4.8.4 Post-marketing start-up check (Check 4)

At the end of the marketing start-up period (for example, six months), a check will be made of the volumes lost through quality problems, with an estimate of the costs involved (in particular, any retrofitting costs). This is clearly the most important indicator for top management. But as far as product improvements and gradual improvements in development processes are concerned, the most important information is provided when the accuracy of each of the graphs used in the previous checks (Figs 4.14, 4.15 and 4.16) is verified on the basis of subsequent events. Verification should help the company improve its forecasting capabilities and discourage certain negative attitudes, of which the most typical is the tendency to meet deadlines but to introduce modifications shortly afterwards.

In this connection, companies with target-oriented incentive schemes should ensure their schemes are consistent with the overall goal of optimising the development and marketing process stream (and all interfunctional processes in general). Incentivation schemes that focus on individual results can never provide a basis for global optimisation, in this specific case, for reducing the number of modifications: the product planner, for example, will always be strongly tempted to deliver the documentation by the scheduled date, despite difficulties that are likely to lead to adjustments, if part of his incentive is tied to meeting the deadline. The incentive can turn into a perverse mechanism, which actually impairs the company's global results. No form of control can improve the situation, unless preventive action is taken. The only way to set off a self-perpetuating cycle that leads gradually to the positive results expected is through incentive schemes geared to the overall results of company teams (development, production, marketing, purchasing), which can be assessed for example during the Check 4 phase.

As far as verification of the target profile is concerned, it is best not to wait for the general customer satisfaction surveys (partly because these surveys generally do not provide the depth of detail required). *Ad hoc* surveys on the new product (or new offer) can be conducted with a significant customer sample. A verification profile is thus obtained – a customer satisfaction profile for the product/offer in question – to close a cycle which, if correctly implemented, should prove extremely educational and gradually lead to the improvement of the entire development process.

4.8.5 Process indicators

For Check 1, use of a global process indicator was suggested, to inform top management about certain aspects of the specification-generation process which are of vital importance to the quality of results. This reflects the importance of correct definition of the product target profile; it also takes account of the pitiful state of this process in many Western companies, which is frequently the cause of these companies' weaknesses in relation to their Japanese competitors.

But this is not the only process indicator that top management needs on the new-product development and marketing macro-process. Management indicators should be drawn up for every interfunctional process and for every major segment of these processes, as indicated in sections 3.4 and 4.4; top management should also be regularly supplied with a process chart showing the state of control of each process. Process indicators should be supplied to top management at regular intervals (for example, every six months), independently of the checks performed on products under development, even though the checks on the most important products may be supplemented with information on the state of the processes (in fact, the reliability of every result presented during the checks depends on the quality of the generating process).

Top management may find **process quality profiles** of the kind

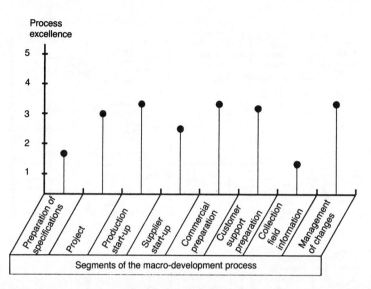

Fig. 4.18 A map of the state of the main development processes puts imbalances and weaknesses into immediate relief. See Table 3.1 for significance of the 1–5 scale.

illustrated in Fig.4.18 useful, especially if the company has a number of different divisions (or different development sectors). Comparisons and the links between the state of processes and results will prove instructive.

The 1–5 scale of the ordinates in Fig. 4.18 refers to the assessment criteria shown in section 3.4, Table 3.1. For interfunctional processes, the assessment should be completed with the criteria described in section 4.4, which reflect the degree of organisational integration among the various segments in the interfunctional process.

4.9 MANAGEMENT INDICATORS IN THE LOGISTICS PROCESS

A second example of process indicator for top management can be drawn from the product logistics process, which is briefly examined in this section.

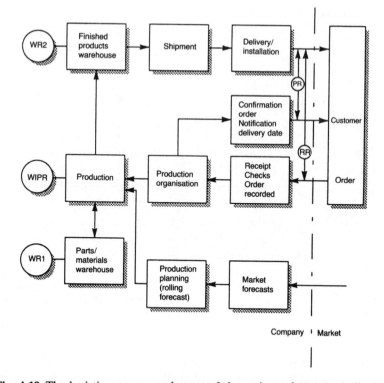

Fig. 4.19 The logistics process and some of the main performance indicators. WIPR = WIP ratio; PR = punctuality ratio = the difference between the actual delivery date and the notified date; RR = rapidity ratio = time between receipt of order and delivery; WR1 = parts/materials warehouse ratio = days of coverage; WR2 = finished products warehouse ratio = days of coverage.

The product logistics process is the process stream that begins with the customer's order and ends with the delivery (and, where appropriate, installation) of the product. Once again, a number of macro-process indicators of interest to top management can be identified.

Figure 4.19 illustrates the stream of processes for a company that produces goods for the market (in other words, not on a contractual basis). The company bases its calculations regarding resources and purchases of materials and parts on a rolling sales forecast, which is drawn up ahead of time, for example, one year. The forecast gradually becomes more precise as the target date approaches and finally becomes a rigid production schedule at a certain point before the target date. This type of forecasting system will affect the specific order-production-delivery cycle because of the inevitable divergences between the sales forecasts and actual orders taken, in terms of both volumes and product mix.

Unlike the new-product development process, the logistics process is highly repetitive. Macro-indicators for top management will therefore be supplied at regular intervals (every month, every quarter, every six months, etc.) instead of being related to checks performed at specific points in cycles.

The main operating indicators with which operating personnel control and improve the process should be identified first, followed by the macro-indicators. The first group of indicators, the most important as far as customer satisfaction is concerned, concerns **punctuality**: first, overall punctuality (PR in Fig. 4.19), that is, punctuality in delivering and – where appropriate – installing the product ready for start-up; then the punctuality of the different functions involved.

The second group of indicators concerns the **costs** associated with the logistics process: personnel costs, warehouse management costs, transportation costs, information system costs, financial costs of stock and factory and trade write-offs. Logistic costs are generally very substantial. Any logistic improvement programme should consider the question from both points of view: customer satisfaction and costs. Very few companies are able to keep account of all the costs listed above. Many simply keep track of inventory levels, which are usually expressed as the number of days of coverage (for the materials and parts warehouse and the finished products warehouse) and, sometimes, work-in-process (WIP). The problem with this approach is that all too often the target number of days of coverage is calculated on the basis of historical data and existing process capabilities, and therefore provides little incentive for improvement.

A third class of indicators is related to the **accuracy of sales forecasts**. These indicators could justifiably be called **frustration ratios**, considering the efforts countless companies have made to improve them, with little success. Back in 1958, J.W. Forrester (1958) observed that erratic sales forecasts are the inevitable consequence of lengthy logistic cycles and associated production start-up and parts/materials purchasing cycles. The only way to improve the accuracy of sales forecasts is to reduce cycle times sharply – the approach adopted by the Japanese.

The fourth group of indicators, in fact, concerns **process times**: overall delivery times first of all (measured in Fig. 4.19 by the **rapidity ratio**, RR), followed by individual process times.

In traditional business management theories, which assess performance in terms of the divergence from goals, the main macro-indicators for top management are punctuality and rapidity (expressed in terms of average divergences from goals and deviation), cost (usually expressed in terms of days of coverage and WIP), and the accuracy of sales forecasts.

In the modern total quality approach, which is geared to continuous improvement, all these indicators retain their import-ance, but the attention of top management focuses in particular on the gradual reduction of process times, month by month, year by year. Reduction of process times will not only improve punctuality and rapidity, variables appreciated by customers (who clearly prefer punctuality on short rather than long delivery times), but also increase the accuracy of sales forecasts and sharply reduce costs.

To conclude, management indicators must, as always, consider two aspects: the attainment of current goals and the improvement of future goals. In the first case, global punctuality and rapidity ratios, costs and the accuracy of sales forecasts are the most significant indicators. In the second case, process times are the most important indicator: not just global turnaround time, but the time of each process segment in the logistics cycle. For this reason, top management will attach greater importance to im-provement rates than to attainment of current goals and will require the goals set by the annual improvement plans to be aligned with the company's goals.

Learning to cope with change and continuous improvement: the education process

5

5.1 A PERMANENT LEARNING PROCESS RATHER THAN SWEEPING TRAINING PROGRAMMES

Corporate **total quality programmes** never fail to include a section on training.

Training usually begins with an awareness-raising phase designed to foster realisation of the urgent need for change and to provide information about what 'everyone else' is doing (where 'everyone else' is usually the Japanese and those Western companies, most of them competitors, that are taken as reference models). A second phase covers the definition of total quality according to the message bearer and a description of the approach, and a third phase gets down to the details.

But these 'details' are usually **lessons** in the use of tools and methodologies rather than an **education about** total quality.

Training is an area in which another of the ambiguities created by the chaotic development of quality today has taken root. When training is seen as information/awareness-raising followed by lessons in methodologies and techniques, training programmes are designed to cover specific target user groups within a specified period of time. And since total quality should involve everyone, the target often becomes a question of quantity: training the greatest number of people in the shortest possible time.

Impressive figures are paraded as indicators of the progress being made towards total quality. The numbers of people who have attended courses are counted and the percentage of coverage per function, per geographic area and so on is calculated. Then the people concerned go back to their jobs, where they find the same organisation, the same management style, the same priorities, the same assessment criteria, and before long everything is just the way it was before, but with an added dose of frustration. Approached in this way, the total quality programme is bound to create higher costs, while the results will be uncertain, if not counter-productive.

Of course, the new approaches to quality require knowledge to be passed on and skills to be developed, for example, in the areas of problem solving, quality function deployment, policy deployment, process management, basic statistical tools and the improvement approach. But the **educational** aspect of training is by far the most important in the total quality field : a **permanent learning process** must be set up within a context of coordinated organisational and managerial initiatives, to promote the spread of the new culture and the development of new attitudes.

It is not easy to define this culture. The main characteristics have been described in the previous pages, for example, the central role of the customer, the imperative of continuous improvement, the orientation towards medium/long-term results, the team and network approach as opposed to the individualist, functional mentality, the need for information based on facts, and so on. But although these are all fundamental components of the total quality culture, two other elements, closely related with one another, are even more important:

- **flexibility**, that is, accepting change as a natural fact in today's – and even more in tomorrow's – world;
- **continuous learning** as a consequence of change (passive aspect), but also as a consequence of the decision to adopt a continuous improvement strategy (active aspect, typical of

companies that want to be protagonists of change). Non-traumatic adjustment to continuous change can only be achieved through continuous learning.

As an essential part of the continuous pursuit of excellence in a changing world (the process conventionally known as total quality), the **education process** must therefore aim first of all to foster **flexibility**, to create a change culture. This means developing the cultural need to learn (intellectual curiosity instead of suspicion of the unknown) and promoting proactive attitudes (a willingness to experiment, to champion change) instead of reactive attitudes (a tendency to conformity, resistance to change). Second, the education process must be designed as a permanent learning process rather than as a series of training courses, even if a fairly rapid succession of initiatives will be necessary during the initial period; the company will have to build something much more difficult, but also less expensive and less ephemeral: an **organisation for continuous learning**. The actual education process therefore becomes part of a broader process designed to promote a total quality culture and, at the same time, to improve specific skills in order to meet the requirements of a constantly changing external environment and the company's strategic policies.

In short, since total quality is not a 'state' but a 'journey', a process, training should focus on creating the ability to work out a route, to keep to that route and overcome any obstacles that may be encountered, before it considers how to handle the countless specific tasks that have to be carried out – and carried out well – at any particular point along the route.

The purpose of this chapter is not to provide 'added value' at the level of the **contents** of training; the contents will deal with the model, self-assessment and improvement planning processes, process management, which are all described in the previous chapters, and with methodologies and techniques, for which the reader is referred to specialist publications (some of which are listed in the Bibliography). Since it does not examine contents, the chapter is short. Its intention is to provide added value in terms of the company's approach, because today the main obstacle to effective total quality training appears to be a misguided approach rather than inadequate contents.

5.2 THE EDUCATION PROCESS AS A MEANS OF OVERCOMING RESISTANCE TO CHANGE

'Who is opposed to quality?' This is a classic rhetorical question, the answer to which is of course 'no one'. In practice, however, the changes required by the total quality approach are so great that many corporate managers are 'opposed to quality', even if their opposition may not be intentional. Resistance to change is therefore the most frequent stumbling block for total quality, more because companies fail to realise it exists or underestimate its importance than because someone has taken a deliberate stance.

The trouble with the word 'Quality' is that while it has many meanings, the concept appears to be immediately clear, so few corporate managers, particularly those who feel they already possess a managerial culture, are willing to submit to a thorough critical review of their ideas in this area. When companies accept quality programmes which in some way merit the qualification 'total', they often fail to realise the extent of the changes required in organisation, attitudes and management style. In other companies, the awareness of the dimensions of change exists, but is limited to a small group of senior managers, who attempt to push change through from the top downwards, without first making sure that lower management levels are adequately prepared.

This is not the place for a detailed discussion of the complex question of resistance to change; as in section 2.2, it is mentioned briefly, in this instance in connection with training, because of its importance in the total quality process. It is an issue that must be fully analysed in advance by companies planning to launch a total quality process, to ensure that **the strategies and tactics designed to overcome resistance to change become an integral part of the plan**, subject to regular monitoring.

Strategies for overcoming resistance to change obviously vary from one company to another, but a number of absolutely general principles should be borne in mind. The first is that the people who will be most affected by change must be involved in the total quality process right from the planning stage, particularly those who will be required to play an active role in the process. **As a mix of information, discussion, training and active participation, the education process can play a vital role here**. It will be impossible to involve everyone from the start, but a progressive approach can be adopted to give the clear impression of company-wide participation. For example, work groups can be set up at senior levels, which in turn can create similar voluntary groups at lower levels to consider specific issues. Information and awareness-raising will be the main concerns initially, after which the company will move on to the proposals stage, where the work groups can make an active contribution.

The work groups will in fact set off the education process as regards change. The chief aim at this stage is to create an active, effective **communications and involvement network** to ensure that, once the company begins to implement total quality, everyone, even in the most far-flung corners of the organisation, knows what is happening and can make his or her views known. Communication in this case is not written communication, house organs, posters, and so on, but verbal communication between the manager and his staff, which costs nothing and uses existing hierarchical structures. In a process of change, frequent manager-staff discussions with an educational content should be the chief means of resolving doubts, anxieties and tension. Only a small part of the massive education process required by change should take place in training centres; most of it should be channelled through the manager (with the assistance of experts), who will regain his fundamental role as an educator.

The work groups can make a valuable contribution by performing organisational analyses, testing out the hypotheses drawn up by top management and the proposals submitted for discussion by the group of experts. They possess the best skills and roles to suggest the strategies and tactics to be used in approaching change: not only can they identify possible passive resistance and propose solutions to overcome it, but in so doing they will

233

identify themselves with the project and resolve any personal reservations. This is the way to transform potential adversaries into champions of the cause and to expose any cases in which this transformation has not taken place, which must be handled individually by top management.

The involvement methods described above can help **create a climate conducive to change**, an important achievement. Struggling total quality projects promoted by an enthusiastic few in the face of widespread indifference or scepticism, with no attempts at creating the climate that alone can lead to significant change, are pathetic sights: not only are they a lost opportunity, they come at a considerable price in terms of cost and frustration. The change-conducive climate will be further strengthened if the company begins the self-assessment and improvement planning process described in Chapter 3 during the transition from total quality planning to implementation. This will extend participation from the work groups to the entire company.

To sum up, when the total quality process of change gets under way – a wide-ranging indefinite change designed to transform the company into a dynamic organisation which pursues excellence in an environment of structural change – creating new formal structures and forcing them on the company is the wrong approach. The right approach is to create the **conditions** in which structural change will be possible, to build a **fertile environment** in which people learn, experiment, become convinced and achieve (and even re-invent the wheel, if this helps to create a feeling of 'paternal responsibility' for change).

This sort of approach will be intrinsically educational if information, training, experimentation and cross-fertilisation are all part of a well-managed process. It will be educational to the extent that it assists the non-traumatic development of new cultural attitudes, at the speed required by the rate of external change and by the company's own particular situation. It will also be educational to the extent that it brings leadership qualities to the fore. In a static environment, good managers may be enough, but in a highly dynamic scenario, companies need leaders capable of taking them into new and unexplored territory.

5.3 CONTINUOUS IMPROVEMENT AND CONTINUOUS LEARNING

The company must therefore respond to continuous external change with continuous internal change. Its ability to do so depends on its ability to become a **learning organisation**, a company capable of listening, of identifying the direction of change, of understanding its causes, of analysing what others are doing and of making its own contribution in terms of added value by playing an active role. A capacity for continuous learning is a key **invisible resource** in the corporate world.

All this may seem logical, but it should not be taken for granted. Past and present quality trends show that very often the managerial mentality is quite the reverse. In the complex area of the new strategic approaches to quality, many companies prefer quick, 'shrink-wrapped' solutions requiring little effort instead of trying to adopt the typical continuous learning approach of understanding, interpreting, distinguishing and experimenting. But since quick solutions are no answer for difficult problems, one solution is abandoned in favour of another, turning quality into the corporate equivalent of high fashion. Quality circles have been followed by the SPC, the Taguchi approach by Benchmarking; all extremely worthy when viewed as part of a much wider whole, but none of them a universal panacea. In the continuous learning environment, the total quality education process is a composite process, which certainly includes but extends far beyond classroom training. Figure 5.1 illustrates the main ingredients of the total quality continuous education process.

The first of these ingredients is the **structured training process**, flanked logically by the **structured information process**. In fact, training, in the form of structured transmission of skills, must be supported by information on external change and on activities in other companies, together with information on the action being taken or planned by the company. Information on external developments and management action will usually predominate at top management level, while the training component will

Fig. 5.1 The ingredients of the total quality continuous education process.

gradually become dominant moving down the organisation, although care should be taken always to provide full information.

The structured training/information components will be particularly important during the start-up of the total quality process, but even at this stage skills and information should be administered in small doses. Special launch events and mega-courses often have very little impact: it is better to plan a series of low-key information/awareness-raising initiatives over a suitable period of time. These initiatives will be followed by the creation of work groups, who will begin to be supplied with information on training issues as they work, while kick-off meetings will be postponed until the groups have completed their tasks.

Formal training can begin when management decides to launch concrete initiatives in a particular sector, but it should never be separated from operations. In this way, training can be geared to the operating needs of process management teams and improvement groups as they are formed and new concepts can be applied immediately – to the teams' actual problems – giving a greater guarantee of understanding and assimilation.

If training is linked to operations, then operating staff will become the vehicles for training. A **cascade** process is thus established, with each supervisor regaining the role of educator, a role typical of cottage industries but more or less non-existent in today's large organisations, where the supervisor's main concern is to manage programmes and resources. Continuous learning restores the educator role, transmitting not only job skills, but attitudes, too. This micro-channelling of education, culture and attitudes is necessary to help the company react promptly to change; without it, the edicts issued by top management are dead letters.

Micro-channelling is also necessary to achieve widespread micro-innovation (section 4.1), without which continuous improvement is not possible.

Two other ingredients of the continuous total quality education process illustrated in Fig. 5.1 confirm the importance of linking training with operations: **process management** and **improvement groups**.

Process management practice is far more educational than any training course, even those held by the leading experts. Once again, while introductory courses on functional and inter-functional process management are essential, their usefulness is nil unless what has been learned can be applied. In this case, it is not just a question of assimilating the new concepts; the educational value of the company's processes is unlimited. Processes are the solid element of the company and it is impossible to improve the company without a thorough knowledge of its processes. Identification of eloquent process indicators and projects designed to improve process capabilities are highly educational experiences.

The **group** is essential for continuous improvement and continuous learning. The stimulus and synergy produced by the group, the spirit of emulation, peer pressure and the enthusiasm that can be generated are vital to achieve results. Improvement groups are therefore a fundamental ingredient of the education process. Moreover, in a structured continuous learning process, groups are no longer set up on a voluntary basis, they are a necessary operating tool. Effective improvement nearly always requires the contribution, verification and support of the group. The ingredients in Fig. 5.1 also include **human resource manage-**

237

ment and the **reward system**. The consistency of personnel management – and specifically of the reward system – with the goals of the education process, in particular the creation of a learning organisation, is vital.

Consistency between words and actions, and among the different components involved is vital to the success of any major change.

The final ingredient in Fig. 5.1 – management support – is also related to the question of consistency. Nothing more need be said about this item, except to repeat that full management support is the bedrock of the total quality process and therefore also of the continuous education process.

5.4 QUALITY EDUCATION IN THE CONTEXT OF CORPORATE TRAINING PROGRAMMES

Even a brief discussion dealing with the approach to, rather than the contents of, quality education should consider a particular aspect of quality structured training ingredient of the permanent education process in Fig. 5.1.

The main specifications for quality training could be summed up as follows:

- development of flexibility;
- continuous learning geared to continuous improvement;
- focus on the customer;
- emphasis on teamwork, on a matrix-based approach geared to processes;
- emphasis on process management;
- acquisition of a factual mentality based on measurement and optimal use of information;
- training in the methodologies and techniques designed to improve the effectiveness (quality) and efficiency (cost and time) of any process.

This is all part of the permanent education process illustrated in Fig. 5.1.

Many of the above specifications are of such general importance that quality education obviously cannot be considered as a
separate element, a specific, specialist area of the wider field of
company training and of management training in particular.
Certain elements can of course be treated as separate disciplines,
but the most important components have to be integrated with
the general company training programme if they are to become
meaningful. The importance of integration is obvious if one
considers that the goals of total quality are indivisible from the
company's general business goals. Training on how to manage a
business and separate training on how to manage it 'with quality'
is a contradiction in terms.

The need for integration is also apparent in companies where
management on a functional approach coexist with total quality
programmes adopting an interfunctional approach. The situation
is disconcerting. The responsibility lies more with business schools
than with companies: business schools have been slower than
companies to embrace the concepts of total quality, and it is
they who usually develop general management training programmes. The integration of total quality training in management training programmes should be a key issue for management
schools in the next few years.

Integration should not, however, be seen as the addition of
quality modules to the general training programme. The concepts
introduced by total quality training are so important they will
necessarily involve significant changes in the entire management
training programme. Reviews of traditional courses in the context of total quality management should lead to complete changes
of emphasis to include:

- interfunctionality: structures and methods for process-based
  horizontal integration;
- vertical alignment: processes for the definition of policies,
  goals and strategies and their deployment/alignment throughout the company; decision-making processes;
- focus on the customer (external and internal); reading/inter-
  preting reality beginning with the customer;
- continuous improvement as a management style based on a

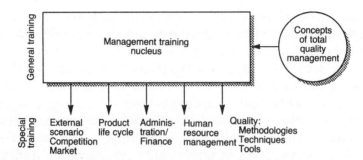

Fig. 5.2 Quality training and management training.

decision to be the protagonists rather than the followers of continuous change;

- human resource management: delegation of responsibility, empowerment, criteria for rewarding results.

Figure 5.2 illustrates this. The concepts of total quality must **permeate** company training, and management training in particular, to which the figure refers. They are therefore an integral part of the central training nucleus, not a separate element. Specific training packages, including a quality package, stem from the central nucleus. But in this case, quality is a set of methodologies, techniques and tools applicable to every company sector and process.

In a continuous education programme, wide-ranging general training – which transmits the fundamental principles of the company's organisation, management style, culture and corporate values – is the only type of training that should be provided through full-time residential courses for set periods of time. Since the courses are intended for widespread participation, attendance will be organised over extended timescales, except when important changes are being introduced, such as the launch of a total quality project. On a much smaller scale, the courses will be held routinely for all new recruits and managers entering jobs where such training is required.

On the other hand, refresher seminars, lectures and talks to bring people up to date on external and internal developments will be held very frequently. These meetings will be brief and organised so as to cause the least possible disruption to work activities.

Specific training, for example in the use of quality methodologies, techniques and tools, should be closely associated with operations. When a sector begins improvement planning, training on self-assessment, planning and policy deployment should be provided; similarly, process management training should be provided when the sector launches process planning, management and improvement activities.

Understandably, the effort involved in the start-up of a total quality project tends to lead to the development of specific quality training programmes (even, in some large companies, to the formation of **quality institutes**). Nevertheless, the habit of separating quality training from general company training should be abandoned and **total quality management** should be integrated with management training, so that **Management** and **Total Quality Management** become synonymous.

The economics of quality | 6

6.1 THE COSTS OF QUALITY: TOO MUCH EMPHASIS AND NOT ENOUGH ANALYSIS

The chapter title 'The costs of quality', as frequent as it is ambiguous and restricting, has been avoided deliberately. With all due respect for the conventional approach to the issue of quality economics, regarded for years as incontrovertible, the time has come for a critical review in this area, too: it is more than natural that the evolution of quality should bring a parallel evolution in the theories regarding the relationship between quality and the company's economic results and a rethinking of measurement and assessment tools.

This chapter does not claim to offer solutions to this vast and complex question. Its aim is more modest: to highlight the inadequacy of traditional views; to suggest alternative approaches; to offer concrete suggestions as regards processes; and to identify areas for further analysis by economic and financial experts.

Quality has a strong impact on corporate economics – and it should have a **positive** impact, in other words, it should improve the company's business results. The point needs to be made, because of the ever-present risk of quality being turned into a bureaucratic procedure, with certain costs and uncertain benefits.

A discussion of the economics of quality, as will be seen below, should first of all move beyond the narrow sphere of traditional quality costs to cover the costs of all the activities that do not generate value, for either the customer or the company (true quality minimises bureaucracy and structural costs!). It should then go beyond costs and consider the impact on revenues and profits (better still, on cash-flow), but it should also extend beyond the profit and loss account to the balance sheet. And as far as company assets are concerned, the impact of quality is not just something that can be quantified in the balance sheet: it also extends to better use of existing physical assets and to less quantifiable assets such as customers or intangibles such as human resources, which, nonetheless, are key factors in company 'value'.

The urgent need for a critical review stems not only from the demonstrated shortcomings of current theories and the 'quality costs' approach, but also from their misapplication. Since the second half of the 1970s, quality costs, like quality circles, have often been peddled as 'miracle cures' for bridging the ever-increasing gap with the Japanese. J.M. Juran's advice that the 'language of money' should be used to attract top management's attention to quality but that the 'language of things' should then be used to achieve improvement has been forgotten, and the mistaken belief has spread that management of quality cost indicators will resolve the greatest areas of inefficiency. Nothing is worse than unrestricted use of an inadequate tool. Information needs to be provided on two fronts today, first to broaden companies' perspectives from the narrow area of quality costs to the wider horizon of value/cost analyses, and second to help companies apply the tool where it can be of use: as a powerful lever for convincing management to adopt the continuous improvement approach, as a 'sensor' for identifying opportunities for improvement as they arise and as a means of illustrating the results achieved.

6.2 THE LIMITS OF THE TRADITIONAL VIEW

The reader is assumed to be familiar with the conventional definition, which subdivides quality costs into prevention costs, appraisal (or inspection) costs and internal and external non-conformity (or failure) costs. Figure 6.1 illustrates the traditional quality costs model. The graph is so widely used that it has

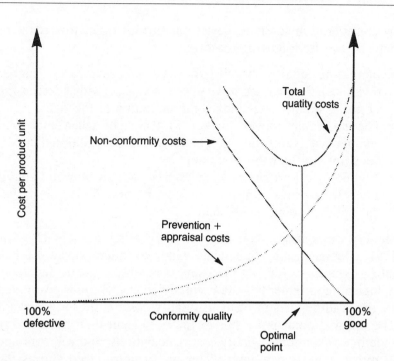

Fig. 6.1 The traditional quality costs model.

become a postulate of any discussion on the subject. Opinions vary as to the details – for example, whether the total quality costs curve should tend to infinite or whether it can have a finite value when non-conformity reaches zero, how the minimum point is affected by other variables such as value for the customer – but there is a certain reluctance to question the actual logic behind the curve, for example, the utility or legitimacy of adding prevention costs to appraisal and inspection costs. It seems to imply disrespect for those who formulated and those who use these curves. But it is simply part of the normal evolution of knowledge to replace old theories that no longer represent the state of the art with new theories.

Without moving away from traditional thinking on quality costs, an article written by Hsiang and Lee (1985) showed that the optimal point of the curve was not the minimum point given by consideration solely of costs, but further right, towards zero defects, for the following reasons:

- Increasing quality usually means increasing sales (higher revenues). A revenues curve which increases (with a decreasing slope) as quality rises moves the minimum to the right.
- The minimum moves further to the right when the 'user perspective' is introduced. The logic behind traditional curves does not consider the customer.
- Technological progress increases process knowhow and gradually lowers prevention and inspection costs. This also moves the optimal point to the right.

Similar views have been expressed by other authors (Bester, 1991), demonstrating that when wider considerations are taken into account – value for the user, competitive needs and technological requirements – the optimal defect rate point postulated by the traditional approach to quality costs is no longer valid. The optimal point is further to the right than that given at any time by conventional quality costs calculations, and will continue to move right as new improvements are introduced and as the company shifts its competitive focus towards value for the customer. A number of points should be considered in moving beyond the traditional approach to quality costs.

6.2.1 Distinguish prevention costs/investments from non-quality costs

The subject of prevention will be discussed later in a broader context. Here, the point to be made is that preventing problems – and therefore unwarranted costs – from arising later (in time and in space) means doing the right things at the right time and in the right place, and doing them right first time. This is true prevention and it cannot be separated from operations (from development work, for example), whereas what the traditional approach to quality costs calls prevention costs can be separated from operations, indeed some authors include them under the heading **controllable non-quality costs** (Harrington, 1987) (the use of the expression 'non-quality' indicates the real nature of

246

this so-called prevention). These traditional prevention costs can be subdivided conceptually into two groups.

(a) Initiatives

These can be likened to investments in that they are expected to bring a return. As such, it is incorrect to include them with recurrent costs such as inspection and non-conformity costs. Investments should be treated as such (see below) and not as operating costs. Initiatives that are normally grouped under the heading 'prevention' are usually of two types: those designed to improve the quality system (as defined in section 2.3, type (c) processes), such as training or the creation of a quality information system, which clearly qualify for the prevention category; and those designed to improve products (for the market or for internal use). Product-improvement initiatives are the more frequent, but whether it is correct or useful to classify them as prevention initiatives is debatable, since the action taken is often designed to rectify products that were not done right first time, at the level of goals or execution. Since the utility of a quality costs system depends on the degree to which the system helps management reach decisions and, in particular, manage improvement, it is advisable to keep entirely separate accounting records. Payback estimates should be made beforehand, when the initiative is planned, while the sums actually invested during the year in **improvement** initiatives, and possibly also the overall return, can be calculated at year-end.

(b) Dedicated resources

These include people involved in process planning/management activities or assigned permanently to improvement (often included in the quality function). In the distributed, process-oriented total quality approach, these tasks should be performed by operating personnel, not delegated to other people. Delegation is tantamount to institutionalising the fact that the job of certain people is to:

247

- put right things done badly by others (typically, problems in development);
- monitor other people to prevent them from making mistakes;
- provide a supplementary contribution to prevent things from being done badly.

These are obviously 'repair' costs for organisational defects, not prevention costs. Including them in the prevention costs category is a dangerous contradiction: it is equivalent to maintaining the **status quo**, the artificial distinction between those who achieve quality and those who plan/check/improve quality.

None of this means that the costs traditionally known as prevention costs should not be measured. Given, however, that quality costs management should be strategic, that is, geared to the company's goals, and not based on routine accounting procedures, then, for the purposes of total quality, these costs (which are often similar to investments) **should not be added** to inspection costs, much less to non-conformity costs, in the search for improbable minimums (quality not quantity should be the criterion for quality costs).

In addition, the term 'prevention' should be rejected in favour of two distinct terms: **planning/control** (where **control** refers to processes, not results) and **improvement**; dividing the group into two may seem an added complication, but it is useful for strategic management of the transition towards total quality.

Process planning and **process control** (for example, of product-specification formulation, product development, production start-up, manufacturing, distribution, sales) are wholly preventive activities and as such must be performed within the processes, not by external functions. Process control is the most important way of checking where and how these activities are performed, but if cost monitoring helps managers understand how many resources are involved and where they are allocated, then it is worth the trouble. Monitoring these costs becomes complicated when prevention activities are conducted, as they should be, at operating level and not by separate functions, but this is a 'happy' problem.

As far as **improvement** is concerned, global closing data in the

248

form of a summary of the costs of the year's improvement initiatives may be useful, but it should be accompanied by an overall assessment of the return on investments. Of course, management must carefully assess the merits of each initiative, but an overall evaluation is useful to measure the sector's global improvement effort. However great the prevention effort, improvement is always a crucial factor in total quality, if only because goals are dynamic. The percentage of total resources dedicated to improvement is a strategic figure for top management.

This is the picture as regards the risks involved in grouping together disparate items, a practice which can prove particularly dangerous in the area of prevention and improvement investments, where the rule of thumb is quality, not quantity. For these costs, the problem is not to avoid spending money but to spend it well, although overall year-end figures are useful since companies usually tend to spend too little.

Companies must also be careful to avoid the risk of grouping together related items in an overly broad context. This applies in particular to improvement, where the most significant evaluations are produced at the level of the individual initiative and its related pay-back, but it applies in general to all categories of quality costs: data is highly significant at process, department and product level, but becomes less meaningful as the field widens.

6.2.2 Use caution in dealing with appraisal costs

Appraisal/inspection costs, which can be expressed as a percentage of the total process or product cost, can vary greatly depending on the nature of the process or product. Appraisal costs may be low for simple products, mature technologies, simple processes and/or processes where great efforts have been made to improve the tolerance/capability ratio (C_{pk}). Conversely, for complex products generated by complex processes, which utilise new technologies, appraisal costs may be high, particularly in the early stages of the product life cycle (for example, the testing times for complex hardware-software systems can only be kept within economically reasonable limits through a carefully managed learning curve and any necessary improvement initiatives).

Both types of situations – low or high percentage costs – are legitimate, although cases where costs are highest obviously offer the greatest scope for future improvements. Where appraisal costs are concerned, therefore, it is important to judge each case individually and to look continually for opportunities for improvement. Their significance should not be lessened by grouping together different processes or different classes; each case should be considered on its own merits. Since the ultimate aim is to eliminate non-quality, wherever this is economically reasonable, appraisal costs will not be cut if this leads to equal or higher non-quality costs; nor will appraisal costs be raised, even if they are very low, unless a benefit can be gained in terms of a reduction in non-quality. In a conventional balance-sheet, every extra pound spent for appraisal should correspond to at least one pound less in non-quality. In practice, the effect on the customer of the product's residual non-quality outweighs the costs measured by the supplier, so that more than one pound can often be spent in appraisal for every pound less in non-quality; but for the company geared to improvement, this will in any case be only a temporary measure, since efforts will be made to reduce appraisal costs and non-quality costs simultaneously.

It is worth repeating however that constant attention must be paid to appraisal costs (which, according to the traditional classification criteria, also hide non-conformity costs such as acceptance controls) and to failure costs. Both types of costs are 'eligible' for reduction: failure costs in any case, as long as the improvement initiative has a reasonable pay-back; appraisal costs when technology, skill and process improvements permit reduction without raising non-quality (preferably lowering it, for example through process capability improvements).

6.2.3 Concentrate on failure costs

Freed from the nightmare of searching for (and from the hope of finding) an 'optimal defect level' corresponding to the minimum level of costs (prevention + appraisal + non-quality), companies can concentrate on the real enemy: failure (failure is just one of the enemies, as will be seen shortly, but in the traditional quality costs approach it is **the** enemy).

This does not of course mean that in any situation and at any time the most cost-effective point is close to zero defects. When work begins on a new product, the defect rate is generally higher than for an established product. Calculation of cost effectiveness will take all factors into account: revenues, costs (global, not just quality costs) and market share. All things considered, it may be worth going ahead even if the defect rate is relatively high (as long as customer relations are correctly handled), but zero defects must always be the ultimate goal: the cost effectiveness of another step towards zero must be **weighed up continually**, evaluating all the opportunities that only a determined pursuit of improvement will indicate.

The optimal point exists when a hypothesis is formulated, but the continuous pursuit of improvement, process analysis and technology will continually suggest new hypotheses, so the optimal point will move further towards zero non-quality. It is better to spend time on improvement rather than on finding the optimal point (which moves as soon as it has been identified . . .). Weighing up the cost-effectiveness of another step towards zero involves investment pay-back calculations of the kind shown in Fig. 6.2 (other factors may be considered, such as variations in 'revenues'), where the first improvement initiative, which brings non-conformity costs from C_0 to C_1, has a pay-back, t_1, of less than two months. The second initiative, which brings non-conformity costs from C_1 to C_2, has an even better pay-back of just over one month. The third initiative has an eight-month pay-back and may not be considered worthwhile in relation to the product life cycle.

Use of the curves shown in Fig. 6.2 is highly recommended to calculate non-conformity costs at closure (referred for example to unit-of-product), to assess the cost-effectiveness of improvement initiatives and to calculate the actual pay-back of each initiative implemented. Since significant improvement initiatives – those that affect process capability – often provide reductions in non-quality and also lessen the need for inspection/testing, it

251

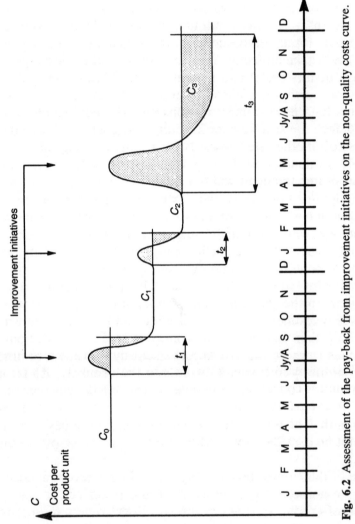

Fig. 6.2 Assessment of the pay-back from improvement initiatives on the non-quality costs curve.

may be worth adding appraisal costs to non-conformity costs to create ordinates. This is an example of flexible quality costs management, where costs are kept separate or added together as required. It confirms the thesis of this chapter, that quality costs should be not be regarded as an accounting tool, a bureaucratic procedure to be handled by the administrative department, but as valuable information for the purposes of strategic improvement management.

6.3 THE ECONOMICS OF QUALITY IN RELATION TO TOTAL QUALITY: MAXIMISE VALUE AND MINIMISE COSTS

An analysis of the economics of quality should begin with processes, the links in the chain of value and costs, and with the customer, for whom the value is generated. Before reading this section, the reader is advised to re-read the first part of section 1.4 on added value and added cost in the process, paying particular attention to Figs 1.11 and 1.12.

Figure 6.3 goes to the heart of the problem of the economics of quality, which is basically a question of **value** (to which pricing and market shares are related) and **costs** (which measure the efficiency with which the company generates value and, together with value, determine the company's business results). 'Costs' in this case covers only costs to the company. As far as the supplier is concerned, non-quality costs for the customer are part of the value of the offer. From the supplier's point of view, products that provide lower defectiveness offer greater value. From the customer's point of view, lower defectiveness means lower costs, that is, a reduction of the denominator in the value/cost ratio (section 1.1); this produces a positive perception, which raises the global factor creating customer satisfaction (value for money).

As will be seen in greater detail below, the 'value' category includes all value generated by the company processes: in other words, value not just for external customers, but for the company, too.

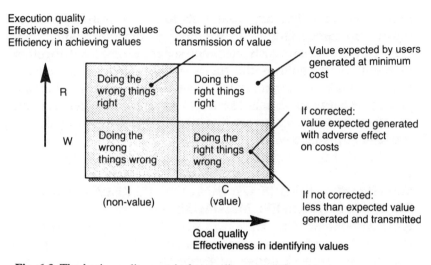

Fig. 6.3 The basic quality matrix for quality economics.

One of the most interesting questions concerning value generated by improvements in process quality is how much value should be transferred to the customer without an immediate return for the company and how much should be transferred at an additional cost to the customer (in other words, how greater value should be distributed between the company and the customer). This is a marketing question, related to competition at the level of quality. One of the chief characteristics of the Japanese competitive approach is the transfer of greater value to the customer at equal prices: this is a strategic policy, which ranks increased market share as a higher priority than higher profits.

In Fig. 6.3*, the traditional view of quality is basically covered by the vertical axis (quality of execution), that is, doing things well or badly (see also Fig. 1.2); the corresponding quality economics approach focuses on the non-quality costs of execution (non-conformity) and on the costs of preventing and inspecting

---

* The four-quadrant grid concept used as the basis for this analysis takes its inspiration from a presentation to Olivetti management by ODI (Organizational Dynamics Inc., Burlington, MA, USA) at Mazzè Castle near Turin in November 1989.

254

execution errors. The total quality approach introduces and gives priority to the quality of goals, that is, doing the right things (Fig. 1.2): in Fig. 6.3, the horizontal axis introduces the distinction between correct goals and incorrect goals. The vertical axis no longer considers costs alone, but also effectiveness in maintaining value (loss of value in relation to goals).

The horizontal axis – quality of goals – is fundamentally the 'value' axis. The company's goals define the values to be generated: value for the customer (for example, a feature to simplify use of the product, better delivery service, higher reliability) and value for the company (higher market share, better price control). The vertical axis still represents chiefly 'costs' or efficiency, although it, too, is a value axis, since the degree to which the target values are actually incorporated in the product depends on effectiveness – or quality of execution.

A discussion of the economics of quality must therefore begin with the **target values** the company intends to achieve through its processes – values for customers and values for the company – and will then consider the effectiveness with which these values are achieved (depreciation of customer and company values during execution) and efficiency (costs of achieving value).

The most important question, how to measure value, is evidently still far from being resolved, indeed it is still not clear whether satisfactory solutions will be found; but this does not lessen the need to analyse all aspects of value and cost associated with quality. Companies drawing up the quality profiles of new products do not always analyse value for the customer (value that differentiates the company from its reference competitors), nor do they assess how much of that value should be transferred free of charge (and conversely how much should come back to the company in the form of higher prices/lower discounts) and what impact this could have on market share.

The analysis of value and cost elements described below should therefore be viewed as a more detailed illustration of the concepts introduced and only in part – as regards the company processes – as a concrete application guide; the comments on the economic consequences of quality in terms of market share and increased company value are simply qualitative conclusions for the reader's

255

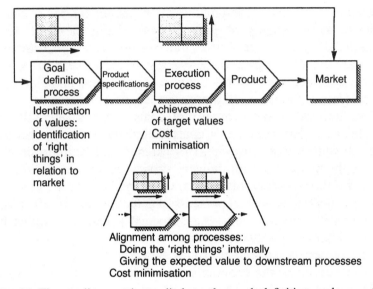

Fig. 6.4 The quality matrix applied to the goal definition and execution processes.

consideration. The chapter closes by indicating possible areas for further investigation.

6.3.1 Analysis of value and costs

This section looks at value and costs analysis in relation to the two processes (or process streams) of the model in Fig. 2.4, reproduced in Fig. 6.4: the new-product goal definition process and the execution process. The matrix of Fig. 6.3 can be applied to both the first and the second process stream and to every single integrated process they contain.

The **goal definition process** should guarantee that the goals fall in the right-hand side of the matrix: identification of the 'right things' for the market and of value for the user. Market surveys, value analysis and quality function deployment techniques should be used when checking and attempting to quantify value. Analysis of value for the user is still a rudimentary science, however.

The **execution process** should aim to achieve the target values at the lowest overall cost, in particular minimising non-quality costs (vertical axis). Similar effectiveness and efficiency goals should be shared by each integrated process in the macro-execution process (or process stream). Since the corporate process chains often lose sight of the final goals and communication between adjoining processes is often impeded, **alignment** among processes is the most important goal, from both the economic and the functional points of view. 'Alignment' here means 'doing the right things' from one process to the next: transferring to downstream processes **all and only the value they expect**. As seen in section 1.4 and emphasised below, the chief losses arising from non-quality are usually caused not by 'doing things badly' but by doing useless or the wrong things, which generate no value for either customers or the company.

The value/cost analysis can now be conducted at the level of the individual processes in a chain of execution processes (a similar analysis can be conducted for the goal-definition processes, where analysis of value for the user, touched on only briefly here, is the main consideration).

Figure 6.5 examines the concepts introduced in Fig. 1.11 in greater detail. Beginning from the top, the **first three blocks** represent the added value of the process: value for end users (external or internal), which is by far the most important, the process's *raison d'être* (value for the end user has a return value for the company); value for downstream processes (the input needed by processes to enable them to generate their own share of value, for example, documentation); and value that increases the company's assets. This last item is often neglected, but it has an important role in process value and costs analysis. The construction of a total quality system, for example, requires adequate, well-focused resources, so the portion of the process's added value that raises the value of the quality system must be carefully monitored and safeguarded. Similarly, quality initiatives designed to improve use of physical assets (machinery utilisation rates) or to modify the organisation in order to improve structural efficiency (for example, just-in-time) should be encouraged and safeguarded by highlighting the increment in value.

The **fourth block** of Fig. 6.5 covers the costs of non-quality

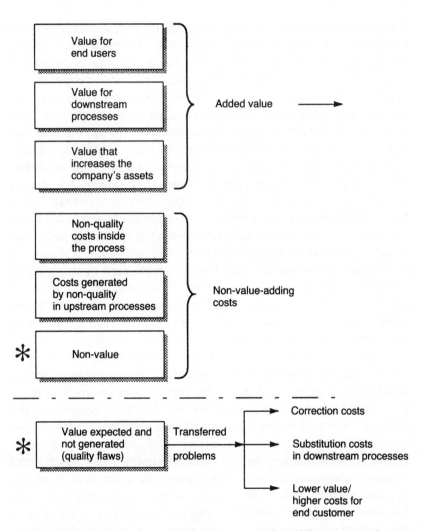

Fig. 6.5 Process economics: added value, non-value-adding costs, value expected and not generated.

inside the process, attributable to the process itself. They include the costs of internal failures, plus appraisal/inspection costs, or at least that part of such costs that would disappear if the process were able naturally to generate the quality required.

The **fifth block** represents the effect on the process of shortcomings in upstream processes, which are shown in the seventh block.

The **sixth block** ('non-value') represents activities that do not add value, even though they do not cause errors or defects. The output of these activities is of no use either to end users or to downstream processes, for example, useless or superfluous information and documents. These activities can easily be spotted through joint supplier-customer analyses. The block also includes conspicuous activities created in exceptional circumstances and never dismantled, activities that uselessly repeat action already taken upstream or downstream (typical of the sectorial organisational approach), or activities designed as stop-gap solutions for chronic errors. In short, it includes all those activities that increase structural costs, which no cost-reduction programme seems able to eliminate. If the cost-reduction programme takes a functional approach, the heads of function are unlikely to admit the futility of their work and dismantle their defences; so management searches desperately for ways to cut costs, assigning indiscriminate reduction targets, and fails to realise it is sitting on a hidden 'gold mine'**.

Only a global analysis of the process stream conducted by the management team with the support of the process guarantor (section 3.9) will identify the pockets of inefficiency which slow process streams and cause the greatest discrepancies between added value and costs (Fig. 1.12).

Given the efficiency improvements possible with this type of analysis, companies that confine themselves to traditional quality costs are just scratching the surface instead of penetrating to the heart of problems. Of course, the results achieved will depend not only on the accuracy of the team's analyses (for which specialist support will frequently be necessary), but on time and determination, too. Resistance to change is extremely strong in this area (entire sectors of staff will have to be gradually

---

** The 'gold in the mine' concept is taken from Juran (1979), who uses it to highlight the possible economic benefits of reducing non-quality. It is a 'reverse' mine, in the sense that when the company begins to dig it will excavate non-quality and therefore reduce costs and raise margins. Here the concept is extended to 'organisational non-quality', which is buried even deeper than product and process non-quality.

removed, although they will offer a thousand reasons to justify their existence) and the actual changes required are difficult and delicate.

The **seventh block** in Fig. 6.5 (value expected and not generated) is also extremely critical. It belongs neither to the added value category nor to the category of non-value-adding costs, but to the category of work that was not done, was done poorly or was left unfinished.

Work done poorly will have to be corrected by a process further downstream, while a substitute downstream activity will have to perform work that was not done or was left unfinished. In both cases, a downstream process will have to sustain correction or substitution costs, with the amplifying effect described below. The alternative to downstream correction or substitution is the transfer to the end user of lower value or higher costs.

Even so, it is hardly ever possible to remedy a 'quality hole' in downstream processes (they are not the appropriate sites and often do not possess the necessary knowhow or resources); so the end result, apart from higher costs for the company, will almost always be lower value or higher costs for the customer. This situation is inevitable when the last link in the chain, the process that directly interfaces with the end customer, is the process that fails to generate all the value expected.

6.3.2 True prevention

The above considerations on value and costs lead to a more appropriate concept of prevention. True prevention, as noted at the beginning of this chapter, is an integral part of an activity, not additional to it: it means performing the activity so that customers are supplied with **all and only the value expected**, minimising non-value-adding costs. **Value expected and not generated** is particularly critical as far as prevention is concerned. The 'value hole' sets off a negative chain, which transfers flaws in value and costs downstream, gradually amplifying the costs involved (Fig. 6.6).

An interfunctional, team approach to process management helps the company to spend money at the right point and at the

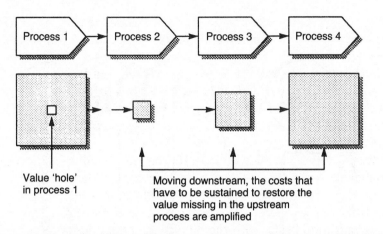

Fig. 6.6 Prevention means generating expected value in the right place at the right time: the 'value hole' in process 1 causes a dispersion of value in the downstream process which has to 'repair' the hole; the further downstream the process, the greater the dispersion.

right time and to avoid short-sighted sectorial cost reductions, which create the conditions under which non-quality costs are amplified.

Prevention is the only way to optimise the blocks in Fig. 6.5 (except the fifth, which depends on upstream processes), but the negative power of non-prevention is particularly significant in the last two blocks (marked with asterisks), where the costs of non-quality can reach double-digit turnover percentages. And careful and constant interfunctional process management is the only way to ensure alignment and the global optimisation of process effectiveness and efficiency; in other words, to guarantee true prevention.

6.3.3 Areas for further investigation

One area for further research suggested by the above considerations is the correlation between the measurable results of quality initiatives and their impact on the company's short and medium-term business results.

Figure 6.7 illustrates the basic concepts involved, beginning in

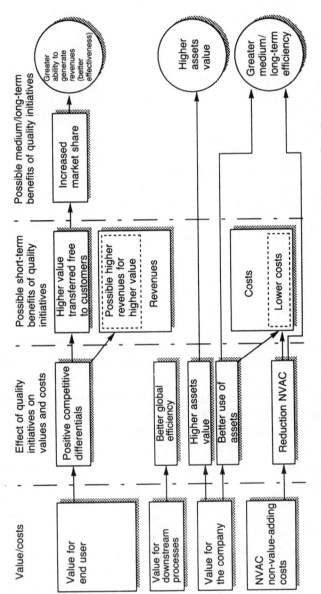

Fig. 6.7 Benefits expected from quality initiatives over the short term and the medium/long term.

the first column with a simplified version of the value/costs categories of Fig. 6.5. The second column shows the expected effects of quality initiatives: positive competitive differentials at the level of perceived value, a rise in company assets (for example, an improvement in the quality system), better use of assets (for example, a higher capital turnover factor), a reduction in non-value-adding costs (NVAC). In this column, to repeat a point already made in this chapter and elsewhere in the book, efficiency improvements, in particular cost reductions, are the most easily measured element today; assessment of added value for the customer is still little understood: a first area for analysis therefore is **value for the customer**.

The relationship between quality and increased assets value is a wholly unexplored area, partly owing to the considerable problems that arise when the traditional area of corporate assets is widened to included 'customer assets' or intangible elements such as human resources or the quality system.

The efficiency improvements obtained through better use of assets (for example, a higher capital turnover factor or better use of equipment) are easier to quantify, though rarely quantified.

Clearly, a prudent approach should be adopted when assessing the business results of quality initiatives (in the case of quality awards, for example). A credible assessment today cannot go much further than efficiency (lower costs and shorter execution times) at least until more accurate tools have been developed for assessing the various aspects of 'value'.

The third column in Fig. 6.7 shows the economic benefits possible over the short term: the most immediate benefits of quality initiatives – benefits with a short-term pay-back – arise from reductions in costs and better use of assets. Greater value generated in the offer (positive competitive differential) can in part be used to raise revenues (through price increases/lower discounts), in part transferred to customers; in the first case, short-term benefits are possible, in the second case, benefits will arise over the medium/long term, in the form of larger market share. Short/long-term strategic use of greater value for the customer is an interesting area for research (Garvin, 1988). Studies on the approaches adopted over the last twenty years by Western and Japanese companies could provide interesting material on corporate strategies.

The fourth column is the most important, because the benefits of the most effective quality initiatives emerge over the medium/long term. In the medium/long term, a 'structural' ability to generate competitive differentials turns into higher, consolidated market share, that is, a greater ability to generate revenues. A structural ability to improve processes turns into a constant and lasting improvement in efficiency.

As far as an increase in the value of company assets in general is concerned – still an entirely unexplored area – the long-term benefit of a consistent total quality strategy is an increase in 'company value'. This is the value considered for example when a company is assessed with a view to acquisition or as a long-term investment, but it is not easy to assess with the usual economic-financial indicators. Quality is one of the intangible factors that can make the most significant contribution to company value.

Assessing company quality: self-assessment, certification and quality awards

7

7.1 THE FIRST STEP: ESTABLISH WHAT IS BEING ASSESSED AND BY WHOM

The question of building total quality has been discussed in the previous chapters, but it may be useful to conclude with a look at an issue currently of great importance: company quality assessments.

A quality assessment of a company or of a part of a company may be conducted for various reasons. The most frequent are listed below:

1. The assessment is commissioned by the customer, who needs to acquire **confidence** regarding the supplier's **ability** to meet his quality requirements. This is known as **second-party** assessment, because the party that commissions and owns the results is a customer of the company concerned. The company is assessed in relation to a customer-specific or a sector-specific standard, or in relation to a general standard (for example, the ISO 9000 standards).
2. The company submits to an assessment by a **third party**, that is, by an independent agency which does not answer to either the customer or the supplier. The company may request the assessment in response to customer demand or on its

own initiative, in anticipation of likely market requirements. Certification of conformity with the international ISO 9000 standards comes under this category.

3. Top management wishes to assess the company's situation as regards quality. This may be because it intends to implement a total quality programme and needs to know where to begin; or because a programme has already begun, but an independent assessment of progress is required; or, more simply, because management wishes to conduct a preliminary internal audit prior to a second- or third-party assessment. This is a **first-party** assessment, and can be conducted by the company's internal resources or by an external agency. In this case, top management is the party that commissions and owns the results of the assessment. President's audits come under this category.

4. The assessment is an integral part of the corporate improvement process. This is **self-assessment**, a fundamental stage in the move towards total quality and the starting point for strategic improvement planning. Self-assessment is described in detail in Chapter 3.

5. The company submits voluntarily to an independent third-party assessment in order to gain public recognition of excellence (national and international quality awards).

This chapter will show that assessment criteria vary greatly depending on the purposes of the actual assessment and the aims of the assessment owner, and that the tendency to extend the use of criteria suitable for standards-conformity certification to total quality and national quality awards is extremely dangerous.

The chapter suggests a number of criteria to enhance the significance and reliability of assessments in general, and of third-party assessments in particular. In fact, assessment becomes increasingly complex when moving towards the area of total quality and assessment reliability consequently tends to diminish.

For the sake of simplicity, not all the categories listed above will be discussed here. The most important categories for the present and near future are 2 and 5 – typical third-party assessments, also referred to below as **external assessments** – and 4, self-assessment, also referred to below as **internal assessment**. In the proactive context of total quality, self-assessment is the cornerstone of improvement, the vital element to which all other kinds of assessment must refer if they are to guarantee reliability.

7.2 STANDARDS-CONFORMITY ASSESSMENT AND ASSESSMENT IN RELATION TO THE TOTAL QUALITY MISSION

Figure 7.1 illustrates the basic company-market model for the quality mission developed in Chapter 2. Figure 7.2 presents the model as a tree chart, down to the second-branch level, on which the **assessment reference model** shown in Fig. 7.3(a) is based. The model in Fig. 7.3(a) reflects the concept that company quality assessment involves assessment of all three components in Fig. 7.2 – **results**, **processes** and **quality system** – and an appraisal of the consistency of the results of the three assessments.

Results are the basic component of the general assessment model in Fig. 7.3(a). They provide irrefutable proof of the company's capabilities, of the progress made towards total quality and of improvement trends; they also provide an accurate basis for verifying the other two components, which must be consistent with results. The logical assessment sequence moves from results to the **processes** that led to those results, and from there to the **quality system** beneath those processes.

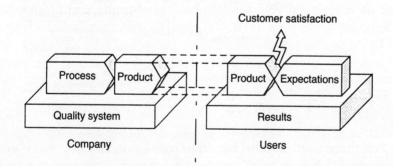

Fig. 7.1 The reference model.

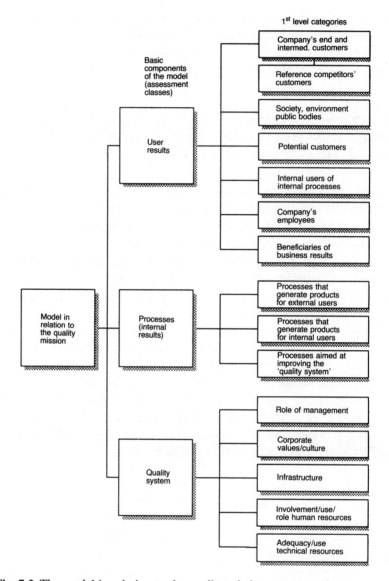

Fig. 7.2 The model in relation to the quality mission, as a tree chart.

All three components are therefore necessary for a correct assessment. Nevertheless, in certain instances, assessments are concerned only or mainly with the quality system (Fig. 7.3(b)). This type of assessment, which has proved its historical worth

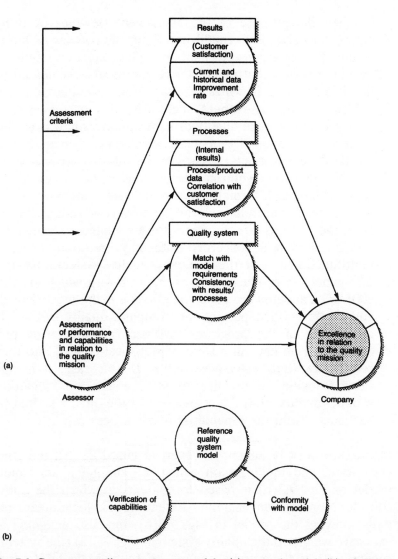

Fig. 7.3 Company quality assessment models: (a) general model; (b) simplified model.

and continues to play an important role today because it includes ISO 9000 certification, is covered by categories 1 and 2 in the previous section.

The legitimacy of the simplified assessment model in Fig. 7.3(b) is based on the following assumptions:

269

1. The specific purpose of the assessment (second- or third-party) is to give users **confidence** about the company's future results through *a priori* evaluation of the company's ability to deliver products that meet user requirements. By definition, this is a situation in which results are not – or may not – be present, so the assessment necessarily focuses on **how** the company ensures the quality of its results (this **how** is usually illustrated in a **quality manual**, which has to meet certain standard requirements). Assessments of this type are frequently an **entry requirement** for new suppliers. Once the supplier has been formally approved, a full capability assessment is performed, through the use of **vendor ratings**. In this case, too, 'results' are necessary for a complete assessment.

2. The assessment is concerned with only one area – even if multifunctional – of the company quality system, the area that generates products. This is the area with which the ISO 9001/2/3 standards are concerned, and it is the most tangible and easily verified part of the company quality system. In fact, some of the processes involved (manufacturing processes) can be kept in a state of statistical control and their **results are statistically predictable**. In this case, it is considered legitimate practice to infer conclusions regarding product quality from the assessment of the quality system (in particular, from the **capabilities** of the processes).

Great care must be taken, however, to guard against the tendency to extend the logic on which the simplified assessment model of Fig. 7.3(b) is based to contexts in which the above considerations no longer apply. Extending this logic means not only applying the model in Fig. 7.3(b), but also assigning an excessive weight to the quality system in Fig. 7.3(a) (the system's capabilities), to the detriment of results. In the Malcolm Baldrige Award model, 1991 edition (Fig. 7.5), customer satisfaction results have a 7% weighting (plus an additional 7% in comparison with competitors) and internal results have an 18% weighting; the weight of the quality system is nearly 70% (and was as high as 80% in the original model). The suspicion inevitably arises that long familiarity with second- and third-party assessments for standards conformity lies at the root of the priority given to the quality system, or capabilities, over results.

When the purpose is self-assessment or assessment for an award (categories 3, 4 and 5 of the previous section) rather than *a priori* assessment of capabilities (categories 1 and 2), external results (from the user perspective) and internal results (processes/products) must evidently be available (consideration 1 is therefore not valid). Moreover, as the quality system becomes more complex and the number of intangibles grows, consideration 2 becomes increasingly arbitrary. Although many people refer optimistically (or rashly) to '6σ' (in other words, to situations in which processes are assumed to be in a state of statistical control) for processes in which human, social, communication, organisational and political variables are significant factors, it is best to avoid all forms of determinism, even of a probabilistic type, where total quality is concerned. In the present stage of development of total quality models, a positive match between the actual quality system and the theoretical model is, at best, a necessary though certainly not sufficient condition to ensure reliable results.

7.3 CONTROL-ORIENTED ASSESSMENTS AND IMPROVEMENT-ORIENTED ASSESSMENTS

To sum up so far, the closer the company moves towards total quality the lower the objectivity of the quality system model and the smaller the possibility of extrapolating results from the degree of conformity with the model. This means assessments must have access to real, appropriately weighted results. A good balance must be established between the three components (quality system, internal results and external results).

A second requirement is that the three components must be **consistent** with one another. A lack of consistency indicates incorrect assessment/measurement of one or more components. The three components are in fact intrinsically linked with one another in a cause-effect relationship (apart from timescale discrepancies, for which allowance must be made). The fact that these correlations are often not obvious – or, given their complexity, not sufficiently obvious for quantitative deductions to be made – does not mean they do not exist. On the contrary, an analysis of the cause-effect chains that emerge from assessments will bring these correlations to light and enable the company to improve both its process indicators (for better alignment of internal results with user results) and its quality system model.

Verifying the **consistency** of the three components is a fundamental part of the assessment process. Verification can begin with the quality system (categories and items of the model in section 2.3, the Malcolm Baldrige model or other models) and end with results. This is the approach adopted by the Malcolm Baldrige model, even for internal assessments. The logical sequence is:

quality system item → company's specific approach → deployment (that is, extension of the approach to the company) → results.

Alternatively, consistency can be verified in the opposite direction, beginning with user results (for each user class and each branch in the customer satisfaction tree, see section 3.3) and then moving backwards through the generator processes to the quality system. In this way, the cause-effect chains are followed through, beginning with effects (Fig. 7.4). This is the self-assessment approach adopted in this book. Chapter 2 stresses the importance of **results** as the focal point of the model and Chapter 3 proposes a **results-based** approach to self-assessment as the basis for improvement planning.

The first type of assessment therefore begins with the quality system, more precisely with a reasonably accurate model of the quality system (possibly just a working hypothesis). Since the Malcolm Baldrige Award is an important example of an assessment approach which begins with a quality system model (a conceptual model, not a prescriptive model for implementation), it is used for reference here (Fig. 7.4(a)). For each item in the model, the conformity of the actual situation with the requirements of the model is checked, assessing the company's specific **approach**; next, the degree to which this approach is applied

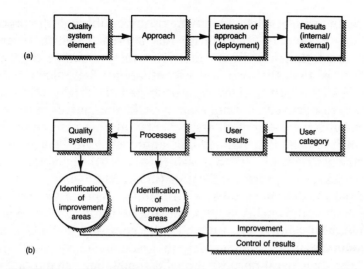

Fig. 7.4 The two approaches to assessment: (a) from the quality system to results (control-oriented assessment); (b) from results to processes to the 'quality system' (improvement-oriented assessment).

within the company is verified (**deployment**); finally, **results** are assessed. But results are not necessarily user results. Results exist at the various levels of the cause-effect chains and the assessor will often be forced to end his appraisal at an inter-mediate, internal-results level, and be unable to reach the user results at the ends of the process chains.

The second assessment approach (Fig. 7.4(b)) begins with results and works back along the chains to the quality system. In other words, it begins with data that, by definition, is real – user results – not with models of reality, and its purpose is diag-nostic: to identify the causes of deviation from expected results and therefore pinpoint the weaknesses and strengths of the com-pany's processes and quality system in order to permit adjust-ment and improvement.

As noted above, **results** are the cornerstone of the model described in this book (based on a **customer-centric** rather than **company-centric** perspective). This produces a strategic but at the same time concrete approach to improvement (**results-driven** improvement); the expression 'reading reality from right to left', beginning with results and moving upstream through the process stream, is used to characterise this approach, which reverses traditional thinking on quality. The thesis submitted in this section is that the two assessment approaches illustrated in Fig. 7.4, the 'left-to-right' approach and the 'right-to-left' approach respectively, are not equally valid alternatives in the case of improvement-oriented assessments; in this case, only one option is open, the 'right-to-left' approach. Only the typically diagnostic 'right-to-left' approach (Fig. 7.4(b)) highlights inconsistencies in the process indicators (incorrect alignment between internal and external results), shortcomings in process capabilities and flaws in the quality system (missing or insufficiently weighted items). But, above all, it enables the company to build a customised quality system model, to gradually move away from the usually general-purpose model assumed beforehand or from the equally general-purpose models of the Malcolm Baldrige National Quality Award or the European Quality Award, towards a specific corporate model. In other words, the criterion of continuous improvement based on reality, on facts (and results are facts, the quality system is just a model of the causes), is applied to the quality system, too.

For these reasons, the assessment illustrated in Fig. 7.4(b) can be termed an **improvement-oriented assessment**, while Fig. 7.4(a) is a **control-oriented assessment**. This second type is perfectly adequate for checking that everything is going according to plan, in particular that the quality system and process improvements planned after an earlier diagnostic self-assessment have been implemented. The Malcolm Baldrige approach, therefore, is suitable for external award assessments, but not for self-assessments.

This is a conclusion of some significance, in view of the extremely widespread use of the Malcolm Baldrige model for improvement-oriented self-assessment; a practice motivated by the award and regarded as the route towards the model of excellence stipulated by the award. The risk of a model-driven view of improvement developing rather than a results-driven view is all too real.

The interpretative, diagnostic **results → processes → quality**

system process bears some logical resemblance to the **reverse engineering** process, which companies sometimes apply to their competitors' best products in order to trace a path back from the measurable results given by a product and its parts to the planning decisions that made those results possible. In the current phase of total quality development, a great deal of reverse engineering needs to be carried out to improve understanding of the planning decisions which, in the development of the company system, lead (naturally, not in a deterministic fashion!) to excellent results. The widespread use today of benchmarking is an evident indication of the search for suitable planning solutions at the level of processes and the quality system. Reverse engineering should not, however, be restricted to other companies, to the best competitors; it should be applied systematically inside the company, too, to assess the consistency between external results–process measurements–quality system and consequently to improve indicators, processes and the system.

7.4 ASSESSMENT RELIABILITY

It is also useful to examine the question of assessment reliability. The first point to be made is that reliability is closely linked with the range and nature of the quality characteristics being assessed. It decreases as the range widens and quality becomes increasingly 'total'.

As noted earlier, and with reference to Table 2.2, the presence of user results and process/product measurements significantly raises assessment reliability. The quality system is always the most critical component: even at the level of the most tangible and easily controlled subsystem, product generation, the quality system is a critical factor whose weight increases exponentially as the system broadens to embrace the entire company and a growing number of intangibles.

A second factor affecting reliability is 'who' controls the assessment, who commissions and owns it. A self-assessment commissioned by the company for its own purposes, to monitor its situation and plan improvement, **is by far the most reliable**

275

assessment. The company's aim is to **understand**: it has nothing to gain by creating ambiguities or distortions.

This is the aim of the company, but not necessarily of those delegated to perform the assessment or of those asked to express their opinions. The company must therefore study the methodology with great care to ensure the greatest possible impartiality.

As a general rule, external parties should be appointed to conduct the most delicate phases of the assessment – such as the interviews – and to evaluate the main intangibles. This will create an image of impartiality and confidentiality and ensure that the assessment is conducted by people with the necessary skills and experience. Self-assessment has been examined in some depth in Chapter 3, to which the reader is referred for greater details on the conditions needed to ensure maximum reliability.

The reliability of assessments by second parties (customers) and third parties (independent certification organisations or independent award-assigning organisations) is low: the company tends to assume a defensive attitude in second-party assessments, or feel it has to pass an exam in third-party assessments. If the 'external assessment' factor is combined with the 'increase in complexity' factor, reliability drops sharply. This is why this book has strong reservations about the utility of extending to total quality those approaches that already involve an element of risk when applied to less complex situations (certification). How, for example, can intangibles such as leadership, customer culture, the team spirit and respect for people, which are such important factors in determining corporate excellence, be assessed on the basis of a report submitted by the company's management (the application reports used by the awards) and a three/four-day site visit by a group of examiners?

Reliability also depends on a third factor, 'the people who make judgements'. Here, the situation varies according to which of the model's three components is being assessed: results, processes or the quality system.

No difficulties arise as far as results are concerned: opinions are expressed by the customer (in the extended sense, see section 2.3). Customers have 'expectations' and are therefore qualified to judge the degree to which 'products' (in the extended sense) meet their expectations: this is why results are considered the most reliable data and why it is suggested that a very high, predominant weight should be given to results if an award is to be credible. For processes/products, assessment reliability is potentially high because it deals with measurements. In practice, as explained in section 2.3, measurements are reliable only if the process is in a state of control and aligned with user results. It is possible, however, to evaluate this reliability and raise it to high levels by adopting the approach described in Chapters 3 and 4. The 'voice of the processes' is indispensable for a serious assessment of processes, and the reliability of this voice may be very low or very high, depending on the state of process management within the company. To ensure assessment credibility, the company must allow its processes to 'speak' through proper indicator systems.

Assessments of the quality system are conventionally made by management, in reports frequently based on audits. But audits are potentially objective only when they deal with tangible characteristics; where intangibles are concerned, the assessment is often opinion-based, and the opinion of management tends to be optimistic (section 3.5). Management, in particular top management, is the 'supplier' of the quality system and as such is inclined to have a favourable opinion; management also tends to believe that the situation is 'as it should be' and not 'as it is', particularly in the case of the main intangibles, with which management is often directly concerned (leadership, the atmosphere in the company and decision-making).

Assessments of the quality system are much more reliable if the **system users** are asked to express a judgement (company personnel at all levels, from blue-collar personnel to management). It must be made clear that the assessment is not an internal user satisfaction survey, but a 'fitness-for-use' survey in which employees are the users of the quality system (section 3.4). This approach is consistent with the **quality philosophy**, which evaluates every 'product' in terms of its fitness-for-use.

Assessment by the user also goes a long way to solving the problem of assessing intangibles. As a group, the people who live and work in the company have an intimate understanding of its intangible characteristics, even if the maieutical skills of external specialists are usually needed to collect this information in a suitable form.

To conclude, assessment reliability requires judgements from a variety of sources, expressed in formal management reports, audits (for tangible characteristics) and employee questionnaires/ interviews (for less tangible characteristics).

7.5 THE CENTRAL ROLE OF SELF-ASSESSMENT

The central role of self-assessment in the total quality process and in the improvement planning process in particular has been stressed repeatedly (especially in Chapter 3). Self-assessment should also play a central role as a compulsory basis of reference for external assessments, especially assessments of excellence in the field of total quality, for practical reasons first of all. If it is true that results and processes are always vital to ensure reliability, above all in total quality assessments, then no external assessor could afford to conduct an independent survey of customer satisfaction; nor could it check the reliability of process measurements, because that would require precise audits of their state of control, or verify their alignment with user results. The external party needs information summaries, comparisons and assessments of results and processes, which can only be obtained through a systematic, complete and detailed self-assessment procedure conducted for the company's own purposes.

Moving from results and processes to the quality system, the low reliability factor of external assessments becomes predominant. Even in simple assessments concerned solely with the product quality assurance subsystem, defensive attitudes or the 'exam syndrome' can impede understanding. When the quality system is extended to the entire company and intangible characteristics predominate, it seems unwise to imagine that external assessors can understand and assess the state of the system on the basis of a report by the company's management or a site

278

visit. Similarly, it is unwise to count on the frankness and objectivity of people whose sole aim can only be to 'pass the exam'.

This is the 'Achilles' heel' of awards like the Malcolm Baldrige, which consider the application report a self-assessment simply because it was drawn up by the company itself, naturally on the basis of all available data, when in fact it is an *ad hoc* report, prepared with the intention of competing for the award.

Self-assessment as described here is entirely different. It is a much broader, more detailed process than that set in motion by an *ad hoc* report (which has to follow the guidelines laid down by the external organisation and not exceed a certain number of pages); above all, it is an integral part of the company's total quality process.

The thesis submitted here is that all external assessments should be based on the self-assessments performed by the company (improvement-oriented self-assessments, which begin with results). In the case of awards, the availability of self-assessments (referring to at least the previous two years) should be a requirement for companies applying for an external assessment (Conti, 1991c, 1992).

7.6 QUALITY AWARDS: THE POSITIONING PROBLEM

Before examining the three main quality awards in the light of the above considerations, the **positioning** concept should be introduced. This concept clarifies what is actually being adjudicated by the award, quite apart from the organisers' declared intentions.

Section 2.3 describes the assessment model as a tree, with two tiers of 'branches': the first and hierarchically superior tier consists of the assessment categories, the second tier of items or specifications. Figures 7.5, 7.6 and 7.7 illustrate the categories and an example of second-level deployment for the Malcolm Baldrige National Quality Award (1991 edition), the Deming Application Prize (1989) and the European Quality Award (1992), respectively, which will be referred to from now on with the abbreviations MBA, DAP and EQA. The assessment model

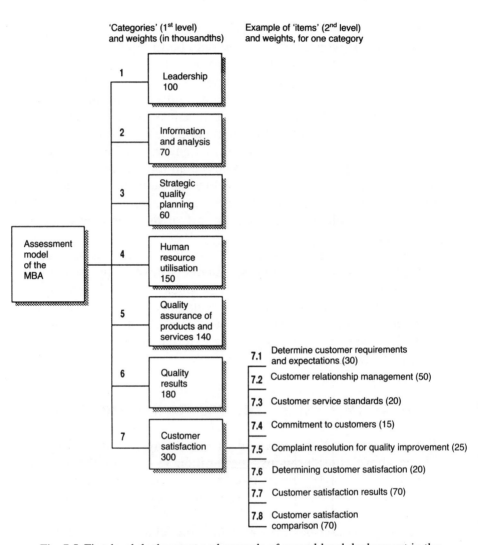

'Categories' (1st level) and weights (in thousandths)

Example of 'items' (2nd level) and weights, for one category

1 — Leadership 100

2 — Information and analysis 70

3 — Strategic quality planning 60

Assessment model of the MBA

4 — Human resource utilisation 150

5 — Quality assurance of products and services 140

6 — Quality results 180

7 — Customer satisfaction 300

7.1 Determine customer requirements and expectations (30)

7.2 Customer relationship management (50)

7.3 Customer service standards (20)

7.4 Commitment to customers (15)

7.5 Complaint resolution for quality improvement (25)

7.6 Determining customer satisfaction (20)

7.7 Customer satisfaction results (70)

7.8 Customer satisfaction comparison (70)

Fig. 7.5 First-level deployment and example of second-level deployment in the assessment model of the Malcolm Baldrige Award (MBA) (1991).

proposed in this book, in the tree chart of Fig. 7.2, is used here as a basis for comparison. Compared with the MBA and the DAP, this model introduces another tier at a higher hierarchical level, the three classes or components of the model: results, processes, quality system. Figure 7.2 illustrates just the two

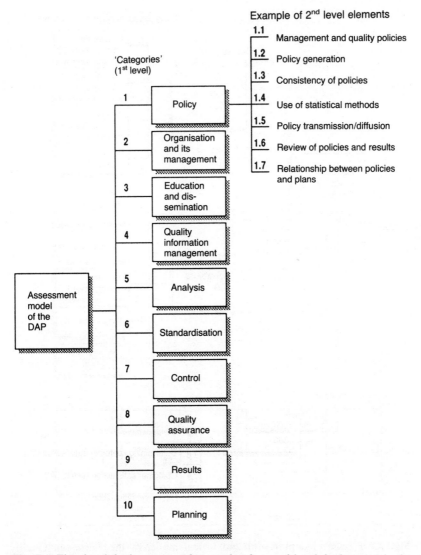

Fig. 7.6 First-level deployment and example of second-level deployment in the assessment model of the Deming Application Prize (DAP) (1989).

highest tiers: the classes and the first-level categories in each class; for simplicity, the next deployment level, shown in Fig. 2.23, is not illustrated.

The MBA gives weights to each branch, at both first and

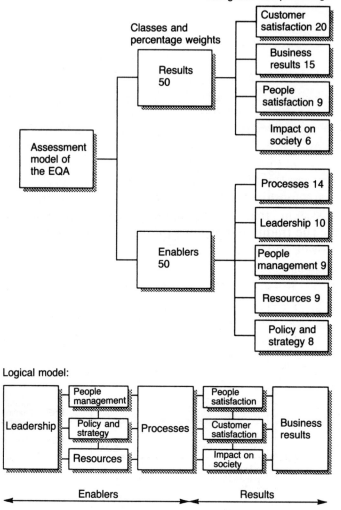

Fig. 7.7 First-level deployment and logical model of the European Quality Award (EQA) (1992).

second levels; the EQA weights just the first-level branches; the DAP does not explicitly attribute weights. The EQA (Fig. 7.7) makes a clear distinction between results and **enablers**, that is, the features that make these results possible – the quality system in the terminology used in this book – and allocates its weightings equally between the two blocks. The MBA mixes external results (part of category 7) and internal results (category 6) with the quality system categories. In the DAP, results are one of the ten categories.

A look at the menus of the three awards highlights in some cases significant differences, but it is difficult to understand the particular nature of each award, its chief purpose, and what it aims to reward. The concept of **positioning** can help to clarify the intentions of the awards and their particular features, and avoid the multiple interpretations that have led to so much debate about the MBA, to take just one example.

The **first positioning** concerns the comprehensiveness of the quality system, that is, its proximity to the ideal limit of total quality. The traditional product quality system can be positioned at the lower end of this scale. The upper end is an ideal quality system covering the entire organisation and everyone working in it: in other words, the system that responds in full to the total quality mission.

In Fig. 7.8, this positioning is represented by the horizontal axis, even though such a simplified representation is wholly

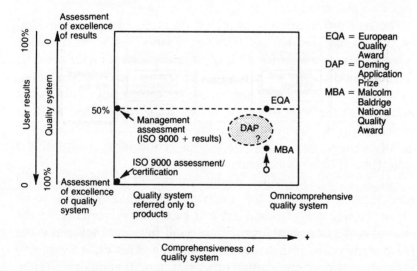

Fig. 7.8 The positioning of assessments and awards.

283

inadequate. An award can only be accurately positioned on the comprehensiveness scale if its quality system tree is analytically compared with a **universal** or **omnicomprehensive** tree of the type described in section 2.3 and illustrated in Fig. 2.23. This would make it easier to highlight the particular options and goals of each award (for example, the EQA's emphasis on 'society and the environment' and on people, the DAP's focus on a widespread statistical culture and on standardisation/stabilisation as a necessary complement to improvement, and the MBA's attention to strategic planning and benchmarking).

A global and inevitably subjective assessment indicates that the three awards should be positioned more or less at the same point in relation to the horizontal axis of Fig. 7.8, with some reservations about the DAP, given the lack of information about its assessment criteria and weighting system (see below). Nevertheless, it seems correct to place the three awards in the same area as regards the comprehensiveness of their quality systems.

This positioning is therefore not a differentiating factor: all three awards, in the current phase of quality development, are well positioned as regards total quality. If they were placed further towards the right, assessment would be even more complex and less reliable.

The true differentiating factor of the three awards is provided by the **second positioning**, between quality system and results (vertical axis in Fig. 7.8). This positioning is best understood by considering the extreme case of an award focused solely on company excellence in achieving customer satisfaction: this award would be at the top end of the scale. In theory at least, another award might be geared solely to the excellence of the company's quality system, and would be placed at the bottom end of the scale (like ISO 9000 assessments in Fig. 7.8).

The key role of results in any assessment has been stressed repeatedly in this book, but a conceptual distinction needs to be drawn between self-assessment and external assessments. In the case of self-assessment, results are vital because they represent the starting point of the assessment and the yardstick for verifying the other two components, processes and the quality system (**results-driven** assessments oriented to improvement). At the next stage, however, the improvement planning and implementation stage in which the company aims to create the conditions for better future results, the roles are reversed (that is, the focus shifts to the quality system and processes).

In the case of external assessments, results must always be predominant, not only for the reasons mentioned in the previous sections, in particular as regards assessment reliability, but because their presence and use demonstrate that the company is moving correctly towards total quality (reading the situation 'right-to-left'). In the total quality field, external assessment of the quality system is such an uncertain business that it is always best, even for awards for the excellence of the company approach, to wait until excellence is reflected in results, rather than risk giving an award to an apparently perfect system, which fails to produce the expected results.

Today, an optimal positioning would give a 50% weighting to the 'voice of the users' (results) and a 50% weighting to the 'voice of the company' (quality system + processes). In Fig. 7.8, the EQA occupies this position. Despite the apparently high weight given by the MBA to the customer satisfaction category (30%), only 14% is actually given to results (7% each for the company's own results and results as compared with competitors, Fig. 7.5)*. The positioning of the DAP is not clear, since the weights given to the assessment categories and items are not known.

The second positioning offers significant clues to the objectives of the awards. The primary aim of the EQA clearly is to give ample scope to users in assessing company excellence and to give credit to a total quality management system that has already proved its effectiveness. The objective of the MBA seems to be recognition of the excellence of the quality system: indicating national TQM models which can be imitated (with the risk, explained earlier, of inconsistency with results). The vertical positioning of the DAP is not clear, for the same reasons its horizontal positioning is uncertain. The origins of the prize and

---

* The text refers to the 1991 edition of the MBA. The 1992 edition has further increased customer satisfaction results, from 14 to 15% (its own and in relation to competitors).

the information available suggest that, like the MBA, the chief purpose of the DAP is recognition of the excellence of the TQM system; there is reason to believe, nevertheless, that in practice, if not in theory, significant weight is given to results.

7.7 A BRIEF CRITICAL ANALYSIS OF THE THREE MAIN QUALITY AWARDS

Some comments on the DAP, the MBA and the EQA have been made in the previous pages. The chapter can be concluded with a brief critical analysis of each award in the light of the theories discussed in this book – and in this chapter in particular – regarding the criteria to be used in assessing companies' progress in relation to the total quality mission.

Too little is known about the Deming Application Prize to permit any reliable judgements. The following remarks, based on the limited amount of material published in the West and on the information supplied by the very few Western companies that have taken part in the DAP in Japan or in their own countries, are therefore largely subjective. The DAP was set up more than forty years ago and its objectives have gradually evolved in line with the development of quality concepts and practices in Japan. Its declared intention is to 'recognise success arising from the implementation of CWQC on the basis of statistical quality control' (Deming Prize Committee, 1989). Over the years, the award has moved from QC (quality control) to CWQC (company-wide quality control), although it continues to focus on a statistical culture and statistical tools, at all company levels and in all company sectors. The DAP's examiners, selected by the Japanese Union of Scientists and Engineers (JUSE) from a small group of scholars and other distinguished experts associated with non-profit-making organisations, share a deeply rooted and culturally uniform approach to quality. This has apparently created a situation where codification of values – the weights and relative attribution criteria of the other awards – is unnecessary; in comparison, the examiners of the MBA and the EQA are a much

286

larger, open and culturally mixed category, which does not have such a long cultural tradition of total quality.

Given the importance of the expert's personal judgement, the assessment is based almost entirely on the findings of the site visit; the application report has little significance (in the other awards, the application report must be approved before the site visit can take place).

The comments made earlier as regards assessment reliability, the need to base external assessments on self-assessments, the positioning between results and quality system, appear to indicate a number of shortcomings in the DAP. But since this award is linked more closely with traditional culture, the skills of the examiners and the application approach, it is not possible to judge how far characteristics that would be inadequate in the West are in fact acceptable in the Japanese environment. Greater information is needed on the procedures adopted by the DAP, with real case histories and explanations of the criteria used by the examiners in their quantitative appraisals.

The most significant comments on the Malcolm Baldrige National Quality Award have already been made. They concern the award's **assessment approach** and its **vertical positioning** (as shown in Fig. 7.8, that is the relative weighting of results and quality system). The two issues are separate but conceptually related with each other. The 'left-to-right' assessment approach (correct for external award assessments and for verification assessments, but not for improvement-oriented self-assessment) produces a 'model-driven' assessment; attribution of a high weight to the quality system puts even greater emphasis on the model in relation to results. The objection to the MBA stems from the key importance of results, as explained in this book. The focus on results means, first of all, allocating a high weight to results and, second, requiring the company to provide evidence of use of a 'results-driven' 'right-to-left' self-assessment procedure. As has been seen, the first edition of the MBA allocated an even lower weight to results than the current edition (10% to external results, 10% to internal results, since raised to 14% and 18% respectively). This seems to indicate a cultural conditioning in the original formulation of the award – a model-driven view of assessment – and a gradual realisation that insufficient weight had been given to results.

A second comment concerns **assessment reliability**. For the reasons explained earlier, *ad hoc* application reports and site visits do not offer sufficient guarantees of reliability. Only an assessment based on the company's self-assessments, together with a high weighting allocated to results, can ensure a reasonable level of reliability.

The European Quality Award incorporates some of the concepts described here, which stem from the proposal reported in the article quoted earlier (Conti, 1991c). In particular, it adopts the principle of self-assessment as an entry requirement for companies applying for the award and has assumed an optimal positioning (equal weighting for results and quality system). Nevertheless, the EQA still has a number of weaknesses, which hopefully will be eliminated during the planned annual improvement process. The first weakness concerns the business results category. In theory, it is correct to include in the customer satisfaction block a category covering the satisfaction of the class of users identified in Fig. 7.2 as the beneficiaries of the company's economic/financial results. In practice, however, the reliability of the assessments made by these users is low, partly because the users have visibility on the results shown in the company's financial statements but not on the long-term returns produced by quality initiatives, and partly because economic/financial results are the outcome of many variables, which the users are certainly unable to pinpoint (and for consistency with the model in Fig. 7.7, the results concerned must be due to the enablers, that is, to quality and not to other causes). It may therefore be concluded, correctly, that business results should be assessed by experts, not by users. But finding a solution to the second problem, how to separate business results produced by quality from those produced by other variables, is still extremely difficult, even for the experts (Garvin, 1991). The best solution, until more is known about the influence of quality on income statements and company value, is to limit the assessment to areas that can be measured today (Chapter 6). The business results category need not be eliminated, but it should be limited, at least for the time being, to questions of efficiency, such as the effect of quality initiatives in reducing costs and cycle times; it could also examine variations in market share, with careful analyses of the various factors involved.

The second weakness of the EQA is the apparent absence of the fundamental **internal results** category (or **processes**, Fig. 7.1). In some people's view, internal results is implicit in other categories, but it is inadmissible that such an important category (one of the three main components of the model described in this book, and a first-level category of the MBA, with an 18% weighting) should be absent or implicit in some other category. In the EQA application guide, processes are considered solely by 'how' questions, which concern the quality system, and not by 'what' questions, which look at results.

The third problem arises with the assessment approach. An award that puts so much emphasis on results and, above all, makes **self-assessment** the basis for the external assessment process cannot then confine itself to the MBA's 'left-to-right' approach. Apart from anything else, this immediately creates difficulties: since the EQA considers results as a separate assessment class, its organisers decided they could not adopt the typical MBA 'approach → deployment → results' sequence, but would have to stop after the first two steps. But in fact even a control-oriented assessment (left-to-right) has to apply the full sequence, from the quality system through processes to results, although it will often stop at internal, intermediate results and be unable to follow the entire chain to user results. Apart from this ambiguity, since the assessment performed by the EQA's external examiners should look first of all at the results of the self-assessments conducted by the company, the award ought to emphasise the results-driven improvement approach.

One final observation about the three awards. The DAP is not competitive: every company whose application is accepted receives the award. The MBA is competitive: it is given to not more than two companies in each of its three categories (industry, services and small businesses). Competing companies naturally have to reach the pass-mark. The EQA is essentially non-competitive, because every company that reaches the pass-mark (not known) receives a 'Prize'; but the 'Award' is given to the best prize-winner. This is an ideal solution: it does not make participation in a competition (which can lead to distortions) a condition for achieving recognition, yet a competitive 'climate' is maintained with a 'prize-winners' prize'.

The question of company assessments and quality awards, currently one of the most hotly debated issues in the total quality field, closes this book. By raising general awareness and providing information, the national and international quality awards are contributing to the development of valid total quality management models. It is important, however, that research should not be impeded by chauvinist attitudes towards the national models or by the importance attached to the competitive and public relations value of the awards, to the detriment of their core value, true and lasting quality growth. Only through open comparison of cultural developments and experience will the transition be made from a phase of tumultuous development geared to a mythical total quality towards the organisation of knowledge and the methodical assimilation of concepts and attitudes within the main body of the corporate sector. This book will succeed in its attempt at clarification and organisation if, apart from helping the daily work of colleagues engaged on quality development, it fuels fresh debate and further investigation, perhaps by those who disagree with its analyses. In particular, further discussion is needed on the total quality management model (specifically, the quality system model) and the resultant approaches: results-driven quality (the 'pull' approach) or quality geared to a model or to the opinions of management or experts (the 'push' approach). The future of total quality depends on thorough comparisons and constructive debate.

Bibliography

Abernathy, W.J., Clark, K.B. and Kantrow, A.M. (1981) The New Industrial Competition. *Harvard Business Review*, September–October.

Akao, Y. (1990) History of quality function deployment in Japan, in *The Best on Quality*, Vol. 3, International Academy for Quality, Hanser, Munich-Vienna-New York.

Beer, M., Eisenstat, R.A. and Spector, B. (1990) Why Change Programs Don't Produce Change. *Harvard Business Review*, November–December.

Bush, D. and Dooley, K. (1990) The Deming Prize and Baldrige Award: how they compare. *Quality Progress*, January.

Camp, C.R. (1991) *Benchmarking*, ASQC Quality Press, Milwaukee.

Cowling, K. and Cubbin, J. (1970) Price, quality and market share. *Journal of Political Economy*, November–December.

Deming, E.W. (1967) What happened in Japan? *Industrial Quality Control*, August.

Deming, E.W. (1986) *Out of the Crisis. Quality, Productivity and Competitive Position*, Cambridge University Press, Cambridge.

Drucker, P.F. (1971) What we can learn from Japanese management. *Harvard Business Review*, March–April.

Feingenbaum, A.V. (1983) *Total Quality Control*, McGraw-Hill, New York.

Gerstfeld, L.W. (1982) The price-quality relationship revisited. *Journal of Consumer Affairs*, Winter.

GOAL/QPC Research Committee (1989) *Hoshin Planning: A Planning System for Implementing Total Quality Management*, GOAL/QPC, Methuen, MA.

GOAL/QPC Research Committee (1989) *Total Quality Control Education in Japan*, GOAL/QPC, Methuen, MA.

Hardaker, M. and Ward, B.K. (1987) Getting things done. *Harvard Business Review*, November–December.

Hauser, J.R. and Clausing, D. (1986) The house of quality. *Harvard Business Review*, May–June.

Hayes, R.H. and Wheelwright, S.C. (1984) *Restoring our Competitive Edge: Competing Through Manufacturing*, Wiley, New York.

Hiromoto, T. (1988) Another hidden hedge – Japanese management accounting. *Harvard Business Review*, July–August.

Ishikawa, K. (1976) *Guide to Quality Control*, Asian Productivity Organization, Tokyo.

Ishikawa, K. (1984) Quality and standardization: program for economic success. *Quality Progress*, January.

Juran, J.M. (1964) *Managerial Breakthrough*, McGraw-Hill, New York.

Juran, J.M. (1978) Japanese and Western quality: a contrast. *Quality Progress*, December.

Juran, J.M. (1979) *Quality Control Handbook*, McGraw-Hill, New York.

Juran, J.M. and Gryna, F.M., Jr (1980) *Quality Planning and Analysis*, McGraw-Hill, New York.

Juran, J.M. (1981) Product quality: a prescription for the West. *The Management Review*, June (part I) and July (part II).

Juran, J.M. (1989) *Juran on Leadership for Quality*, The Free Press, New York.

Kane, V.E. (1986) Process capability indices. *Journal of Quality Technology*, January.

Kobayashi, K. (1986) Quality management at NEC Corporation. *Quality Progress*, April.

Kogure, M. and Akao, Y. (1983) Quality function deployment and CWQC in Japan. *Quality Progress*, October.

Kondo, Y. (1990) The development of quality in Japan, in *The Best on Quality*, International Academy for Quality, Hanser, Munich-Vienna-New York.

Kotter, J.P. (1990) What leaders really do. *Harvard Business Review*, May–June.

Koura, K. (1990) Survey and research in Japan concerning policy management. *Acts of the XLIV Annual Quality Congress*, American Society for Quality Control, San Francisco, 14–16 May.

Kume, H. (1985) Business management and quality cost: the Japanese view. *Quality Progress*, May.

Kume, H. (1986) Business management and quality economy. *Acts of the XXX Congress of the European Organization for Quality Control*, Stockholm.

McClaskey, D.J. (1990) Baldrige Award and Overseas Deming Prize: a basis for improvement. *Acts of the XLIV Annual Quality Congress*, American Society for Quality Control, San Francisco, 14–16 May.

McCollen, D.J. (1966) An experimental examination of the price-quality relationship. *Economica*, February.

Mizuno, S. (1989) *Company-Wide Total Quality Control*, Asian Productivity Organization, Tokyo.

Mizuno, S. (ed.) (1988) *Managing for Quality Improvement. The 7 New Managing Tools*, Productivity Press, Cambridge, MA.

Nadler, L. (1984) What Japan learned from the US that we forgot to remember. *California Management Review*, Summer.

292

Natayani, Y. (1987) The 7 management tools and the applications. *Acts of the International Quality Control Congress*, Tokyo.

O.D.I. (1989) *Total Quality Improvement System*, Organizational Dynamics Inc., Burlington, MA (educational publications).

Ohmae, K. (1988) Getting back to strategies. *Harvard Business Review*, November–December.

Phillips, L.W., Chang, D.R. and Buzzell, R.D. (1983) Product quality, cost position and business performance. *Journal of Marketing*, Spring.

Scherkenbach, W.W. (1986) *The Deming Route to Quality and Productivity: Roads Maps and Roadblocks*, CeePress, Washington.

Shewhart, W.A. (1931) *Economic Control of Quality of Manufactured Products*, D. Van Nostrand, New York.

Stalk, G., Jr (1988) Time, the next source of competitive advantage. *Harvard Business Review*, July–August.

Sullivan, L.P. (1984) Reducing variability: a new approach to quality. *Quality Progress*, July.

Sullivan, L.P. (1986) Quality function deployment. *Quality Progress*, June.

Taguchi, G. and Wu, I. (1979) *Introduction to Off-Line Quality Control*, Central Japan Quality Association, Nagaya.

Wheelwright, S.C. (1981) Japan: Where operations really are strategic. *Harvard Business Review*, July–August.

Wheelwright, S.C. and Hayes, R.H. (1985) Competing through manufacturing. *Harvard Business Review*, January–February.

Xerox Corporation (1984) Quality office, competitive benchmarking: what it is and what it can do for you, January.

Yamada, Y. and Ackerman, N. (1984) Price-quality correlations in the Japanese market. *Journal of Consumer Affairs*, Winter.

References

Abegglen, J.C. and Stalk, G., Jr (1985) *Kaisha. The Japanese Corporation*, Basic Books, New York.

Akao, Y. (1990) *Quality Function Deployment*, Productivity Press, Cambridge, MA.

Bartlett, C.A. and Ghoshal, S. (1990) Matrix management: not a structure, a frame of mind. *Harvard Business Review*, July–August.

Bester, Y. (1991) Quality economics and productivity, in *The Best on Quality*, Vol. 4, International Academy for Quality, Hanser, Munich-Vienna-New York.

Block, P., Hababou, R. and Xardel, D. (1986) *Service compris*, Editions Jean-Claude Lattès, Paris.

Carlzon, J. (1990) *La piramide rovesciata*, Franco Angeli, Milan.

Charan, R. (1991) How networks reshape organizations for results. *Harvard Business Review*, September–October.

Conti, T. (1988) Dalla Qualità dei prodotti alla Qualità dei sistemi aziendali. *L'Impresa*, no. 3.

Conti, T. (1989) Process management and quality function deployment. *Quality Progress* (12), **22**, December.

Conti, T. (1991a) Considerations on process management, in *The Best on Quality*, Vol. 4, International Academy for Quality, Hanser, Munich-Vienna-New York.

Conti, T. (1991b) Mantenere la rotta nel lungo viaggio verso la Qualità Totale. *Qualità*, no. 71, April.

Conti, T. (1991c) Company quality assessments. *The TQM Magazine*, June and August.

Conti, T. (1992) A critical review of the correct approach to quality awards. *Proceedings of the EOQ 36th Annual Conference.*

Deming Prize Committee (1989) *The Deming Prize Guide for Overseas Companies*, Union of Japanese Scientists and Engineers (JUSE), Tokyo.

Desatnick, R.L. (1987) *Managing to Keep the Customer*, Jossey-Bass, London.

Drucker, P.F. (1988) The coming of the new organization. *Harvard Business Review* (1), **66**, January–February.

295

D'Egidio, F. (1989) *Il Global Service Management (GSM)*, Franco Angeli, Milan.

Feigenbaum, A.V. (1956) Total quality control. *Harvard Business Review* (6), **34**, November–December.

Feigenbaum, A.V. (1961) *Total Quality Control, Engineering and Management*, McGraw-Hill, New York.

Forrester, J.W. (1958) Industrial dynamics. A major breakthrough for decision makers. *Harvard Business Review*, July–August.

Garvin, D.A. (1988) *Managing Quality*, The Free Press, New York. In Chapter 5, the author makes an interesting analysis of the links between quality and other elements, including price. According to the results of surveys, the links are weak, but so far little data is available and refers to situations where suppliers have not yet developed a 'value-price-advertising' strategy and where customers lack information about quality.

Garvin, D. (1991) How the Malcolm Baldrige really works. *Harvard Business Review*, November–December.

Godfrey, A.B. (1991) Information quality – a key challenge for the 1990s, in *The Best on Quality*, International Academy for Quality, Vol. 4, Hanser, Munich-Vienna-New York.

Harrington, H.J. (1987) *Poor-Quality Costs*, ASQC Quality Press, Milwaukee.

Hsiang, T.C. and Lee, H.L. (1985) Zero Defect – A Quality Costs Approach. *IEE, Communications in Statistics* (11), **14**.

Imai, M. (1986) *Keizen – The Key to Japan's Competitive Success*, Random House Business Division, New York.

Ishikawa, K. (1985) *What is Total Quality Control – The Japanese Way*, ASQC Quality Press, Prentice Hall, Englewood Cliffs, NJ.

Juran, J.M. (1954) Universals in management planning and controlling. *The Management Review*, November.

Juran, J.M. (1982) *Management of Quality*, Copyright J.M. Juran, New York.

Juran, J.M. (1988) *Juran on Planning for Quality*, The Free Press, New York.

Kast, F.E. and Rosenzweig, J.E. (1985) *Organization and Management. A Systems and Contingency Approach*, McGraw-Hill, Singapore.

King, B. (1989) *Hoshin Planning – The Developmental Approach*, Bob King, GOAL/QPC, Methuen, MA.

Kume, H. (1990) Quality management. Japan and the West. *Quality*, May.

Malcolm Baldrige National Quality Award (1991) *Application Guidelines*, US Department of Commerce, NIST, Gaithersburg, MD.

Marquardt, D., Chové, J., Jensen, K.E., Klaus, P. and Strahle, D. (1991) Vision 2000: the strategy for the ISO 9000 Series standards in the 90s. *Quality Progress*, May.

Norton, D. (1988) Breaking functional gridlock. The case for a mission-oriented organization. *Stage by Stage* (2), **8**.

Pall, G. (1987) *Quality Process Management*, Prentice Hall, Englewood Cliffs, NJ.

Pall, G. (1990) *Quality Process Management*, Prentice Hall, Englewood Cliffs, NJ.

Peters, T.J. and Waterman, R.H., Jr (1982) *In Search of Excellence*, Harper & Row, New York.

Tosalli, A., Conti, T., Pettigiani, A. and Pettigiani, M.G. (1990) *La qualità nel servizio*, Bariletti Editori, Rome.

Index

Page numbers appearing in **bold** refer to figures and numbers appearing in *italics* refer to tables.